Fishnets in the Far East

Fishnets in the Far East

A Dancer's Diary In Korea
(A True Story)

Michele E. Northwood

"A story told is a life lived."
(Willoughby, the Chinaman. Outlander, Season
3, episode 9)

An ode to all non-British readers.
This poem is to apologise/apologize.
I do not wish to offend your eyes,
But I'm a Brit and you may think
My spelling's completely on the blink. (fritz)
My sombre/somber poem's for you to see,
You do not write the same as me.
You use a 'z´ when I use 's´
In cosy/cozy and idealised/idealized. I
guess...
I add a 'u´ when you do not,
In honour/honor and colour/color (It
happens a lot!)
Ambience/ambiance and travelling/traveling
Our difference in spelling is a curious thing!
So as you manoeuvre/maneuver through this
book,
And at these differences, you look,
Mistakes for you are not for me,
(It's the way that I was taught you see.)
I need to emphasise/emphasize this well...
Before you assume I cannot spell!
I hope you'll enjoy this book you've bought,
and not give these differences another
thought.
Kind regards, Michele xx

Contents

1   "KOREA? ... THERE'S A WAR ON, YOU KNOW!"   1

2   MOVING TO KYONGJU   10

3   A PICNIC, A PERVERT AND A PAGODA   30

4   MAFIA, MOTORBIKES AND MILITARY LEADERS   43

5   MOVING BACK TO SEOUL   59

6   ARABS AND AQUARIUMS   94

7   A PARTY, A PRACTICE AND A PREGNANCY TEST   121

8   TOWERS, STADIUMS AND APARTMENTS   163

9   SHOOTING, MODELLING AND
    HOSTESSING   186

10 FILLINGS, FIGHTS, FIRES AND
    FLASHERS!   223

11 TWO WEEKS IN TAEJON   266

12 BACK TO SEOUL   307

13 TWO WEEKS IN CHUNCHEON   327

BIBLIOGRAPHY   351

Chapter 1

"KOREA? ... THERE'S A WAR ON, YOU KNOW!"

Mid-March, 1989.

The three of us stood to attention like soldiers during inspection- rather than the dancers we actually were - as our agent and choreographer, Marion, marched past our beds like a sergeant major, casting a suspicious eye over our luggage. We had just finished ten days of rehearsals and were due to fly out to South Korea the following day.

Both Louise and Sharon - the two girls with whom I would be spending the next six months of my life - received a dismissive nod of approval, but I was less fortunate. Marion stared in disbelief at my two suitcases, make-up case and hand-luggage bag, all stuffed to bursting.

"You can't possibly take all that to Korea!" she exclaimed theatrically. "One suitcase, and don't put a lot in that either. Everything is SO cheap over there that you might as well buy a whole new wardrobe!"

I stared in dismay at my luggage, laden with everything but the kitchen sink, trying to imagine how on earth I was supposed to reduce the contents. Up until now, I had worked on holiday centres as part of the entertainment's team, where it was customary for me to set off for each summer season by filling my dad's car to bursting and unloading it all with his help, at the other end. (Personally, I thought I'd downsized considerable well!)

Dad, my trusty roadie, looked as vexed as I did. He stood with his hands on his hips shaking his head and looking utterly defeated.

"Look at Sharon, she's brought just a small suitcase," Marion continued, seemingly oblivious to our dilemma. "Heaven only knows what on earth possessed you to bring so much stuff. You'll never get all that on a plane!"

Sharon stood to attention, with a slight smirk on her face, coupled with an expression of sheer unadulterated complacency. She had been made head girl on the first day of rehearsals purely because she had worked for the agent on a previous contract. In Marion's eyes, despite Sharon being

2

the youngest of the three of us, she was thought to know the ropes and therefore deemed to be the best girl for the job. Or, in other words, the one least likely to do a runner!

Dad unexpectedly dropped to his knees. For a fleeting moment, I thought he was going to plead with Marion to let me take all of my treasured possessions, but he bowed his head, unzipped the first suitcase in slow motion and sighed.

"Come on then, Michele, let's get organized."

Half an hour later, my luggage passed Marion's approval and we all dispersed, arranging to meet at the airport the next day, to begin a six-month tour of South Korea.

* * *

The following morning as Dad was driving me to the airport, and I was growing more nervous with the passing of every mile, I sat in the passenger seat, quietly ruminated on the events which had led to my imminent departure to the Far East.

I had been eating my evening meal at the dining room table, blissfully unaware of mum's imminent statement:

"I've just found out about an agent who is looking for dancers to work in the Far East ..." she informed me from her position of authority, at the head of the long dining table. "And, I've arranged an audition for you this Saturday morning."

"I don't know..." I muttered, automatically starting to feel apprehensive.

"You go first," mother said, ignoring my reservations, "And if it all turns out okay, I'll let your little sister go out on a later contract."

Not relishing the thought of being the family Guinea pig, I frequently voiced my misgivings, general lack of enthusiasm and fear of impending doom over the next few days, but it all fell on deaf ears.

Saturday came around all too quickly and I was bustled off to audition in London. Despite my misapprehensions, the audition went well, and I was further reassured to find another group of five dancers there, who were in the midst of rehearsals. It appeared that they were also heading off for Korea and would be leaving in a few days. The girls were chatty and friendly, and a couple of them had worked for the agent before, which helped to qualm my fears of gullibly allowing myself to be sold into the sex trade and unwittingly becoming the latest victim of human trafficking!

A week or so later, I was summoned back to London to start rehearsals. With apprehension mounting, I arrived at the boarding house with the words of my next-door neighbour ringing in my ears.

"Korea? What do you want to go there for? There's a war on, you know."

"Well, it's not like I'm going to live there permanently! And, anyway, it's only for six months," I said, trying to convince myself more than my neighbour. "Besides, I've always wanted to visit Asia."

"Well, I've heard of people going to Korea, but they never come back," she said. -Hardly the type of words to instil confidence when I was heading off to the other side of the world!

The two girls with whom I was destined to spend the next six months of my life were already installed in the boarding house when I arrived, so I took the remaining bed.

"Hello," I said with a shy smile as I busied myself with my belongings.

"Hi!" They replied, eyeing me curious interest from recumbent positions on their beds: one eating packets of crisps and the other flicking through a magazine.

Conversation between the three of us was stilted at first, but as I unpacked, the three of us continued to tentatively assess each other, chatting with cautious, trying to discover what we had in common and what other dancing jobs we had done.

I found myself comparing the three of us with the quintet I had previously met, and it had to be said that we were hardly the epitome of the perfect dance trio. Sharon stood five foot four inches tall, rounded and plump, with long, straight, blond hair. Louise was five eight, buxom, with a mane of shoulder-length, curly, black hair and the most impressive pair of breasts I had ever seen! Then there was me; five foot seven, long, ginger hair, built like a beanpole and totally flat-chested!

Despite these dissimilarities, the agent, in her ultimate wisdom, had seen fit to sling us all together. Over the next ten days, she worked with diligence, moulding us into some semblance of a trio, teaching us two twenty-minute shows, which, according to Marion, would be sure to 'wow' the Koreans.

Our motley threesome was christened 'The Collier Dancers'. This proved to be rather unfortunate, not only because it made me think of three coal miners clomping about on the stage but also as Koreans, like all Asians, constantly struggle with the difficulty of pronouncing the 'L' or the 'R', the chances of being announced as the Collier trio were bordering on the impossible!

We diligently rehearsed our two shows from dawn to dusk. Each 20-minute spectacular contained an average of six routines and consisted of an opening number with feather headdresses, back-packs (the mass of feather boas which hang from the shoulders of the dancers) two solo performances, and a variety of duets and trios to finish each show. Two of these were 'playback´ numbers, which involved one of us miming to a song, while the other two danced behind her.

I was chosen to mime or 'lip-sync´ to 'Finger on the trigger´ by Donna Summer and also to perform one of the solo routines. I was to dress like a Bond girl and whilst brandishing a gun, I would dance to the 007 Theme tune – I have no idea why everything I fronted had to be related to guns!

Once all these routines had been memorised, we prepared for the final dress rehearsal. This was no easy task. At specific points in every dance routine, one or two of us had to sprint off stage and make a mad dash to the corner of the studio where all our clothes were laid out; one on top of the other, in preparation for each ridiculously quick costume change.

We battled through the dress rehearsal various times, to master the art of tearing off the existing costume and replacing it with another in thirty seconds flat, while the end of the previous routine's music drew to a close with increasing rapidity.

Each change consisted of replacing one entire costume for another: bikini and feathers for a dress, dress for a leotard, a leotard for lycra tights and a sequined top, plus the compulsory 'Marion accessories´: gloves and headdresses or hats accompanied by different shoes or boots.

Every time one of us failed to complete the change, we faced the wrath of Marion. The tape recorder would be snapped off and our agent would turn to us with a face like thunder. She was tiny compared to Louise and myself; we towered over her, however, what she lacked in stature, she more than made up for in attitude. No-one wanted to be in her bad books and face the barrage of abuse she deemed fit to holler in our direction, every time a sequin caught in our fishnet tights and we failed to complete the marathon quick change.

"Come on, come on! What are you playing at? And mind the costume. If you tear it you'll have to repair it!" she would bark then head off towards the tape recorder again, shaking her head and muttering something inaudible - but most likely expletives - under her breath.

When we had succeeded in completing all the quick changes required for two full shows, Marion deemed us ready for Korea. Her husband, Mike, stood in the doorway to assure a bird's eye view as we repeatedly ripped off our clothes and struggled in our G-strings and fishnet tights to dress ourselves again. When we had finished, he gave a sharp cough, I suppose it was to get our attention, but we were well aware that he was there!

"Right girls, you need to follow me back to our flat, as you have got contracts to sign. You can also have a look at the photos I took from the photoshoot a few days ago. I need to fax some of them to the Korean agent."

This all sounded very amiable to me, yet at the back of my mind, I could not abate the lingering feelings of doubt which I harboured when it came to signing the contract. The silent voice of reasoning inside me seemed to vociferate daily, silently niggling away at me as I became more and more enmeshed in the intricacies involved in the proceedings until I reached a stage where I was so entrenched, I felt that I could no longer back out.

Back at the flat, once the signing of the contracts was completed, Mike informed us that, for some reason, the photos he was obliged to fax straightaway to the Korean agent, were arriving blurred and fuzzy at the other end.

"Never mind," he said. "I'm going to send fliers with pictures of Sharon's original dance group on them instead. It won't make any difference."

This struck me as a bit odd and rather deceptive, but I did not voice my opinion. The deed was done. I had signed the paperwork, so all I could do was let fate take its course.

Chapter 2

MOVING TO KYONGJU

The next day, March 28th, we began our 24-hour journey to South Korea. We set off all bright, alert and excited and on arrival, we groggily made our way through the airport feeling jetlagged, dishevelled and disorientated. As our sleep-filled eyes looked around, at the multitude of people meeting and greeting each other with tears, laughter or austerity, we spotted two young, Korean men marching purposely towards us.

With no attempt at any sort of introduction, either formal or otherwise, they came to a sudden halt in front of us.

"Dancers, you come!" they said, in a brusque, authoritarian manner with no hint of a smile.

They seemed to speak no other English than the phrase they had just uttered, and we certainly did not speak Korean so through a process of exaggerated gesturing and waggling of paperwork under our noses which we could not read, we followed them to the exit, struggling to keep up and carry our huge amount of luggage.

As the doors opened, the thickness of the air that hit us momentarily impelled us to stop. Oppressive and oven-like, we gulped in the heady oxygen, pungent with a fusion of aromas, a bittersweet blending of flora, car fumes, food and sweat.

The two men strode ahead, oblivious to our predicament, as we traversed the car-park in silence. We concentrated on following the two dictatorial Koreans who made no attempt to help us as we dragged all our personal belongings, plus a huge suitcase and a smaller one containing all the costumes, towards a waiting van.

As the men stood watching us, we began throwing our luggage inside and were just about to climb in behind it when a third Korean arrived with another group of three Australian girls. We surmised their nationality from the passports they still clutched in their hands. The trio refrained from speaking and merely eyed us up and down with expressions of contempt mixed with curiosity.

The Koreans exchanged words, more papers were waggled and checked, then all of a sudden, everything changed. Our luggage was unceremoniously dumped in the car park and we were shooed away like a pack of mangy dogs.

The Australian trio, who continued to ignore us, let out various supercilious sighs at the inconvenience as we shuffled aside, allowing them to sulkily take our places inside the van.

"Tteonana," the three men said, barely glancing in our direction.

"What?" we answered in unison.

"Tteonana, tteonana!" (Go away!) The men repeated incessantly, whilst shooing us away with their hands and flapping the paperwork.

"Huh! It appears that we are not the trio they thought we were," Louise said. "I think we were about to leave with the wrong guys."

"Bloody hell!" was the only interjection I could muster. "I wonder where we would have ended up if we had left with them?"

"Don't go there!" Louise replied. "I don't even want to think about it!"

Dejected, we retraced our steps, dragging our entire collection of luggage back towards airport arrivals where, on our return to the airport lounge, it became more than apparent that nobody was waiting to meet us.

We sat about for over an hour, talking intermittently and biting our nails with nervousness until it finally dawned on Sharon that she had been given the Korean agent's telephone number. After managing to change some money into Korean Won, she scuttled off to find a phone.

"The agent is running late," she told us, returning with a smile. "But, don't worry, he's on his way!"

"Talk about state the bleeding obvious!" Louise muttered under her breath.

"This isn't a good sign," I said, my nerves getting the better of me.

"Yeah, he's not exactly making a good first impression, is he?" Louise replied.

We sat for almost two hours before a little, squat, rotund minion of a guy waddled into the airport. Sporting a dark brown suit and glasses, and sweating profusely, he spotted us huddled together and beckoned us towards him.

"I'm late, I'm late!"

"For a very important date," Louise sang quietly as we gathered all our belongings once again and dragged them in his direction.

When we came to a stop in front of him, we jumped in surprise, as he abruptly shot his right arm forward, holding it aloft. For a brief second, I thought that he had mistaken us for Germans and was about to give us a German salute, but his arm bent inwards at the elbow towards his face so that his wrist stopped directly in front of his right eye. We realised that he was checking his watch. (We would later learn that he had almost lost his eye in a fight when his assailant had stabbed him with a pencil!)

Patting his cheeks and rubbing his brow with a grubby looking handkerchief, he introduced himself as Mr Lee – a surname which we were to discover was one of the three most common in Korea and used by more than half of the population, (Park, Lee and Kim). He ushered us outside, towards what was locally known as a 'Bongo van': a similar vehicle to the one from which we had previously been ejected.

"Come, I will tell you the plan," he said as we struggled again to load the luggage without any help.

We were to be taken to a hotel in the centre of Seoul in the province of Chong-y-Chong, where we would be allowed to stay for a couple of days to recover from our jetlag. Later, we would be driven to the province of Kyong-ju (also known as Gyeongju) to work in a hotel there.

As we left the airport and joined the motorway, I felt excited yet decidedly nervous and more than a little vulnerable, but I tried to banish any misapprehensions and enjoy my first impressions of Korea. These turned out to be a mixture of surprise and disappointment. In my naivety, I had assumed that the only buildings I would be likely to see would be traditional Asian pagodas, not the huge, cosmopolitan metropolis with high rise buildings, wide, snaking motorways and towering skyscrapers which met my eyes. I scanned the landscape for a traditional building but by the time we reached the hotel, I had not seen a single one.

Roughly forty-five minutes later, the Bongo van pulled up outside the Hotel 'Central', which was a large, rundown, decrepit looking building, smack bang in the middle of a busy town centre. The hotel seemed eclipsed by the myriad of elevated expressways, an elaborate swirling mix of six lanes of traffic leading off in all directions around it. The incessant flow of vehicles seemed never-ending. Every few seconds, impatient drivers were honking on their horns, constantly battling to change lanes, in a vain attempt to arrive at their destinations a little quicker.

We followed Mr Lee to the reception, dragging all our belongings with us once more. Then we waited while he negotiated with the reception staff and finally booked us a room. We were taken to the fifth floor and shown a small, basic room, which once we had deposited all our belongings inside, left us little floor space to move around.

Sharon and Louise took first pickings of the beds and I took the remaining one. It was hardly the Ritz, but we were so tired at that point, we did not care. Mr Lee said his goodbyes and half an hour later, we were dead to the world, sleeping off the jetlag.

When we regained consciousness, we found that we had slept for almost sixteen hours and were momentarily unaware if it were night or day. It turned out to be mid-afternoon so being excited and anxious to explore the city; we headed outside to experience life in the Far East.

After becoming accustomed to the air-conditioned hotel, stepping outside in the heat was, once again, overwhelming! Within seconds, we were covered in a thin sheen of sweat and dust. The streets were satiated with a frenetic cacophony of sounds from shouting and music to sizzling food, motorbike engines, honking horns and the tinkling of bicycle bells.

Every available space seemed littered with people, all pushing and shoving their way forward, virtually oblivious to everyone else - everyone except us, it seemed. Men, women and children came to a complete standstill and stared at us, mouths agape as we walked by. Some stopped to openly gawp; the women pointing and laughing behind their hands; the men guffawing and shaking their heads in complete incredibility.

Our physical appearance and attire of jeans and t-shirts seemed to be highly amusing to them. (However, I should point out at this point that Louise was wearing a pair of jeans with the knees ripped out as was the fashion in the UK at the time. And it was she who seemed to get the brunt of the ridicule!) Louise's Levi's seemed to cause no end of mirth for the cackling Koreans. After ten minutes of constant ridicule, she lost her cool.

"What IS your problem?" she shouted into the fore, stamping her foot and clenching her fists in frustration.

Unfortunately, this outburst only enticed the Koreans to laugh even louder.

We walked on, trying to ignore the sniggering and pointing, but we soon learnt that stepping out on Korean streets was not as straight forward as one would imagine. The few pavements in existence were almost impossible to traverse, as cars were parked with haphazard abandon across them. People tended to sidle around them, reminding me, to some extent, of a colony of ants. They moved ceaselessly, striving forwards with a hidden goal of which no one else was aware.

Motorcycles were also being driven on the sidewalks, by nonchalant riders who weaved in and out of the hoards of pedestrians. The entire scene appeared chaotic. It almost seemed safer to walk in the road among the six lanes of traffic! There were also bicycles everywhere, leaning against shop windows or up against trees, yet, to my surprise, none of them seemed to be padlocked to prevent theft, unlike at home.

On almost every street corner there were little pushcarts, where elderly weather-beaten women were selling their wares. These ranged from fruit and nuts to baked potatoes, and what would become a favourite of mine, an 'eggy bread sandwich. A slice of bread and a few very finely chopped pieces of cabbage and carrot were dipped in a beaten egg, then the whole thing was thrown onto a hot plate. Once it was cooked, it was rolled up like a Swiss-roll and deposited into a grease-proof cone. It was simple, tasty and cheap (300

Korean won, or around 25p). I would end up live off them for the next few months.

There was also a candy-floss stand, but we purposely avoided the old man selling it, purely in the interest of hygiene! The sleeves of his jacket were so encrusted with the remains of years of old sugary brown residue, we had to assume that health and safety inspections most likely didn't exist here.

Along the sides of the road there appeared to be several workmen's tents. At first, we thought there must be innumerable road works taking place in Seoul, but on closer inspection, these turned out to be little bars selling beer and snacks.

Although I was enamoured at being in the Far East and was drinking in the surroundings with eager eyes, absorbing the language and getting my first tastes of Korean culture, a sinking feeling hit me like a freight train as I contemplated my plight. I looked straight ahead. All I could see, as I was elbowed in the ribs and jostled from left to right, was a sea of black hair. I equated myself to wading through black treacle and slowly drowning! I felt so alienated from these people and so unprepared for what I was about to undertake. It was an overpowering, oppressive emotion.

What am I doing here? What have I done? I inwardly screamed.

After a couple of hours of wandering around, in which being laughed at had progressed to being poked and prodded in various parts of our anatomies, we had all had enough and returned to the sanctuary of the Central Hotel.

Several minutes after our arrival, we received a telephone call from Mr Lee.

"Plan change," he informed Sharon. "Tomorrow you all go Kyonju province."

* * *

Our driver arrived the following morning and kindly helped us transfer our entire luggage collection into the Bongo van before we started the four-hour journey. Once again I perused the area for a traditional pagoda, but I was unsuccessful and I felt strangely disappointed.

On arrival at the Hotel Kyongju-Chosun, we were more than a little impressed and delighted to see an extensive eight-storey construction with panoramic views overlooking Lake Pomunho.

Mr Lee booked us into the hotel, and we dragged all our belongings unaided to the lift and along a corridor, following three able-bodied men who did not attempt to help us. They showed us to our room, where Louise and Sharon squabbled over the beds again, and I took the remaining one. I dumped my bags on the floor and pulled back the curtains expecting to see the beautiful lake, only to find that our view was the car-park! There were several lush, green mountains in the background though, so it was not all bad.

We were told to settle in - or at least that is what we assumed they were saying. In fact, the only part we understood in its entirety was when one of them pointed an index finger in our direction and spoke one sentence in English.

"Tonight, you work. Show start 'ereben´ o'clock."

That evening after arriving at the venue, being shown the stage and the location of the dressing-room, the daunting task of what we were about to do finally dawned on us. It was all very well doing a dress rehearsal in London, where running to the corners of the dance studio to change costumes took all of four steps. Here, we would be expected to leave the stage, run down a corridor and into a dressing-room, before we could even think about changing!

Half an hour later, we stood at the side of the stage, waiting to perform our 'debut´ in the Hotel's nightclub. The disco music came to an abrupt end, the lights dimmed, and the room took on an ominous stillness as the clientele waited in silence. A Disc jockey cleared his throat audibly over the microphone and announced us:

"... The In-ger-land dancing team... Col- ree-arse -Tree Show", he babbled into the microphone and before I knew it, we were walking onto the stage.

Our opening routine was a bikini and feathers number so we took up our starting positions with our backs to the audience. On cue to the music, each girl turned and lifted her arms to a high 'V' over her head. As the first chords of music bellowed through the loudspeakers, Louise turned first and there was an audible gasp. The Koreans clapped in appreciation of her impressive cleavage which threatened to burst out of the bikini top. Sharon turned next and received similar appreciation. Then I turned... There seemed to be a slight pause while everyone registered that I had less up top than even the Korean girls had, then everyone burst into laughter! It seemed to go downhill from there!

The only positive aspect of that first performance in Korea was that, despite our apprehension, running on pure adrenalin, the three of us managed to accomplish all the costume changes, although I honestly do not know how!

As the night wore on, the all-male audience became increasingly more inebriated and much more daring. By the time we performed the second show around midnight, the stage resembled a battle-ground. We were dancing under constant fear of being attacked.

Several younger members jumped up and down in front of the high fronted stage in a frenzied need to try to touch us. Whenever we got too close, they grabbed at anything, in a desperate attempt to pull us down to their level. The thought of being dragged into the drunken mob was, to be honest, extremely frightening. Their alcohol fused brains meant that nothing was out of bounds.

After the two shows had finished, when we assumed we would be able to calm down and relieve our built-up tension, we found ourselves standing behind the dressing-room door, pushing with a hidden strength than none of us previously knew we possessed, in an attempt to prevent any member of the male-only audience from getting inside the room.

The corridor teemed with innumerable drunken contenders whose main priority seemed to be to gain entrance to the dressing-room. We dreaded to think what they would do if they got inside!

As the combined weight of several men pushed yet again on one side of our only means of exit, and we shoved with all our might on the other, telling them in no uncertain terms to go away, we became aware that amidst all this confusion, someone was formally knocking on the door! We looked at each other in surprise.

"Girls, girls. Please, open door! I am Yoyo. I have manager here."

We did not have the slightest inkling as to whom Yoyo was, but we stood aside as the door crashed open into the wall and a slightly dishevelled, highly enraged manager fought his way through the drunken bevvy of his clientele. As bouncers held back our marauding fans, he entered clutching a fistful of Sharon's scrunched up fliers featuring her original group. His disgruntled expression as he looked us all up and down did nothing to calm our nerves. He traversed the dressing-room, marching from left to right, waving the fliers under our noses, sniffing and snorting like a trapped bull. A barrage of Korean shot from his mouth before he threw the fliers with dramatic abandon onto the floor.

"Err, solly. This is Mr Lee," Yoyo, who turned out to be the DJ, explained as the manager continued snorting. "He is manager. He not happy. You not girls in photo."

The three of us froze. We stood there like novices under their first spotlight, feeling more than a little stunned. After a long pause, when we were all lost for words, Sharon slowly bent down to retrieve a flier and turning on her charm, she pointed to herself in the photo.

"Well. . . this is me," she said, flashing her most seductive smile. "And. . . that's them," she added, with rather less invincibility as she waved a loose hand across the flier and over in our direction. Louise and I stood together and flashed the manager a weak smile. It was blatantly obvious that we were not the same girls in the photo, and the manager was not buying it. He snorted, hurled us with a barrage of fast-fire Korean, then coughing up a wodge of phlegm, he spat it out onto the floor and fought his way outside between his bouncers and the throng of dipsomaniacs.

"Solly, solly, don't worry!" Yoyo whispered, followed in his wake. Giving us an apologetic bow, he scurried away as we focused on the slimy glob of mucus deposited at our feet.

"Charming!" Louise commented.

* * *

After work, the following evening, where we once again spent the first fifteen minutes after the show leaning against the dressing room door, Mr Sol, the hotel owner, entered in much the same dishevelled predicament as the manager had done the night before. He told us to get changed, as he was taking us out to eat. (Or we gleaned as much from his miming gestures). Little did we know what he had in store for the three of us.

Mr Sol had decided to introduce us all to the Korean equivalent of a Japanese Geisha establishment. As sliding doors opened out into a large room resembling a restaurant, we were obliged to remove our shoes before we stepped inside. Taking in our surroundings, we surveyed the scene. Men sat around low tables on thin, multi-coloured cushions, drinking and eating as Geishas wandered from table to table or sat with the clientele. Traditional, tinny music echoed through the loudspeakers and a female singer's shrill voice reverberated around the room.

With a smile, Mr Sol edged us along to a second set of sliding doors which led into a private room. This also housed a low table in the centre and an assortment of cushions liberally thrown around it.

"I don't know about you two, but I think this is a whore house!" - Louise said, expressing what I had been thinking.

"Deep joy!" said Sharon - (an expression which stuck´ and we used incessantly during the next six months.)

As we took our places, two more men entered who appeared to be friends of Mr Sol. Bringing up the rear were three Korean 'Geishas' with white painted faces and wearing traditional, Korean costumes. They entered bowing and smiling. After introductions were made, the Geishas took their places between each man and then began to serve us all.

For Mr Sol and his friends, the main requirement was whiskey. As shot glasses were dealt to each person, and I realised that whiskey appeared to be the only beverage, I screwed up my face.

"I don't like whiskey. I can't drink that!"

"Just pretend to drink it," Louise said. "Otherwise, we'll be drunk in no time!" Despite her caution, she chose not to heed her own advice. Putting a glass of the amber liquid to her lips, she took a swig. "Actually, that's pretty good stuff!"

One of the Geishas, Miss Han, spoke some English and had understood our conversation.

"This is the most expensive whiskey we sell. Each bottle costs $170 and is one hundred per cent proof."

"What!" We cried in unison.

"Don't worry," she assured us. I will have some Coca-Cola brought in and you can pour the whiskey into that."

As the hours passed, and the whiskey continued to flow, Mr Sol, his male colleagues, and the Geishas became increasingly more inebriated. Miss Han explained that it was considered the height of bad manners for Korean Geishas to refuse whiskey from a man, and there was a process, or custom, to go through, in order not to offend the male of the species. After a Geisha is asked to drink with the man, she must:

1. Hold out her shot glass in her right hand.

2. Her left hand must be held out straight, palm facing inwards, with her fingers touching the side of the glass.

3. The man pours the whiskey.

4. The Geisha drinks it down in one.

5. The Geisha passes the glass to the man.

6. The man holds the glass up in his right hand.

7. The Geisha fills the glass.

8. The man drinks it down in one.

Despite being the foreigners, we were still expected to drink the whiskey when offered it, but we soon realised that if we pulled faces to express how strong the alcohol was, the men would laugh, lose interest and leave us to drink it in our own time, giving us a slight reprieve.

As the night progressed and the men became inebriated, I managed to pour most of my whiskey discreetly into a big, almost empty glass of coke under the table, but as the hours ticked away, I was forced to keep sampling it, as I was thirsty and there was nothing else available.

Around three o'clock in the morning, when we were all anything but sober, the sliding partition doors opened and an abundance of food began to arrive. There were nuts and fruit, noodles, rice, a type of fish served with peas in a batter and a Korean-style pizza which consisted of egg, vegetables and fish. Everything was eaten with chopsticks – including the pizza! The Geishas fed the men. We fed ourselves, hoping to be able to soak up some of the excess alcohol we had all consumed.

Throughout the night, more and more vitals arrived which the Geishas continued to feed to their men whilst intermittently removing their client's shirts to massage their backs. This seemed such an intimate action that it made me feel more than a little uncomfortable. I perceived myself to be intruding.

At some point during the night, the sliding doors opened again and in came a guitarist to play for us. Later each Geisha did her party piece. One sang; one played a Korean musical instrument called a kayagum (gayageum), a twelve stringed instrument similar to a zither, whilst the third danced.

When we were told to take the floor, we did, literally! We decided to try out some break-dancing moves and were soon swivelling about on our backs like disorientated crabs.

Mr Sol, who by this point in the proceedings was finding it difficult to even stand up, decided that he wanted to dance with me. Not wanting to offend, I complied, but I was hardly sober myself and trying to hold him up became impossible. Consequently, we collapsed in a heap on the floor and everyone ended up having a cushion fight.

I have no recollection whatsoever as to how we all got back to the hotel that night, but I do remember Mr Sol escorting us down the corridor with a staggering gait and telling us that he practised Martial arts. All of a sudden he jumped up in the air and kicked a light fitting on the ceiling which smashed to the ground with a resounding crash. We were all shocked and expressed great stupefied admiration for his antic.

"Wow, Mr Sol! Very good!" We exclaimed, bursting into rounds of applause, which boosted his drunken ego no end. In retrospect, our enthusiasm was probably too encouraging, as he then proceeded to smash a second light fitting, then a third, further down the hall. How he was able to achieve that when he could just about stand up is still beyond my comprehension!

Chapter 3

A PICNIC, A PERVERT AND A PAGODA

A couple of days later, on the 4th April, Mr Sol banged on our door at ten o'clock in the morning, dragged us out of a fitful slumber and told us to go down to reception.

As we had not gone to bed until 4:45 am, we were not particularly pleased to be loaded into a Bongo van and driven to an unknown location. The vehicle came to an abrupt stop at the edge of a forest, where Mr Sol told us to get out. We begrudgingly trampled after him, three; disgruntled souls following this man into the depths of woodland without the slightest idea of where we were going, or why.

"Where the hell is he taking us?" I whispered.

"God only knows!" Sharon sighed.

"It's a good job he's so jovial," Louise said. "If not, I guess it would be safe to assume that we are being taken into the woods to be shot and left to die. Our crime being that we were not the original girls on the fliers!"

The three of us burst into laughter, not just at Louise's comment but also at the ridiculous situation in which we had found ourselves. Although, Louise voicing what we had all been thinking, left us all feeling uneasy and tinged with incertitude. Nevertheless, we blindly followed Mr Sol until the trees thinned out, and we found ourselves in the middle of a woodland clearing.

We were pleasantly surprised - and more than a little relieved - to find that all the band members and bouncers from the club were in the clearing too. Everyone was lounging around with nonchalant abandon, stretched out in recumbent positions on the grass or sitting on rocks which bordered a little stream.

We took in the stunning scenery, chastising ourselves for not bringing a camera. Behind the stream, a mountain range stretched before us, and the majestic height of the tall trees behind us created a scenic landscape to which a painter's palette probably could not do justice. It was a beautiful sunny day; the sound of the stream and the birds singing in the trees were a welcomed surprise and helped us to relax almost immediately.

"Well, this was definitely worth getting up early for," I voiced. The girls nodded in agreement.

The hotel staff had made little fires with twigs, using firelighters and some sort of rolled up coloured paper as kindling. Over this, they had placed wire meshing with pieces of tin foil on top. Beside each little fire was a plastic bag that contained thin slices of beef, which they were cooking on the makeshift barbeques. There was also an assortment of vegetables (mainly lettuce, spring onions and garlic) which were washed in the stream and then cooked. Refreshments in the form of cans of beer and lemonade stood in crates, cooling in the river.

It was a great experience. As we 'chatted' with the others and learnt a few Korean words, I began to feel that we had been accepted as part of their team. I sensed that we had begun to bond, not only with the Koreans but also with each other. Furthermore, it was evident that only living and working in the country would warrant experiences like this. I felt extremely privileged to be a part of it.

As the day wore on, and the makeshift barbeques wore down, I had to laugh when I realised that the source of kindling being used to boost up the fires was none other than Sharon's fliers! She was far from being impressed. Louise and I, on the other hand, found it highly amusing – and strangely cleansing!

As the sun began its descent behind the mountains, the afternoon drew all too soon to a close, and everyone began to put out the fires and tidy up. It was at that juncture that I had a profound sinking feeling in my stomach. The realisation that we were due to go back to work was a daunting thought, one which filled me with dread.

* * *

Our late-night show schedule meant that we did not finish working until the early hours of the morning and then. More often than not, we would go out to eat. This meant that we didn't go to bed until around 4:30 am. Therefore, being woken up for the second, consecutive day, at eight o'clock in the morning by the ringing telephone, meant that we were not particularly impressed! Sharon picked up the receiver and yawned.

"Hello?"

"Hi, I'm Jeffrey, I work for the United States Army. I saw your show last night and I'd love to meet y'all. Would you like to go out for coffee?"

As we had been in Korea for ten days, had not seen our agent since he deposited us in Kyongju, and we still had not been paid, the thought of anything for free was not to be turned down. We were not slow in accepting the invitation and arranged to meet him in reception in half an hour.

Unfortunately, Jeffrey wasn't a man used to being kept waiting, so twenty minutes later as we fought for the bathroom and hurried to get dressed, he knocked on the door. Sharon opened it and was so shocked to see a huge, overweight, six-foot-tall, African American standing there, she spoke without first putting her brain into gear.

"Oh my God! It's a big fat fucker!" She exclaimed.

Louise and I stopped, like startled rabbits under headlights, unsure how to continue. As we stood there, cringing inwardly, wishing we could turn back time, Louise was the first to regain composure. She strode towards the door with her hand outstretched.

"Hi," she said, shaking hands with the big fat fucker. "I'm Louise, this is Michele, and this is Sharon."

"Hello," I grinned.

"Hello," Sharon mumbled, eyes downcast, as she tried wit desperation to hide behind the door.

Fortunately, Jeffrey chose to ignore Sharon's first expletive, and as our invitation to coffee was still being offered, we followed him to the cafeteria. This progressed to him inviting us all to spend the day at his apartment in Taegu province. Again, we accepted, secretly hoping that we may be fed for free too!

During the car journey to Taegu, we established that Jeffrey was a high ranking Army official who lived in an apartment off base – or so he said. He had his own driver, another tall, six-foot-two GI called Nuller, whose muscled physique also made him someone not to mess with. There was something about Jeffrey that filled me with a sense of foreboding, but despite my apprehension, I figured there was safety in numbers. And I had to admit that it was a pleasant variance to be able to talk to someone other than ourselves in English for a while.

On arrival at his apartment as Jeffrey opened the door, the first thing our eyes were drawn to was a huge four-poster bed in the centre of his bedroom and as time passed, we realised that Army official or not, Jeffrey was a man totally obsessed with sex.

"Here, have a look at these!" he said, giving us a blue coloured folder as we sat nervously on the sofas in the living room. "A blue folder for my blue movies," he purred. "Pick one, which one do you want to watch?"

The three of us cast frantic glances at each other.

"We're not really in the mood to watch TV today," Louise replied.

Sharon and I nodded in frenzied agreement.

"But, I recorded them all myself!" he proclaimed proudly.

"This is a very nice apartment, Jeffrey," I said, hoping to change the subject.

"Yes, it is, isn't it?" He replied. "Here, have a look at this." He beckoned me over to a shelf where a figurine was poised in a sexual position.

"Oh, yes, interesting," I said, not sure how he was expecting me to react.

"Look Louise, darling," Jeffrey crooned. "Here's another one."

"Yep, there sure is."

There seemed to be a number of ornaments dotted around the apartment in a variety of sexual poses. Another, which looked innocently like a man's head, on closer inspection was composed of men and women in various sexual positions.

As the hours dragged by, it became more than evident that Jeffrey had a strong crush on Louise. His remarks and sexual innuendos became more and more obvious, and Louise became more and more uncomfortable – as did Sharon and I. We could not help but wonder how we were going to successfully get out of this situation.

"I have a yacht. Would you like to be the captain of my yacht, Louise?" he crooned, sidling towards her. "I could take you out sailing one day. You would make the perfect captain."

"I've never really been into sailing," Louise replied nonchalantly.

"Shame, I've always liked my women with a bit of meat on their bones," Jeffrey grinned, edging closer. "I like something to grab on to. Then I can shout: 'hold on baby I'm coming! '"

Nice," said Louise, trying her best to keep the breakfast bar between the two of them.

Nuller, the driver - who for the most part had stayed in the background and had not really spoken - informed us that he had to go back to base. This prompted Jeffrey to invite us to write a list of provisions.

"Put down whatever you gals need, and I'll go back with Nuller and get it from the PX," he said.

After establishing that PX, short for the 'Post Exchange´ meant the 'Commissary´, or army base 'Store´, he pushed a pen and paper into my hand and told me to start writing.

This seemed like a good idea to the three of us, as we could kill two birds with one stone. Primarily, we would have a reprieve from Jeffrey and his lecherous advances and furthermore, he could help us solve a couple of problems that we had had since our arrival in Korea. Firstly, the matter of deodorant; it did not seem to exist here, and we were seriously running out. Secondly, the only sanitary products we had been able to find were a form of Korean tampon which would not have stopped a nosebleed!

Jeffrey wandered off to talk to Nuller, and as I was given the task of writing the list, the girls watched, nodding with approval as I wrote 'three deodorants´ in big letters at the top of the list. However, when the beginnings of the word 'tampons´ appeared, there was a sharp intake of breath.

"You can't ask for those!" Sharon whispered harshly.

"That's SO embarrassing!" Louise said.

"No, it isn't," I argued. "If you ask me, I think this will be right up Jeffrey's street."

The girls had to agree and after I jotted down a few other necessities, off went Jeffrey with a smile on his face to complete his errand.

As soon as he left, I headed for the bedroom. Ever since I had seen the bed, I had been thinking about my younger sister. She had always dreamed of having a four-poster, and I was determined to get a photo of myself in a recumbent position, among the silk sheets and cushions.

"Quick! Take my picture on here," I said, pushing my camera into Sharon's hand and jumping onto the bed.

Unfortunately, the process of taking a photo turned out to be much more difficult than I had originally imagined. All at once, the bed started undulating, swishing up and down and rocking from side to side.

"Shit! It's a bloody water bed!" I exclaimed.

"Oh my God!" Sharon giggled as I jiggled up and down like a boat at sea.

Louise doubled over with laughter.

"Ha! You look so funny!"

"Stop bloody laughing and help me!" I shouted as all the silk cushions, matching silk sheets and throws in rich reds and pinks began sliding into the centre of the bed or dropping onto the floor as I struggled to remain in one position.

Despite this predicament, the photo was eventually taken, but as I tried to extricate myself from the bed, I spotted something ominous in the corner of the room.

"Bloody Hell!" I said, pointing to a video-camera that Jeffrey had set up on a tripod and had conveniently aimed directly at the bed. I think this is arranged for us!"

"Or for you, Louise," Sharon said.

"Not bloody likely!" Louise sniffed.

Remembering an earlier conversation, I gasped.

"Oh, my God! I bet when he said he'd recorded all the porno films himself, he meant in this room, with that camera!"

"Bloody Hell!" Sharon exclaimed.

As we struggled to put the bed into some semblance of its original order, we devised a plan as to what to say to our host on his return, in order to make a quick exit. Feigning forgotten rehearsals and a meeting with our agent, we managed to escape unscathed, with three new deodorants and enough sanitary products to last for a couple of months!

* * *

We had been in Korea for twelve days before I saw my first pagoda. The ever so obliging Mr Sol invited us out again for the day. As usual, we had no idea where we were actually going, but as we read the signpost for the Pulgaska Temples written in English, all became clear. We pulled into the car-park and there it was: my first pagoda!

"Finally," I grinned, reaching for my camera. "Let's get out of the Bongo van and take some photos."

Mr Sol did the honours, taking several photos with each camera, whilst simultaneously laughing to himself.

"Semyŏnso, ha ha ha!" He kept repeating as he clicked the cameras. "Semyŏnso."

The three of us were puzzled. We could not understand why he found it all so amusing. Shrugging it off as an idiosyncrasy, we carried on posing. When the impromptu photo session came to an end, Sharon immediately crossed her legs and started jumping up and down.

"I need the loo!"

"Me too," Louise replied.

Still jiggling up and down, Sharon looked at Mr Sol. "Toilet?"

Mr Sol guffawed even more and pointed to the pagoda.

"Semyŏnso... Toiret," he said chucking to himself and shaking his head from side to side.

"Great!" I replied. "We've just taken a hundred photographs of a loo!"

Despite this unpropitious beginning, we had a pleasant day out. We were fortunate to visit the temples when we did. The cherry trees were in full bloom, resplendent with perfumed pink and white blossoms which permeated the air and smelt divine. The combinations of temples and cherry blossoms made everything appear so quaint and much more picturesque.

We wandered around the ancient site, not really appreciating or understanding the wealth of information and historical significance the sacred place held for the Koreans. We visited various temples, to see statues of Buddha. He was either sitting or standing and varied in size and material, from enormous figures in granite to small images in gold or bronze. We viewed artefacts which dated back to AD 7 and stopped to pay homage before tombs of Great, Korean Kings who were buried inside small mounds resembling little hills. I later discovered that Great, Korean military leaders were also buried there, but at the time, all of this was lost to us, due to the extremely limited Korean language we possessed at that time.

Later that day, Mr Sol drove us to Pomunho Lake which was part of a Tourist Complex. There, we discovered that our hotel nestled in the middle of this successful conglomerate. We went sailing in little boats in the form of swans, had a drink in the cafe and generally wandered around.

As we were leaving, we stopped at a little souvenir shop, and I managed to buy a book about the temples, which was written in English. Later, I read it from cover to cover and I was so glad I did. Mr Sol was obviously proud of his ancestry and felt it was important for us to see such an ancient place. The oldest temple was constructed in AD751 at the foot of the T'ohamsan Mountain. On its completion, more than eighty buildings had been constructed around it. The site became one of the biggest Buddhist temple complexes in East Asia. More recently, due to the number of artefacts and ruins which have been found there, it has been given the nickname of 'The Athens of East Asia´.

We expressed our thanks to Mr Sol for a lovely day out and headed back towards the Bongo van. The only negative aspect for me was, again, the thought of returning to work.

Chapter 4

MAFIA, MOTORBIKES AND MILITARY LEADERS

April 5th, 1989.

After only one week in Korea, doing the shows at the end of each day was something which I now dreaded. I loved to dance, but in Korea, from my limited experience, I deduced that dancers seemed to be little thought of and certainly neither appreciated nor respected.

In the nightclub, the audiences had become so unruly that we needed bouncers constantly positioned at either side of the high stage to remove unwanted customers while we trod the boards. The inebriated men continued to gather around the front of the stage, rather like fans at a pop concert venue and asking friends to hoist them up so that they could clamber onto the stage in an attempt to touch us had also become a common occurrence. When they were caught by the bouncers, they would be unceremoniously flung back into the marauding mass of male drunkenness which constituted our audience below us. These scorned rejects, angered and humiliated, would seek their revenge by throwing paper projectiles or orange peel at us and onto the stage.

One evening, when I stupidly got too close to the edge, a young guy jumped up and tried to set my costume on fire with his lighter.

Every quick costume change resulted in finding two or three Korean men sitting in the dressing-room, waiting to watch us get undressed. We would order them to leave, but they never complied, and we just did not have time between the changes to physically attempt to manhandle them out. I often wondered if one of the bouncers had struck a deal with certain clientele. I believe, he was charging a fee for guys to sit there and observe a peep show in which we involuntarily played the leading role.

After the shows, more often than not, we would have to stand with our shoulders to the dressing room door as we had done on our first performance, in an attempt to keep other groups of men from gaining entrance. It was hardly what I would call an ideal venue, or what any of us thought we had signed up for.

When it was safe to leave the dressing-room, we invariable went out to get something to eat. This usually meant that, more often than not, we were accosted on the street or at the very least stared and laughed at before we reached our chosen destination. After a while, we became oblivious to the staring but constantly being poked, prodded or grabbed was not so easy to ignore.

Each time we entered a bar or café, we became accustomed to being presented with either a glass of water - which we were dubious to drink as we had no idea as to its origin, or Ginseng tea, which resembled dirty water, and we were also dubious about drinking! This was usually accompanied by either a small basket of popcorn or crisps. If we were fortunate, we might be able to eat our meal without interruption but more often than not, that wasn't the case.

One evening, as we were leaving a café, we were approached by three middle-aged men who were holding out a stack of Korean money, jiggling from one foot to another and giggling like adolescent schoolboys. It soon became apparent that they assumed we were prostitutes and wanted to know how much we charged! We were momentarily stunned, deeply shocked and offended. I made a grab for the money, as I intended to throw it back in their faces but, unfortunately for me, they assumed I was accepting the monetary offer and were ecstatic! They laughed even louder and patted each other on the back, in expectation of their proposed deal. Louise declined their offer on my behalf and steered me away from the situation.

Another evening, after a rough night's work, Louise and I were sitting eating our meal, minding our own business when a young Korean asked us in perfect English if he could join us. Not wanting to be disturbed, Louise immediately adopted a thick Scottish accent.

"Och, ya ken but I dunna think ya should. Yall nee understand me."

Unfortunately for Louise, the young man said that he could and proceeded to sit down. Anything he didn't understand, he just asked me to 'translate'. Poor Louise had to keep up her Scottish twang for an hour and a half before we could finally get away! I thought it was hilarious. Louise, on the other hand, did not.

That same evening, as we set off back to the hotel, a young, Korean man ran up behind me and grabbed hold of my ponytail, yanking my head so far back that my head was almost touching my knees. I screamed and shouted but he refused to let go, even when I managed to swivel myself around and took a tantrum. I continued shouting and then swung my arms, punching him, stamping my feet, and pulling his hair but he *still* held on. This time it was Louise's turn to find it highly amusing, whereas I, did not. I guessed that this was karma's way of paying me back for laughing at Louise in the restaurant.

On arrival at the hotel, we met up with Sharon, who had taken a liking to one of the Korean DJ's, Park Hyun (their surnames are always pronounced before their given name). She had been out on a date with him and had just arrived back at the hotel.

"Goodbye, goodbye, I love you," he said, blowing her a kiss as Louise and I looked at each other and cast our eyes heavenwards. We all turned to go into the hotel, but Sharon's date seemed reluctant to leave. He lingered conspicuously in the entrance to the hotel, walking up and down with a nonchalant gait, his hands thrust deep into his pockets.

"Do you think he wants me to invite him in?" Sharon whispered.

Louise shrugged. "Probably."

I hope not! I thought.

Park Hyun sensed Sharon's uncertainty and turned to her.

"Go, go," he said, smiling whilst shooing her away with one hand and blowing a kiss with the other. As we followed his orders and were heading for the doors, we heard a small car drawing up. We turned as one, to see Park Hyun clambering inside and sitting between two giggling Korean girls, while a third drove and a fourth sat in the passenger seat. As the vehicle pulled away, Park Hyun saw Sharon's vexed expression and leaned across one girl to roll down the window.

"Sharon, it's business, just business," he shouted. "Don't let me be misunderstood."

Louise and I exchanged knowing glances while Sharon looked on in consternation, watching the little car as it drove off into the night.

* * *

We had been asleep for about an hour when we were awoken by a loud banging on the door. Instinctively clambering out of bed, wondering who on earth would be knocking on the door in the early hours of the morning, we looked at each other in alarm. Sharon reached the door first and peered through the spy-hole.

"It's Yoyo and another little man," she whispered.

"Move out of the way," Louise ordered. She also looked through the spy-hole then putting the chain on and drawing herself up to her full height, she slowly opened the door.

"Yesss...?"

Standing in front of us, was a little, rounded Korean, covered in gold rings and chains, wearing an expensive suit, and smoking a cigar. Despite his diminutive stature, he held a certain air of authority about him; an arrogance that implied he was used to getting his own way and that now would be no exception. Next to him, stood Yoyo who was looking decidedly sheepish.

"Hello, this Mr Kyong, he very important man in Seoul," Yoyo explained.

"Oh Yes...?" said Louise with dubious suspicion as Sharon and I crowded in behind her looking over both her shoulders.

"Er... he want to speak with all of you," Yoyo continued, avoiding eye contact, wringing his hands and looking extremely uncomfortable.

"It's four o'clock in the morning!" Louise replied. "Tell him to come back tomorrow – during the day!"

"No, you don't understand." Yoyo's face was the picture of discomfort. "He watched your show and now he wants to sleep with one of you."

"Well, that's not going to happen, so goodnight." Louise started to close the door but Yoyo grabbed it, holding on with both hands as though it were a lifeline.

"Listen, you have to do what he say. He is chief of Korean Mafia!"

"No, YOU listen!" Louise barked as Sharon and I looked at each other in alarm. "I couldn't care less if he's the bloody Queen of Sheba, He's NOT coming in here!"

The door was slammed shut in their faces, and all three of us leant against it; an automatic response, I suppose, from our nights at work in the dressing-room. Apart from our beating hearts, silence fell on both sides of the door for a few moments as we frantically looked at each other in panic, then all hell broke loose.

We took turns to peep through the spy-hole, to watch this irate little Korea who was having a major tantrum just because he had not got his own way. He snorted and bellowed, stamped up and down the corridor and then began kicking the door and pounding on it with angry fists. In the meantime, Yoyo bowed over and over again, cowered and mumbled things barely audible, maybe in fear of his life! We just looked at each other in disbelief.

"Quick! Let's put a chair under the door handle," Louise said.

"And, let's move away from the door," I added. "He might have a gun."

"Shit!" exclaimed Sharon. She made an instinctive jump into the adjacent bathroom. "I hadn't thought of that!"

We swiftly positioned the chair and moved away from the door in case of gunshots. Then we waited. After an endless twenty minutes, the shouting and banging on the door abruptly stopped and the duo left. However, it became impossible for us to sleep. Over the next few hours, the miffed Mafia boss phoned our room in fifteen-minute intervals. Louise answered every time and told him to go away... or words to that effect!

Once the phone finally stopped ringing, we were still unable to sleep, for fear of further reprisal. However, fortunately for us, we never saw or heard from him again.

* * *

The following evening between shows, Mr Sol decided that he was going to take us out to eat. This time his restaurant of choice was a strip club, but we were unaware of that at the time. While we tucked into large dishes of exotic fruit, we waited unsuspectingly for the entertainment to begin.

Just to the left of our table was a small round stage which was completely behind glass.

"That's a very tiny stage," I pointed out. "The floor slopes and there's a drain in the middle of it. I wonder what that's for..."

"It looks like a shower but it can't be, can it?" Sharon replied. "Why would there be a shower in the middle of a nightclub?"

In our innocence, we could not understand why there would be a need for such a thing but we were soon to find out.

Three Korean girls walked into the glass-enclosed stage wearing nothing but a thin kimono each and white, platform soled, knee-high boots with five-inch heels. Once inside the glass stage, the music started and they dropped their kimonos. We almost choked on the fruit when we realised that they were completely nude apart from their boots!

Mr Sol grinned and watched our faces expectantly as the three-girl lesbian act began gyrating on top of each other, going through a whole gamut of sexual positions while we continued chomping on our fruit. Mr Sol was highly amused as we tried to feign indifference – much less successfully than the girls feigned their orgasms.

"I feel so uncomfortable for them," I said, with a mouthful of papaya. "It must be awful to have to do this in front of us."

"I agree. I suppose they'll be used to doing it in front of men but somehow, this must seem even more degrading." Louise replied.

"It must be awful having to do it at all!" Sharon remarked. She was, of course totally correct.

As soon as they finished their 'act´ and had left the stage, a shower came on, washing away any residue that may have been left behind. Hence the sloping stage and drain.

There was a smattering of disco music then a minute or two later, the DJ began announcing the next act.

"I honestly can't tell you how I feel at this point," Louise said.

"I know," I replied. "I'm partly intrigued to see what's next but dreading it at the same time!"

"Me too," said Sharon.

We tried to focus all our attention on the remaining tropical fruit, as three men and a young girl walked onto a bigger stage in the centre of the club. Their act consisted of each man lashing a cat-o-nine-tails across the floor, then flicking it out towards the poor girl who was constantly whipped, lassoed and tied up. Her mid-drift was covered in scars from previous performances. Mr Sol and the rest of the audience seemed to enjoy it. For me, it was definitely a better choice than the first act - especially as we were trying to eat!

* * *

After almost two weeks in Korea, I had to admit that the novelty had worn off. As far as I was concerned, it was a male-orientated country, where women were treated as second class citizens. I did not know if this was purely because of the working environment I found myself in but I seriously doubted it.

The men's favourite pastime seemed to be coughing up phlegm! They either hacked it up and spat it out, or snorted it back up their noses. Another trick, which was performed outside, was to bend forwards, press their index finger into one side of their nose and blow until long stringy lines of mucus hung from their nostril. A quick shake would send it flying through the air, a snotty projectile ready to attach itself to anything: walls, the floor or poor unsuspecting passersby.

Work continued to be a constant nightmare. It was not possible to dance for the mere pleasure of dancing. We needed to be alert at all times for a mob type 'invasion´ or a lone 'attack´ on stage.

One particular evening, a young, inebriated man jumped up and sat on the edge of the stage. Sitting with his back to us, he swung his legs backwards and forwards over the edge like a child, making silly faces and hand gestures to the rest of the audience while we performed. As I danced past him, he turned his head, his eyes narrowed in contempt and he spat at me. Without thinking of the consequences, I leaned forward and pushed him off. He immediately sprang back up and ran forwards to attack me. Fortunately, a vigilant bouncer had second-guessed the retaliation attempt. He came running to my rescue and threw the client back into the rapacious crowd.

That same evening, in the same show, Sharon and I found ourselves doing a duet, as Louise didn't make an appearance for the finale. As the music droned on and there was still no sign of her, Sharon lost her patience.

"Where the hell is she?" she complained.

I shrugged. "I hope she isn't being accosted in the dressing-room! The man I pushed off stage looked pretty peeved."

As the music finished and we took a bow, we hurried off stage, mentally preparing ourselves for whatever situation we were about to encounter. We ran down the corridor with half of the audience following at speed at our heels. We threw open the door, and as we assumed our positions behind it, Louise joined us.

"Sorry, girls. My zip broke," she said as we pushed against the buckling door.

"Deep joy!" Sharon replied sarcastically.

* * *

After the show, we went out to eat and at around 2:30 am as we were heading home, one of the guys from the club pulled up on his motorbike. We had christened him 'medallion man´, as he always wore his shirt wide open to show off a gold trinket on a thick gold necklace, which would have put a Lord Mayor's livery chain to shame. We guessed he was proud of his motorbike, as he stopped and ran his hands all over the bodywork chattering away in Korean.

Without thinking of the consequences and being an idiot, I threw my leg over the saddle. Before I knew it, he was zooming off down the road with me hanging on for dear life behind him. I was stupefied!

At the end of the road, he swung the bike around and headed back to the girls. As we screeched to an abrupt halt, I breathed a sigh of relief and gingerly tried to make my escape by extricating myself from the contraption. Unfortunately, he realised what I was trying to do, and he shot off again! I was forced to cling to his jacket in fear of falling off as he sped away at break-neck speed, leaving my startled dancing companions in a state of vexation and panic.

They were not the only ones panicking! As the bike drew us further and further away from civilization and down a myriad of country lanes, to say I was frightened would be an understatement.

"No, no. Hotel, hotel, jeh-bahl." (Hotel, please, I'm begging you!) I shouted, constantly pulling on his jacket but to no avail. It was pointless. Medallion Man jabbered something which I could not understand, his words being whipped away by the wind as he continued driving at an alarming pace.

When he came to a stop in a heavily wooded area, in the middle of nowhere and told me to get off the bike, I was close to tears and berating myself for my own stupidity. He grabbed my elbow in a vice-like grip and marched me into the forest.

You're going to be raped! He's going to kill you! I silently chanted my sombre mantra over and over again as he led me deeper and deeper into the forest.

"No, Hotel!" I repeated continuously, trying to drag my arm from his tight hold but to no avail. He pointed ahead and gestured that I should keep walking. With my heart almost beating out of my chest, I did as I was told and reluctantly followed him into the darkness of the woods.

All at once, he dropped my arm, pointed ahead, gabbled something and set off running in front of me. I froze, unsure whether to follow him or make a run for it. The problem was that I knew I could never find my way back to the hotel. It was a moonless night, nebulous, misty and eerily dark. I had no idea where we were, so I followed him blindly, even further into the darkness. I tried to think rationally, despite the gamut of horror films this sinister scene cruelly reminded me of and decided that if his intentions were heinous, he was hardly likely to have run off ahead of me and left me ample time to try and escape.

A few seconds later he halted and beckoned me towards him. Every ounce of my being was telling me to run away as fast as possible in the opposite direction, yet I approached with apprehension, still extremely anguished and uncertain that I was doing the right thing. He took my arm again and dragged me towards a stone. I was instantly relieved to find that he was trying to show me the tomb of General Kim Yushin, (AD 595-673) one of the most famous Korean military leaders.[1]

At that point in time, however, I didn't have a clue as to who this general was, and I really did not care. I did, however, feel slightly less apprehensive. I was more than a little relieved to discover that Medallion Man's motives for driving me all this way were to show me a tomb and not to put me in a fresh one!

After trying to show as much enthusiasm for the General's final resting place as I could muster, Medallion Man smiled and marched me back to the motorbike. Once there, he yanked a flower

---

1. *(General Kim Yushin, (AD 595-673) had provided so much military support throughout his life that it allowed Kim Ch'unch'u to ascend to the throne and become the next King. The General helped to unify two kingdoms and drove out Chinese forces from Korea, making the Korean peninsula unified for the first time under one political leadership. For his distinguished contribution to the country and possibly for his relationship with the royal family, he was posthumously honoured with the title of king in AD 676. On his death, his tomb was built on a grand scale, comparable in size to other deceased kings of the past.)*

from a nearby bush and presented it to me, helped me get onto the motorbike and drove me back to the hotel as I breathed a huge sigh of relief!

When I finally reached my room, I found Louise and Sharon sitting on their beds, biting their nails and looking as worried as I had been.

"That was a really stupid thing you did, Michele," Louise reprimanded. "We didn't know where you'd gone, or what to do. We thought you were going to be raped – or worse."

"I know, I know," I said. "So did I!" Then I sat down and told them all about my adventure.

Chapter 5

MOVING BACK TO SEOUL

On Saturday 8th April, three hours after my motorbike adventure, we were startled awake when the phone rang at 6:30 am. Sharon answered it.

"Yes, Mr Lee. No, Mr Lee..."

"Ooh! I wonder who it is!" I joked.

"At a rough guess, I'd say it could be Mr Lee," Louise replied sarcastically. Turning to Sharon, she whispered: "Tell him we need some money!"

Sharon raised her hand in Louise's direction, silently gesturing her to wait. "Yes, Mr Lee. Oh and Mr Lee...." Sharon turned to face us. "He's hung up!"

"Great!" Louise replied.

"Well, what's he ringing at this ungodly hour for? What did he want?" I asked.

"Er, he said that we have to get up, er... now, pack everything, go to the bus station and... catch the first bus to Seoul."

"What?"

"Why?"

"Er... because, apparently the hotel is going to be raided," Sharon replied with a nonchalant flick of her wrist.

She explained that, according to our agent, the Hotel manager did not have the required documents to allow foreign workers. We needed to leave as soon as possible because if we were discovered, the hotel would face a huge fine. (Mr Lee had omitted to tell her what would happen to us if we were caught!) Therefore, three hours after going to sleep, we found ourselves frantically packing our belongings in virtual silence, our ears alert for any sound of police activity outside the hotel.

Louise and I finished packing our personal belongings around the same time but Sharon still had a long way to go. Every so often, she seemed to stop mid proceedings and just stare off into space with a vacant expression on her face. Leaving her to it, we headed off down to the nightclub to get the costumes.

"Sharon's in a dream," I said as we ran down the stairs. "I thought she would have been ready before us and sorting everything out. I mean, she's the head girl. She should be taking charge of the situation, but it looks like everything has been left for us to do."

"She couldn't organise a piss up in a brewery!" Louise replied. "She should have asked him for money or, better still, rung him back and told him that unless the manager of the hotel gave us our wages, we weren't leaving."

"You're right," I said. "We are going to have to travel up to Seoul with virtually no money at all."

Gaining access to the costumes became the most difficult part of the fleeing proceedings, as the Nightclub was locked. Eventually, a sleepy member of staff appeared with the keys, and we managed to get inside. As soon as we had finished packing and were doing a final check to make sure that all the costumes were accounted for, Sharon appeared in the doorway and with a casual swoop, she picked up two headdresses.

"Oh, have you finished?" She asked, staring around the dressing-room with an absent expression on her face.

We didn't bother to reply – (talk about state the bleeding obvious!)

A few minutes later, we were bustled inside a Bongo van with all our belongings and whisked away under cover of (relative) darkness to Kyongju bus terminal where we were unceremoniously dumped.

"So, what now, Sharon?" Louise asked, barely hiding her frustration. "How are we supposed to get to Seoul? Who's buying the tickets? I mean, what's the plan?"

"Er..."

"That's just great!" Louise slumped down on the costume case in a huff.

"I'll go and see...." Sharon replied vacantly and wandered off. She returned a few minutes later, just as an unknown Korean was pushing three tickets into Louise's hands and ushering us towards an awaiting bus.

I was sad to be leaving the hotel under such circumstances. It meant we would never have a chance to say goodbye to anyone. Although the nightclub had been a nightmare to work in, we had met some really friendly people. I would particularly miss Mr Sol, who had gone out of his way to make sure we had had a good time. Even if some of his ideas of diversion differed from ours, we had certainly had some unforgettable experiences!

* * *

The bus journey back to the capital was bordering on nightmarish. The distance from Kyongju to Seoul was 350km – as the birds fly – and under normal conditions would take approximately four hours. We, however, were travelling on public transport so the journey took much longer.

We found three empty seats dotted along the aisles of the overcrowded bus and sat down. We were exhausted, but the hustle and bustle of the packed vehicle made any idea of catching a bit of sleep impossible. As the sun rose, the heat inside the bus augmented rapidly. Every available window was sealed shut; an antiquated air-conditioning unit at the front of the conveyance jiggled, shook and wheezed, attempting to cough out cold air that never quite managed to reach us. Only the two tiny sunroofs provided an occasional sliver of breeze.

The air was thick and oppressive and smelt of sticky, fried food, sweat and pickles. We were so thirsty but we had nothing but the clothes we stood up in. I equated our situation to how animals must feel when loaded into a cattle truck heading for slaughter. I could not help but feel as though we were heading for the same fate - comparatively speaking. *What did destiny have in store for us now?*

The bus drew to a stop to refuel and everyone poured off the bus, breathing in gulps of fresh, sun-baked air and wiping sticky brows with handkerchiefs. We rushed off to find the restrooms, then the three of us sat down on the pavement feeling totally dejected. Like our arrival at the airport, once again, we felt like we had been discarded, abandoned, and were surplus to requirements.

Pooling our meagre resources, we gave the remains of our cash to a little old man selling bottles of water and an array of nibbles, from fruit and nuts to cold "eggy-bread" sandwiches. Armed with our inadequate provisions, we boarded the bus again, to continue the rest of the torturous journey back to Seoul.

* * *

On arrival in the capital, we were taken directly to Mr Lee's offices. It was the first time that we had been there, and we took in the surroundings with curiosity. Our Agent seemed to have three secretaries working for him in the front office, while he had a private room at the back. He must have heard our arrival, as he came out smiling.

"Hello! Hello! Nice to see you! Okay, this is the plan. We go now to hotel and tomorrow you work." He said, ushering us out of the office before we had really stepped inside.

"Wait a minute," Louise butted in. "Speaking of work. We want our money for the shows in Kyongju."

"Ah, yes, one moment," he said, extracting a wad of notes from his inside jacket pocket. "Here, take this."

"Thank you, Mr Lee," Sharon said, taking the money and sharing it out.

As I lazily started counting mine, Louise looked up and glared at Mr Lee.

"Where's the rest of it?"

There was only half the amount we had been expecting.

"Ah, well, I can't give you all the money now. Remember, I've had to pay to get you out of Kyongju."

"But, it wasn't our fault that you sent us to work in a hotel that didn't have the correct license," Louise argued.

Mr Lee chose not to reply and in an effort to placate us, he took a handful of letters out of a desk draw and grinned as he waggled then in front of us with an enticing wave.

"Ah! Here, this is the mail that arrived for you all while you have been in Kyongju." He pushed a bundle of letters into Sharon's hands.

The thought of receiving news from home was certainly a way to boost our tired, dejected spirits. Sharon took the stack of mail and began to hand them out.

"Louise, me, Louise, me, Louise, Louise, me, me..."

I did not receive a single letter! That was the final straw. I was tired, hot, hungry, and now, it appeared that nobody at home had even thought about me. I excused myself, went to the toilet and had a good cry.

* * *

Once again, we found ourselves back at the Central Hotel. This time I had decided that I was not going to have the last bed, so I made sure I entered the room first. There were two single beds and a double at the far end. I claimed that one.

Sharon chose the middle one and Louise took the bed by the door, under the air-conditioning unit.

The room was decisively basic. Apart from a TV, built-in wardrobe, a small table, a mirror and a calendar on the wall, there was little else in the room. It was, however, a much larger space than the one we had stayed in before. The bathroom was also basic, with a massive, oily-brown cockroach in the middle of the tiled floor, who wiggling his antennae in surprised greeting. Brown water peppered with rust particles was dribbling uncontrollably from the taps. It was not what you would call home from home.

"I hope we won't be staying here long!" I said, as we all slumped onto the beds and looked at one another feeling more than a little despondent. (Little did we know that this room would be our home for the next three months.)

With the money Mr Lee had given us, we went for a walk around the town centre, on the hunt for food and provisions. It became immediately apparent how much more westernised Seoul was in comparison to Kyongju. Due to the large number of army bases and therefore American soldiers, there were chains of restaurants and shops such as McDonald's, Burger King, Dunking Donuts and Wendy's. We could not wait to get into McDonald's and eat a little western food for a change, even if it was fast- food, after the amount of rice and noodles we had consumed since our arrival.

On the way back, we bumped into the five girl group that had been rehearsing when I went to audition in London. As before, they were very friendly. They said that they were working up to five or six shows a night, they were making a lot of money, and although it was difficult to get Mr Lee to cough up at the end of each week, he did eventually hand over the money. On the whole, they said they were having a great time. This boosted our spirits, imagining that we too would be in the same situation within a couple of days.

The girls offered to take us out that night, so we arranged to meet them after they had finished working, about 2:00 am. They wanted to show us Iteawon, the centre of all the nightlife in Seoul.

I had never really liked discos and nightclubs but, against my better judgement, I tagged along with everyone else, as I did not want to appear rude. We were introduced to 'Kings´, a scruffy looking nightclub full of American GI's out on the pull, then on to various bars with enticing names: the 'Boston club´, 'Soul train´, 'East and West´ and 'The Twilight zone´.

In my opinion, of all the bars, the Twilight zone had the most character and ambience. It was situated about four floors up, and there were a medley of tables and chairs of different shapes and sizes, as well as big comfortable sofas on which one could lounge if one so desired. The lighting was subdued but sufficient to be able to see, as the big windows all around the bar let in the multicoloured lights of Iteawon.

The bar sold a host of drinks as well as food, so throughout the rest of the contract, whenever I went to Itaewon, I almost always chose to stop there. It never closed and even boasted a sign outside which said they were 'Open 25 hours a day'. This meant that depending on the time of day that you frequented, there could be hoards of people or just a few. Sometimes, in the early hours of the morning, (the time when we usually arrived,) there would be people crashed out in drunken stupors on the sofas. The staff conveniently ignored their unconscious clients, whilst they cleaned the tables and vacuumed the floor around them.

On this, our first occasion, we ordered 'Omrice' which was the derivative for French omelette rolled into a sausage shape and filled with a mixture of rice, vegetables and tiny pieces of meat. Being a vegetarian, this was about the only food I could find which did not contain so much meat. I spent about ten minutes picking out all the tiny pieces with the chopsticks and putting them on Louise's plate.

"Here, you must try this!" said Tamara, one of the members of the quintet. "It's called 'Kimchi' and it's served with everything here."

"What is it?" I asked as we all eyed with suspicion the little plate of layered cabbage with a red-orangey colour to it.

"It's fermented cabbage, cucumber or radishes and spiced with red pepper, garlic, green onion and ginger," she explained as we screwed up our faces. "It's very spicy, but it's supposed to be very good for you because it contains every possible vitamin and mineral there is."

Very spicy was an understatement. It nearly blew our heads off! My mouth was on fire – and I'd only eaten a tiny bit!

"It must be an acquired taste," I said, spitting it out into a serviette as discretely as I could, whilst fumbling with watery eyes for my gin and tonic and literally gargling with it, in an attempt to cool my mouth. Tamara shrugged.

"You'll get used to it," she said. "The Koreans swear by it."

"Yeah? Well, it's making me want to swear now, that's for sure!" Louise quipped as she looked for the nearest napkin in which to deposit the contents of her mouth.

After eating, we went back outside. The streets and bars of Itaewon were awash with a myriad of kaleidoscopic lights; music blared from every establishment and guys in bright costumes jangled tambourines or banged drums to entice thrill-seeking customers to enter the bars and nightclubs.

Vendors shouted to sell their wares above the chatter of thousands of people; the perpetual buzzing of mopeds and honking of horns: the unremitting hustle and bustle of a city that never seemed to sleep. Amidst so much activity, it was impossible to take everything in.

Tamara pointed towards several little stalls which, according to her, were selling all types of curiosities on kebab sticks, so we wandered over to investigate.

"Urgh! Look at those; they look like some sort of beetle!" Sharon exclaimed, as the little old lady smiled and nodded a greeting from the other side of the stall, in expectance of a sale.

"God knows what that is, covered in batter," Louise replied.

"Yes, but look at these," Tamara said, revelling in our reaction. "These are baby birds that are fully formed but taken from their shells before they hatch. Look! You can see their baby feathers, their beaks and everything. Then the Koreans skewer 'em, fry 'em and eat 'em."

"Urgh!" we replied in unison. "That's disgusting!"

"Yeah, they eat the whole thing. Feathers, beak, the lot!"

Just then, I heard the distinct tinkling sound of an ice-cream van. I spun around in anticipation but was to be disappointed. I discovered that in Korea, this tinny music announced the arrival of the garbage trucks!

"Wow, it's just SO different here from Kyongju!" Sharon enthused, as another group of GI's swaggered past and she smiled demurely in their direction.

Louise nodded in agreement, "Definitely."

I could not have agreed more but for different reasons. They preferred Seoul for the non-stop frenetic atmosphere that correlated a busy city life. In comparison, I preferred Kyongju for the relative quietness of a little town.

As the night drew on, the quintet of dancers disappeared one by one as they hooked up with their American GI boyfriends. With our dwindling numbers, one of the girls, Amy, jumped up.

"Right, come on girls, I think it's time I introduced you all to 'Hooker Hill´.

This turned out to be a narrow sloping street which was renowned for its assortment of local prostitutes, who would position themselves at strategic points up either side of the hill and wait for passing Koreans or GIs. We strode past them, amazed at how many prospective customers there seemed to be until we came to a stop outside a little establishment which appeared to function as both a shop and a café.

"And this..." Amy announced, slinging her hands out in a low 'V´ to present the premises, "...this is the famous 'Kettle House´."

"Er, it's probably a daft question," I said, "but why is it called 'The Kettle house´?"

"You'll see," Amy replied. "You are all going to try Korean Sodu, (pronounced 'So-d- you'), the typical national drink. It means 'a welcome spring´ but, I have to warn you that it's so strong, it has to be mixed with fruit juice and yoghurt to line your stomach."

Bloody Hell, I thought to myself, *talk about a misleading name!*

We stepped inside the tiny shop and sat down at little, rickety, old tables with a mish-mash of stools and old chairs. A tall, slim, middle-aged woman approached our table. She appeared to be so extremely reserved, serene and cultured that she created the impression of almost floating to our table.

As Amy gabbled the drinks order in Korean, I studied the woman more closely. She seemed so out of place to her surroundings that I found myself ruminating as to how she had wound up serving Sodu up a side street full of prostitutes. The same question I had found myself asking when I passed the young women of the night. What were their stories? What had led them to this?

The name of the bar soon became obvious as all customers were served their Sodu from battered old whistling kettles – not that they were whistling now but they must have done at one stage. The Sodu was drunk from disposable plastic cups, in an assortment of colours with an accompanying little straw. Neat Sodu was similar in appearance to Japanese sake or Greek Ouzo. Totally colourless, it was impossible to drink neat – well, for us girls anyway! However, mixed with fruit juice and yoghurt it was the type of beverage that fooled you into believing you were drinking very little alcohol.

"This stuff is lethal," Amy warned. "So be careful!"

I don't remember much after that!

* * *

The following evening as we were in our room preparing for our first show in Seoul, Mr Lee appeared.

"Tonight you will dance at the USA nightclub!" he announced jovially. "Remember, you must do your very best show because this is like audition."

"So, what are you saying, Mr Lee?" asked Louise, eyeing him with suspicion.

"If you do good show, they will employ you. Maybe one month contract, maybe two!"

"Yeah, so, what are you saying? Are we getting paid for doing the show tonight, Mr Lee or what?" she pushed.

"Of course ... NO! This is audition!"

"Great!" our sarcasm more than evident in our reply.

We were more than a little apprehensive as the Bongo van approached the USA nightclub, as we had assumed that we would be dancing to a room full of American soldiers. Somehow, the thought of performing in front of American men rather than Koreans was, for some reason, decidedly more unnerving, and we had no idea how they would react to our show. However, when we entered the venue, there was not a single GI in sight.

The club was full of Koreans who were ogling yet another lesbian act. As we were being shown through the bar to the dressing-room, we caught part of the performance. One girl was topless, while the other was bottomless. Their act seemed to consist of walking around the audience and sitting on the men's knees. Later, they mounted each other and then whipped each other - nothing that we had not already seen before.

We went into the dressing-room, to set our costumes. Not an easy feat, when we discovered that the light bulb did not work, so the only light source available came from the corridor. It was an exceedingly tiny space, with a few chairs positioned around the wall.

In one corner, there was no floor, just a large 'hole´ which dropped down to a small space about three metres square and a metre fifty deep. It didn't seem to serve any purpose, so we decided to put the case down there to give us a little bit more room.

A few minutes later, just as we had set our costumes and were starting to get changed, the music for our show started playing!

"Shit, I'm no way near ready!" I exclaimed.

"Me neither!" The girls said in unison as we stared at each other in consternation then madly scrambled into our costumes.

Nobody had bothered to tell us what time slot we had, or how soon we needed to be ready.

As the music blared out and the audience stared at an empty stage, I assumed that the DJ would switch off the music and revert to disco tunes but that just did not happen. Consequently, the opening number was a complete disaster! Each one of us ran on stage at different times whenever we had some semblance of the costume on our person.

Despite the debacle of an opening number, the rest of the show went well. However, further problems began when we came off stage. As we were walking back towards the dressing-room, we passed the next act about to perform; a man in a smart suit and tie sauntered past us deliberately avoiding eye contact. I assumed he was a singer, and thought no more about it.

We entered the dressing-room and after changing into our outdoor clothes, I jumped down into the little square where we had left the suitcase to start packing the costumes. Minutes later, the 'singer' came sauntering back into the dressing-room wearing nothing but a furry G-string! All three of us did a double-take and had to look again to check that it was indeed a furry G-string as, at first glance, he appeared to be completely naked! (I guess I had the bird's-eye-view, as I was level to his crotch at that point!)

As we turned away and began the process of packing the costumes inside the case, the man dressed himself in a tracksuit then, without warning, he became very irate. Pointing in my direction, he glared directly at me and began shouting. When he didn't get any response (as I had no idea what his problem was), he picked up a chair and threw it across the dressing-room.

"What the hell's the matter with him?" I asked, confused, quite panicked and at a complete disadvantage being down a hole and on a level with his crotch!

"Panty, panty!" He yelled.

As I looked at him with vexation, Sharon was beside herself from trying not to laugh.

"Oh!" she said. "He thinks you've taken his furry G-string!"

"I haven't got it!" I yelled. "What the hell would I want with your sweaty G-string?"

With fire and brimstone flashing in his eyes, he continued pointing, bellowing and gesticulating in my direction.

"Panty, Panty!" he shouted repeatedly.

Louise instantly began panting like a dog. This sent all three of us into fits of laughter, which didn't help the situation at all.

Another chair was thrown across the dressing-room as he continued his tirade of rants and raves.

Despite the bad lighting, Louise spied the offending object on the floor, behind one of the chairs. Picking it up with the hooked part of a hanger, she held up the furry G-string, hanger and all, then with a look of utter distaste, she swung it under his nose.

"Is THIS what you're looking for?"

The guy snatched his prized possession and stomped off down the corridor with a huff and a snort, while the sound of our laughter echoed after him.

* * *

The following day, Mr Lee informed us that we would have two more auditions that night. The first would be at the 'Valentino´ club and the second at 'The Golden Star´. As there was no mention of the USA club, we rightly assumed that we had not got the job.

"So, I suppose we'll be working for free again, then, Mr Lee?" I said. My sarcastic tone was more than evident.

"Well, do a good show and you will start to earn good money," he replied.

The three of us scowled our contempt, but our agent conveniently ignored us.

The first venue was a stylish looking nightclub which made all three of us feel slightly more optimistic. To reach the main stage, we were required to walk along a catwalk. This made our exits for quick changes seem like a marathon, as we had to sprint up the catwalk, along an extremely narrow corridor, which just allowed two people to pass - if both parties turned sideways and one leant against the wall- then, the final dash into the dressing room. Despite these inconveniences, we managed to complete every quick change, by tearing our clothes off as we ran along the corridor towards the dressing-room.

In contrast, 'The Golden Star´ was a dingy, sleazy dive of a place! It had a decent-sized stage but we were forced to manoeuvre through the orchestra's instruments to reach it, which was no easy feat.

The clientele appeared to be older, middle-aged Koreans and there did not appear to be a single, sober individual amongst them. They were restless and not impressed with either show. During our first performance, one man pulled himself to his feet and staggered towards us accompanied by an encouraging round of applause from his drinking buddies.

"Watch out, there's a drunkard about!" Louise warned.

He approached the stage on doddering legs, and being further goaded by his companions, he poured a full carton of milk onto the stage!

"Is that milk?" Sharon asked, not quite believing what she was seeing.

"Yeah, but what an innocent drink such as that is doing in this den of iniquity is beyond me!" I replied. "Maybe it's a Korean custom to signal dislike or something," I suggested as we tried to avoid slipping on the slowly widening milky mess. (If it was a custom, we never found out.)

"Well," I said as we trudged back to the dressing-room after the show and packed in disheartened silence. "I can honestly say that I hope we don't get this contract, it's awful!"

"Same here," Louise replied. "They made me feel extremely uncomfortable."

"And me," Sharon agreed.

When we arrived back at the hotel, we were all feeling despondent and more than a little disillusioned. To cheer herself up, Sharon decided to go out on yet another date with a Korean she had met in reception, while Louise and I chose to visit the Twilight zone for Om-rice and some alcohol to drown our sorrows.

* * *

The following day, Mr Lee arrived unannounced at the hotel to give us some more mail. Sharon and Louise received several, I received one – but it was better than nothing.

As the girls began to scan their letters and cards and chatter between themselves, without warning, Mr Lee lost his patience, stamped his foot, clenched his fists and told us all to sit down. Surprised by his sudden change in character, we immediately did as we were told and stared inquisitively towards our agent. When he knew that he had our undivided attention, he began to speak.

"Now, I need serious talk with you girls," he began. "You give me many problems, many problems!"

"Like what?" Sharon asked.

"The quality of your music is very bad. Very bad!"

"Well, we didn't record it!" Louise argued.

"Look. You need to choose one show, just one. And make it shorter."

"We'll do mine," Sharon said, choosing the one in which she had the solo routine. (It would be months before I would have to dance the James Bond number again).

Mr Lee nodded, looking slightly peeved. Then his eyes narrowed as he looked at Sharon and Louise. "You two are putting on weight. This is very bad, very bad! Oh, and you all need to do the Can-can," he added as an afterthought.

I looked at him puzzled but decided not to bother questioning how we were supposed to carry out his wishes when we had no access to any sound equipment and no money to buy can-can costumes.

"So, will we be working tonight, Mr Lee?" I asked.

"No, no work today; and no auditions."

* * *

The next day, Wednesday 12th April, was yet another day of forced unemployment.

"Mr Lee said that we can't work today, because it's Buddha's birthday," Sharon informed us as she put the phone down.

"That doesn't make sense! " I said. "The other group's working today."

Sharon curled her lip, gave a nonchalant shrug then delved into a bag of chocolates. I fumed inwardly, feeling exasperated that Mr Lee's words about her weight gain were being ignored. I felt trapped in a grim situation which was slowly spiralling out of control, gaining momentum at every turn, and in which I was at a loss to do anything about.

By our fifth day of forced unemployment, our money was down to virtual nil. I had the grand sum of 9,000 Korean won (approx £7.50) in my purse and was feeling exceedingly low. I was missing home, missing my regular income from the summer season work, missing dancing on a regular basis and particularly missing my mum.

Feeling the overpowering desire to speak to her right away, I headed down to reception and rang home, charging the call to the room. As soon as my mum's familiar voice travelled down the phone-line, I started to cry and related the whole sorry story. Mum managed to qualm my fears, but later, back in the hotel bedroom when I had calmed down, I felt decidedly guilty. I could not get the image of my mother fretting out of my head, so I decided to ring her again. Blaming my outburst on tiredness, I told her not to worry.

(Little did I know, that my fiery-tempered, red-headed mum had already rung the English agent and given her a piece of her mind!)

* * *

Thursday was a repeat of the previous day.

"Mr Lee isn't in his office," Sharon said putting the phone down.

"I take it that means that we're not working again then!" Louise fumed.

"If you ask me, he's avoiding us," I replied.

Sharon shrugged and ate some more chocolate. "I don't know, but I'm not feeling very well," she said.

I inwardly screamed. It was blatantly obvious that our agent was having trouble finding work for us but I should not have been surprised. There was an abundance of foreign dancers in Seoul. The clubs had their pick of dance groups and we were hardly prime merchandise.

As we all contemplated yet another day of unemployment and no money, there was a knock on the door. Two of the girls from the other group, Tamara and Amy stood there in kimonos, with sunglasses on their heads and Central Hotel blankets under their arms.

"Hi! We're all going sunbathing on the roof of the hotel. Do you want to join us?"

Louise and I accepted. We had nothing better to do. Sharon declined, saying she had a date with

Charlie, an African American GI she had met in Itaewon.

Ten minutes later, seven of us were laying out, in a line, on hotel blankets, on the Central hotel roof.

Sunbathing as a dancer is a complicated process. There is nothing worse than tanning yourself and later wearing dancing costumes with great big, white strap marks from bikinis or sun tops. Consequently, donned with just our G-strings, we sunbathed topless. I would like to say it was a secluded spot but it would be far from the truth! The hotel was overlooked by other high rise buildings whose occupants would have had a bird's eye view. (Mind you, perhaps in my case, onlookers would have needed a pair of binoculars!)

Despite being overlooked, I was so glad I had accepted the invitation. Even though we were just sunbathing and chatting, the five girl group always lifted my spirits, they were full of fun. Their light-hearted banter flowed easily amongst them and they seemed to be embracing the Korean lifestyle. Obviously, having regular work and regular money was a definite plus to their happiness but it was always enjoyable spending time with them.

When the sun went down, I went in search of cheap food with my remaining 9,000 won and found a little shop behind the hotel which sold two kinds of noodles: one called 'Chajang', which was in a small brown coloured pot and a second in a slightly larger container, called Ramen noodles. They were the princely price of 200 won each; (about 16p) so I knew I could feed myself for a few days before I was forced to starve!

* * *

On Friday afternoon, tempers were wearing thin. Louise and I were becoming exasperated with our so-called 'head girl' who never seemed to be in. Whenever Mr Lee phoned, he would always ask to speak to Sharon, and when he was informed that she was not there, he would hang up, saying that he would call back later. It was irritating that he would not discuss something which clearly involved us, without speaking to Sharon. When our head girl returned from yet another date, Louise confronted her.

"Has Lee phoned?" She snapped. (Due to his lack of success in finding us work, his status had been reconsidered. At that moment, he didn't merit 'Mr´ before his name.)

"Not that I know of, but I've been out most of the day."

"Great!" I said, sarcastically.

"Well, don't you think you should ring him?" Louise said, barely hiding her impatience.

"He just never seems to be in!" Sharon replied, in a weak attempt at defending herself.

"Perhaps if you spent less time socialising and more time doing your job, you'd actually be here when he called!" Louise yelled.

"Well, keep bloody trying for God's sake!" I said. "This is getting ridiculous! We're all skint. Can't you try ringing him now and ask him for some money?"

Realising that she was under attack, Sharon plonked herself down on the bed with a sigh and picked up the phone.

"Hello, this is Sharon; can I speak to Mr Lee, please? ... Oh, okay, thank you." She hung up and shrugged. "He's not there," she said, picking up a packet of crisps.

Louise walked out, slamming the door behind her.

* * *

The following day, as Louise and I returned from sunbathing on the roof, we found Sharon sitting on her bed eating crisps and grinning. Our confrontation seemed to have worked and she had stayed in the room all day.

"Good news! We're working tonight!"

"Yeah? Where?" I asked.

"We will be working in three clubs," Sharon grinned. "We are going to do one show at the 'New Seoul´ Hotel, another at a nightclub called 'Mugan´ and a third one here."

"Here?" I said, screwing up my nose.

"Yes, apparently, they have a show right here in the Central Hotel."

"Right, well, I think you should ask Lee for money," Louise said.

"Oh, and we're going to do two disco spots at the Mugan too," Sharon said conveniently ignoring her.

"What's a disco spot?" I asked.

"According to Mr Lee, we have to dance on a podium to the disco music for fifteen minutes. Every time we do it, we get paid extra money."

"Huh! Let's hope it's true," I muttered.

That night as we put on our make-up and prepared for work, our spirits were high. We were all looking forward to treading the boards again and hopefully boosting our severely dwindling economy.

The first show at the New Seoul went well. It was a rather sophisticated venue, with a long covered tunnel at the entrance to the building which housed a host of red, twinkling lights running the length of it. Not that we had any time to actually contemplate it – or anything else for that matter! We were bustled inside and as soon as we had finished the show, our driver was urging us to hurry up and climb inside the Bongo van so that we would not miss our slot at the second venue, which was back at our hotel.

It felt weird doing a show at the Central Hotel. It was such a dilapidated old place that I doubted its calibre of clientele would be in the least bit interested in any type of entertainment at all.

The first show there didn't go so well. Firstly we were announced as: 'Made in England, Korea-Try-o', then when Sharon went on to do her solo, which was a mixture between a slow modern dance routine, with some acrobatics thrown in for good measure, she performed a 'walkover' and fell, landing with a loud thud on her backside. I was standing at the side of the stage waiting to make my entrance, so I glanced through the curtains to see the audience laughing hysterically, while the manager of the club stood at the back of the room with his arms folded across his chest; his face set like thunder.

Once again the Driver herded us into the Bongo van and off we went to the Mugan. The club was huge and nicely decorated, in contrast to the dressing-room.

"What the hell is this!" Louise exclaimed as we peered into a tiny box-like room. The ceiling was so low, that we had to bend forwards to enter it.

"They've got to be joking!" I replied. Unfortunately, they were not. We changed and set our costumes bending forwards at an awkward ninety-degree angle. It was impossible to put on our feather head-dresses unless we knelt down and exited the dressing-room on our knees. Not the best option when wearing fishnet tights. We found it quite amusing to crawl out like three overgrown babies, our feathers tickling the behind of the girl in front of us. However, it was not quite so amusing when we had to return for a quick change.

It was not until after the show, when we were preparing for the first disco spot, that we realised that we had not given any consideration as to what we were supposed to wear. The Korean disco dancers in every club all wore the obligatory knee-high, white leather, platform soled, high-heeled disco boots. We had silver dance shoes. They wore an assortment of leotards. We had only brought our costumes for the show.

"We'll have to improvise," said Sharon, routing about in the costume case.

We botched together three costumes that looked as different from each other as possible and pledged to go out and buy some suitable attire when Mr Lee eventually decided to pay us.

Ten minutes later we were ordered out of the dressing-room, to work our first-ever spot on a podium. As I followed one of the waiters to my allocated spot, I was apprehensive. I had never danced on such a confined space and I was conscious of how unprotected and vulnerable I perceived myself to be without the other two by my side.

Podium Dancing, I decided, was an undeniably strange experience. 'Boogying´ to disco music was not the same as dancing a choreographed routine. As a trained dancer, I was proud to 'strut my stuff´ and show the world what I had practised for years to achieve but those moves were no longer appropriate. Due to limited space, any movement needed to be controlled, small, and - to a certain extent, precise.

Notwithstanding these initial difficulties, after a while, podium dancing became second nature; we all created our unique styles and moves. Most importantly, on that first night, I realised that most of the time, no-one was even watching us, they were too busy drinking and talking to their friends or the hostesses of the club.

To be honest, there was only one way to describe a fifteen-minute disco spot - particularly after months of dancing on a podium - and that was BORING! However, as this was our first time and a new experience, at the end of that day when we had finished for the evening, we were in high spirits. It was good to be dancing again after our eight-day break.

To add to our rising morale, Mr Lee turned up unannounced with some more mail and, more importantly, some money, so the three of us went to Itaewon to celebrate – and to buy a couple of disco costumes each!

* * *

Two days later, just when we had started to become accustomed to our nightly routine of three shows and disco spots, we arrived at the New Seoul Hotel, only to be stopped from entering by one of the bouncers.

"No show. No show," he said, holding his arms out to halt our progress. "Your manager no call my manager."

"What's going on?" Louise questioned as Sharon shrugged her shoulders.

This situation was both annoying and disappointing. I immediately thought about the money we were losing. Nevertheless, as there was nothing we could do to resolve the situation, we continued to the Central Hotel, determined to do a good show.

Unfortunately, it was not to be. When we took to the stage and waited for the opening music to begin, it became apparent, that the Disc-Jockey, for some unknown reason, had started the opening number halfway through the recording. We managed to establish where we were in the routine and started to dance but there were a few seconds where we stood there looking completely clueless!

After the show, as Sharon did not seem to care, I went to speak to the DJ about it. His condescending expression told me that I was wasting my time. He let me struggle through an explanation before he blew his top. He threw a pen and papers to the floor shouted and gesticulated, spat on the floor and as a final gesture, pushed me into a wall.

More surprises were heading our way at our final venue, the Mugan. After the show and between the disco spots, the manager came in with an interpreter.

"He say that show not interesting."

"Well, the show is the show, and that's it," Sharon replied.

"He say that tomorrow, 'Fingel on the triggel' (Finger on the trigger) you must dance topless."

"You what? You have got to be joking!" Sharon exclaimed.

"No way!" Louise and I shouted in unison.

"He say you no do it, you no do disco spots, and you no have money!"

"Then, we won't have money!" Louise replied, folding her arms impulsively across her chest. (I was not sure if this was to make a stand, or to protect her breasts from future exposure!)

* * *

The next morning, Tuesday 18th, in an attempt to brighten our mood, we decided to go shopping in Iteawon. During the day, we were constantly harangued by vendors trying their utmost to entice customers into their establishments.

"You buy Reebok boot, ten dollar!" was a prolific chant and I thought I had heard them all but was won over by a shop owner who beckoned us towards him.

"Hello, ladies, come in! Now, how can I help you spend your money?"

I obliged by buying a kimono for 14,000 won (£11), a white two-piece trouser-suit for 10,000 won (£8) and a t-shirt with 'I've had the Sodu Experience´ written on it for £2. It depicted a cat slumped on the floor with stars around its head, totally inebriated.

After shopping, we decided to try out a café/restaurant called 'Popeye's´ which eventually became a regular haunt of ours, as it sold Western food. Content with our purchases and with our bellies full, we returned to the hotel in good spirits to get ready to work.

As time ticked away and the driver didn't arrive, we became more and more despondent and exasperated. Sharon must have felt quite uncomfortable as she sat on her bed in between Louise and me as we stared at her in stereo and tried to make her realise that perhaps she should phone the agent. – It did not work.

After we had been sitting waiting for an hour, Mr Lee arrived.

"No work tonight!" he said, wafting his hands at us, literally shooing us away before we could even think about counter-attacking.

"You could have rung us and told us!" Louise remarked. "We've been sitting here for over an hour wondering what's going on.

"Yeah and we've put all our make-up on for nothing!" I said.

Annoyed when Mr Lee ignored me, I walked out of the room and slammed the door.

* * *

The following morning, Sharon waited until Louise was in the bathroom then she turned to me.

"Michele, yesterday when you stormed off, Mr Lee told me that we have lost the New Seoul contract because of Louise's weight," she whispered. "He said he is thinking of sending her home or maybe sending us all home."

I thought it was probably more likely that our agent had blamed the two of them and Sharon was trying to shift the blame onto Louise. Although in all honesty, at that point, I was past the point of caring.

"To be honest, Sharon, if that's true, then the way I'm feeling at the moment, I wouldn't mind one bit if he sent us all home," I replied. "This contract isn't what I'd envisaged at all."

Sharon shrugged, curled her lip and turned away.

I did not regret my words. The more time I spent with the quintet and heard that they were now doing up to six shows a night, in big venues, to be honest, I was envious. I had come to dance, not to sit in a hotel room wondering when I would work again and when I'd next get paid.

Chapter 6

ARABS AND AQUARIUMS

April 20th 1989

With each day of forced unemployment, I became a little more disheartened. I was really regretting coming to Korea. I hated the uncertainty, the constant worry about money and food, plus I seemed to be perpetually crying or on the verge of it. I looked across at my companions and they looked as depressed as I did.

"Right, well, I need to go to the post office and get these photos developed," I said, trying to drag myself out of the doldrums. "Anyone fancy a walk?"

"Yes!" Louise replied. "Any excuse to get out of here for a bit."

"No, I'm meeting Dave," Sharon informed us.

"Who's Dave?" I asked.

"Oh, a GI I met the other night in Iteawon. He's taking me to Popeye's. He's going to buy me lunch."

"Oh, okay," I replied, frowning.

Later in the street, as Louise and I headed towards the post office, I was deep in thought.

"Is it just me, or do you think that the amount of men Sharon seems to be going through is incredible?"

"It sure is, but maybe there's method in her madness."

"How do you mean?"

"Well, look at us: We're scrimping and saving to buy noodles and "eggy bread" sandwiches, while she's having a bloody good meal in Popeye's!"

"Yes, but think how she's paying for it in return."

"Point taken," Louise replied.

Our stroll to the post office and photoshop was completed in record time, and became more of a forced power walk, than a gentle meander. This was mainly due to the fact that the city was littered with Military police who appeared to be out in force. There were two or three agents positioned in virtually every street. The air was thick with tension and to be perfectly honest, we did not feel safe. We knew we were being stared at with more hostility than normal but we were unsure as to the cause. Nevertheless, we decided to avoid eye contact with the Koreans, believing that the slightest wrong move could result in us being attacked. We did not relish the thought of being caught in an outbreak of fighting, so we hurried back to the relative safety of the Central Hotel.

That evening, we learnt that there had been a student demonstration down the same streets we had travelled earlier. The protest had turned violent. Tear gas had been released to disperse the throngs of student demonstrators as they ran riot through the streets of Seoul, protesting over the American existence in their country.

* * *

After two days of unemployment, Mr Lee informed us that we would be working again that night. He had told Sharon that we needed to be ready for nine o'clock, but he arrived at eight in a state of agitation.

"Why you not ready?" he grumbled, marching up and down the room.

"Because you said to be ready for nine o'clock!" I barked.

"Yes, but we go now. I take you to eat!"

The thought of any food, that wasn't noodle-based or a sandwich – and particularly any type of sustenance that we would not have to pay for-spurred us into action. A few minutes later, we were following our agent outside to the Bongo van.

We were taken to a nightclub called the 'Samjung´, where we munched on nibbles and exotic fruit, while two Korean girls danced nude then masturbated on the floor in front of us.

"Been there, seen it, bought the t-shirt!" Louise said as we tucked into the provisions. Nothing was going to stop us eating free food!

After the fruit and 'entertainment´, we were taken to our venue. This time the club was called 'Europe´ – which was yet another grotty-looking, fleapit of iniquity! The venue was tiny with excessively dimmed lighting. Our feet sunk into the squelchy, wet carpet and there was a musty, damp smell which pervaded the nostrils and instinctively made me not want to touch anything within my reach.

The stage was in the centre of the scantily sized club. It was round, not much bigger than a podium and was enclosed with glass, so we immediately nicknamed it, 'The Fishtank´. There was a drain in the middle of the sloping stage, however, this time we didn't need to guess why it was there. Strangely, we didn't bat an eyelid at the thought of dancing on the diluted remains of masturbation fluids!

The only original feature here - or rather the lack of it - was the absence of a dressing-room.

"You leave stage; walk past people and change behind them," we were told when we had casually asked where we were expected to get changed.

"You have got to be joking!" I retorted, glaring at Mr Lee.

"They no look. They watch show!"

"Yeah, right!" Sharon replied.

"You do show," said Mr Lee, "and later, I take you to eat."

"Talk about dangle a carrot under the donkey's nose!" Louise remarked as she dumped the costume case and started to unpack.

We begrudgingly did the show. We had no other choice. Work or starve seemed to be the only two available options. As we expected, more men were watching us change than there were watching the show.

"Look on the bright side," said Sharon, when we had finished. "With all that glass, at least they couldn't pour milk on the stage, throw fruit at us or spit on us!"

I consoled myself with the fact that, with our current record, the chances of coming back here again were slim. (Unfortunately, this time, I was wrong.)

After the show, Mr Lee took us to Popeye's, then to a big club called 'The Ambassador´ to see a five girl group of Australian dancers. The stage floor was made of glass and built on top of a real fish tank. As the girls danced, fish swam nonchalantly around under their feet. It looked amazing. As I watched the show, I once again felt envious and wished that I was part of a bigger group and working in classier venues such as this one.

As though a divine being had heard my thoughts, Mr Lee made an unexpected announcement.

"Good news!" he informed us. "You have contract at the Europe club (The Fish-Tank) for two weeks and you will start work here in the Ambassador in five days' time."

I gasped. Shocked that we would have to return to the Fish-tank, yet simultaneously pleased and surprised that we would be working in the Ambassador. I felt like my wish had just been answered.

"Well, at least here, we'll be dancing on top of a fish tank and not inside one!" Louise quipped.

"Do we get paid for tonight's show, Mr Lee?" Sharon asked.

"No. Today, audition," he replied.

* * *

What the elusive Mr Lee had conveniently forgotten to informed us was that we would also not be starting work in 'The Fish-Tank' until the 25th, the same day as the Ambassador. This meant that we had another four days without work and no income.

Sharon packed a bag and disappeared for two of the four days. We had no idea where she had gone but assumed she was living it up with another GI, somewhere. The annoying thing was that we had no way of contacting her! For the second time, Louise and I both felt that she was deserting her post and not doing her job. She was not there to take the agent's calls and by now, we knew how unpredictable Mr Lee could be. His plans were always changing and, as previously mentioned, he did not appear to be comfortable speaking to either of us, as Sharon was the person he was supposed to deal with.

In order to kill time, Louise and I spent the nights in Itaewon and the days in the hotel. In Itaewon, we limited ourselves to one drink a night and spent the rest of the evening being harassed by American GI's, constantly hoping they might buy us a drink without expecting anything in return!

The days in the hotel dragged by and consisted of us being pestered either by the Koreans or a plague of Arabs who seemed to have taken over the seventh floor (our floor) of the hotel. Every time we went to the elevator, they were either getting out of it - and leaving a horrid, strong smell behind them - or getting into it with us (and depositing a horrible smell inside it). Not only that, but they were constantly propositioning us.

"You come my room."

"No!"

"You come. I very good."

"No chance mate!"

After being fondled in the elevator on more than one occasion, we decided that we should exit the hotel via the back stairs, in an attempt to avoid being molested further. On the way back, we usually had to make a run for our room with a string of Bedouins in pursuit.

All hours of the night, Arabians and Koreans were constantly knocking on the door. It was both annoying and frightening. Even the reception staff seemed to find it amusing to open the door with the master key and enter our room whenever they felt like it. We never seemed to have a night's sleep without some type of disturbance or another. We were sleep-deprived, fed up and exceedingly irritable.

One afternoon, after another almost sleepless night, Louise started scribbling on a piece of cardboard.

"Right! Have you got any sticky-tape?"

"Yeah... Why?"

"Good! Help me put this on the door."

Our new sign read:

Fuck off! We are sleeping!
Do NOT disturb!

Unfortunately, it did not seem to make any difference. When we complained to Amy, one of the girls from the quintet, about being constantly harassed and propositioned both in the hotel and outside on the street, she laughed.

"You do know that we're living in the middle of the red light area, don't you?"

"No!" I said. "But that explains a lot!"

"Deep joy!" Louise replied.

"That's why we get groped and spat on so often, whenever we go outside," Amy chuckled. "Everyone thinks we're on the game!"

"Great!" Louise replied sarcastically.

I was lost for words!

* * *

Sharon returned on the 23rd with no explanation as to where she had been, or with whom - and we didn't ask. However, the following morning when the phone rang at 4:00 am and it turned out to be Sharon's latest fling, Louise and I were fuming! Whereas I glared at Sharon, seethed inwardly and turned over, in contrast, Louise blew her top.

"Maybe if I sleep in the F'ing bathroom, I might be able to get some bastard sleep!" she yelled. Barging into the aforementioned room, she threw a blanket and pillow in with her and slammed the door.

Sharon ignored her, continued her call and giggled incessantly into the phone for the next twenty minutes.

Later that morning when Louise had emerged from the bathroom, tempers had calmed down and we were all tentatively talking to each other again, we decided to make a trip to the British Embassy.

Unfortunately for Sharon, as we were about to leave - and to further complicate the proceedings - her early-hours' caller chose that exact moment to turn up in person outside our door, accompanied by a friend.

"Hi!" he said, grinning like the proverbial Cheshire cat. "How's it going?" Sharon, realising she was still in the bad books, tried to convince them to leave but to no avail.

"We're actually just on our way out. We're going to the British Embassy," she told them.

"Oh, yeah. Why?"

"Well, we've been informed that we should register, in case war breaks out between North and South Korea; that way the Embassy will know where to find us."

"Cool! We'll come too!"

I was sitting on my bed, half expecting Louise to blow her top again, but a few hours' sleep in the bathtub seemed to have put her in a better mood. She glanced in my direction, cast her eyes heavenwards and shook her head.

Twenty minutes later, we set off (with two GI's in tow) and began the long journey to the centre of Seoul. This was an arduous undertaking, as it involved travelling on two, overcrowded buses in the heat of the day. On arrival, we were hot, sweaty and not in the best of spirits after being jostled, pushed and insulted throughout the journey.

We were met at the closed gates of the Embassy by two Korean soldiers armed with rifles.

"Hello, we're English. We've come to register," Louise told them, waggling her passport under their noses.

They mumbled together for a moment then, shook their heads.

"No. Come back tomorrow."

"What?" we exclaimed in surprise.

"Look, we've travelled on two buses to get here," I said. "Please, let us in."

"Embassy closed. You come tomorrow."

"Bloody Hell! Turned away from your own Embassy. Good job it isn't an emergency!" Louise exclaimed.

"But, I can't believe this! There are people still walking into the building," I said to the soldiers. "I can see them."

"No, Embassy close 4 pm. Too late, come tomorrow."

"It's a minute past four!" Sharon replied. "What a joke!"

"It's a minute past four now!" Louise said. "It was before four o'clock when we started having this discussion."

"So much for registering," I said. "I bet if war did break out, they wouldn't bother to come looking for us at all!"

* * *

The following day, we attempted 'Trip to the Embassy, take two.' This time we arrived in the morning, without our GI chaperones and were allowed straight through the gates without a problem. As we rounded a corner and walked towards the main building, I spied a plaque on the wall.

"Look at that."

The opening hours were displayed for all to see. They closed each day at 4:30 pm.

"I still don't think they should close at all," Louise replied. "What if there's an emergency?"

"I still don't think they'd bother to come looking for us even if there *was* an emergency," Sharon replied.

To register as English citizens living in Korea was a straightforward procedure. We filled in a form and handed over our passports. The officials, seated behind glass, scrutinized the photo and attempted to validate it with the individual standing in front of them. The passport was then photocopied and stamped. We were curtly informed that we were now officially registered in South Korea. The entire procedure was done in the usual 'English Upper-lip´ fashion, without a smile in sight. I had hoped to receive a warm welcome from our fellow countrymen, but we were generally made to feel like we were lesser mortals than the civil servants, that we were wasting their time, spoiling their day and, as we were not civil servants, were probably of the criminal persuasion.

After registering, we went back to the hotel to get ready for work. We were about to leave the room when the phone rang. As usual, Sharon answered it.

"Yes, Mr Lee. Ok, Mr Lee."

"Money!" Louise whispered, rubbing the tips of her fingers together.

"Oh, about the money, Mr Lee... Mr Lee? Hello?... He's rung off!"

"Great!" Louise said.

"Why am I not surprised?" I asked sarcastically.

"Apparently we are working a third club tonight," Sharon informed us, ignoring our comments.

"Oh, okay. Where is it?" I asked.

"I don't know, he didn't say. He said our driver knows."

We set off for work that evening, each wondering aloud where the mystery club would be. I was more than a little suspicious and feared that as this venue seemed shrouded in secrecy, there had to be negative connotations involved.

We danced first, in the Fish-tank, where the management had finally provided us with a folding screen for us to change behind. It looked suspiciously like it had been stolen from a hospital ward, but we were grateful for a bit of privacy at last! Later we worked the Ambassador club, locally known as the 'Amba´ and climbed inside the Bongo van to go to the third venue. We could not believe it when we came to a stop outside the Samjung strip joint where Mr Lee had taken us to eat five days ago.

"Ha! Maybe our audition was showing how well we could eat tropical fruit!" I quipped, trying to lighten the mood.

"At least we weren't out of pocket doing the audition," Louise replied.

"A strip club! Things are going from bad to worse!" Sharon moaned.

We slouched off to the dressing-room feeling thoroughly disheartened, trying to convince ourselves that at least we were working.

Fortunately, we were told that we would not have to perform in the enclosed fish-tank where we had watched the lesbian act. We were given the bigger stage. As we took our places on stage and looked out at the all-male audience, we heard the DJ announced us and I started to laugh.

"England dancers, Mar-ee-oh-ship-sheo."

Louise looked at me and frowned.

"What's so funny?" she asked as we got into position.

"Sorry! It's just that every time I hear someone say 'Mar-ee- oh-ship-sheo´, I think he's saying 'Marion's- shit show´!"

The girls laughed out loud and we looked surprisingly happy during the opening routine.

This turned out to be a plus, as the rest of the show was a total disaster! Louise's zip broke during one of the routines, so she did not come on stage. Later, in the final number, the zip in that costume jammed. This meant that I only had one backing dancer as I mimed to Donna Summer.

Sharon was fuming. "Honestly, that was like *our* show! We did duet after duet, with a guest appearance from Louise!" she complained as we left the stage.

"Yes, the manager didn't look very impressed!" I replied.

Louise apologised, but the damage was done. We never performed there again. (Not that any of us were particularly upset about it!)

* * *

Next morning, Louise and I took a trip into Itaewon to replace the zips in her costumes. I took the opportunity to have a pair of boots repaired; two new heels and a sole stuck back in place for just 80 pence. We went for an iced coffee in the Twilight zone and then returned to the hotel.

On arrival, we found Sharon's two GI friends - Charlie and Ted who had accompanied us to the Embassy - hiding in the bathroom. They sighed and gave a nervous laugh when they realised it was us.

"What's going on?" I asked.

"They've done a runner from the taxi driver, and now they're hiding in the bathroom," Sharon explained, with a matching nervous giggle. "Every time there's a knock on the door, they hide in the loo!"

Louise and I looked at each other knowing exactly what the other was thinking. The poor taxi driver was trying to make a living, it wasn't right that they had left without paying. Furthermore, to ask the driver to take them to the Central hotel, then run away by entering the very same hotel wasn't what either of us would call a bright idea! Not only that, but it was also annoying that they had come to our room and therefore implicated us in their actions.

The reception staff had guessed who the guys were and whom they had come to see, so it was only a matter of time before one of them knocked on the door with the duped taxi driver and the guys had to pay up.

When the Americans decided to leave, Louise glared at Sharon.

"It's bad enough that your 'friends´ have to come here, but to involve us in this, is totally out of order!"

"I didn't know they'd run off without paying, did I!"

"No, but you eventually found out what they had done. You should have told them to leave."

Sharon ignored her and looked for solace in a bag of crisps.

That night, as we were driven to the Fishtank, there was a distinctly uneasy feeling amongst us. Louise and Sharon were barely talking to each other and I was trying to break the silence, by talking about anything and everything which came into my mind. It did not seem to be working.

During the show, and unfortunately for me, I got my heel caught in the drain in the middle of the sloping stage and fell over twisting my ankle. I felt like a real fool as I tried to extricate the heel from a drain full of black hair and bodily fluids with my bare hands, yuck!

Fortunately, my misfortune lightened the mood between us, as both of my dance partners burst out laughing at my predicament. I was quite pleased that the tension had been broken, even if it meant that I was forced to limp for the next few days and dance with my ankle strapped up in an elastic bandage.

* * *

The next morning, Louise and I did our usual trip to the post office and the photoshop, stopping as we always did at a little convenience store on the way back, so that I could buy an iced lolly in the form of a slice of watermelon.

As we wandered back towards the hotel, we saw a group of around twenty Korean men huddled around a tiny stall, all giggling like schoolboys. Intrigued, we pushed our way forwards to get a better look. On seeing us infiltrating male territory, the guys' mood immediately changed. They became offensive and tried to push us away, but not before we saw the object of their previous laughter. A man had a wooden dowel mounted upright on a flat piece of wood and was slowly unravelling a condom, to guffaws and sniggering from his captive audience.

"He's giving them a lecture about how to use a condom!" Louise exclaimed as we were shoved ruthlessly into the road.

I was shocked to think that these men would not know how to use them, particularly with the threat of AIDS being so prevalent on the news in the UK at that time.

On our return to our room, Sharon informed us that we would be doing three shows again that night; the usual two, plus a third one at the New Seoul Hotel.

I was confused. The New Seoul was the contract which, according to Sharon, we had lost before because of Louise's weight. I glanced across at her with a puzzled expression on my face. Sharon shrugged.

That evening, Mr Lee was waiting for us at the club, all smiles.

"You have six-week contract here. Do good show," he ordered.

"Are we being paid for this, or is it another audition?" I asked, suspicion growing with every passing second.

"Yes, yes, today you get paid," he said, sighing with exasperation, as though I were a complete nuisance.

Afterwards, he took us to Popeye's for dinner and gave us some more mail from home. In my stack of letters, there was one from the English agent. She told me in no uncertain terms that I was out of order phoning my mother and crying. She accused me of 'acting like a child´ and said that I needed to pull myself together and get on with it (or words to that effect.) I was livid and vowed to write her a snotty letter back.

Louise also received a letter, it was from her boyfriend in England.

"Well, girls, it appears I'm young free and single again," she told us.

We had only been in Korea for just over a month. It made me wonder how long my long-distance relationship with my boyfriend, Lenny, would endure.

* * *

On Friday morning, we were startled awake by screaming. We cautiously poked our heads out of the door, in an attempt to establish what was going on. We discovered that another English dance group had arrived during the night. They had been woken up by an Arab who had kicked their door off its hinges. There was a lot of commotion in the corridor as three different languages, English, Arabic and Korean fought for dominance and understanding.

Apart from being surprised that the Arab had succeeded in gaining entrance, we were not overly concerned and chose not to get involved. It was, after all, a situation which we faced on an almost nightly basis, and these girls would have to learn to accept it. As we gathered our things together, walked past them and went onto the roof to sunbathe, Louise smiled.

"Huh! Maybe my door sign works after all," she said.

That night we worked the three venues again. It was half the amount of work that the other groups seemed to be doing, but at least it meant that we should have some regular money coming in for a while – if the elusive Mr Lee could ever be persuaded to pay up!

In the New Seoul club, with the very low ceiling, as we were putting the final touches to our opening costumes, a Korean girl walked into the dressing room, closely followed by a man. For some unknown reason, he was angry and began to do the usual things that we were becoming more than accustomed to when a male Korean was irate: shouting, gesticulating, coughing up phlegm and throwing things. Without warning, he reached out and pushed the girl so hard in her face that she fell backwards onto the floor. Then, for some unknown reason, he became aware that he was being watched and turned his ire on us. His arm shot out and he stabbed Louise in the neck with his index finger.

"Hey! What are you doing you, stupid idiot!" Louise yelled, pushing him away and adopting her aggressive stance. The man glared at her and grunted. He stood in the doorway with his hands on his hips, guarding the entrance like a bodyguard, determined that we were not going to get out.

Then, without warning, our music started playing. We all tried to scramble past this irate Korean to get to the stage on time. Unfortunately for us, he had other plans. He stood his ground, pushing us all backwards each time we took a step towards him. In the end, I just ran at him, head down, like an angry bull so that my feathered headdress went up his nose and in his face. This forced him to take a step backwards. Taking advantage of his weakness, we pushed him towards the wall and charged past, managing to make it to the stage just in time!

Throughout the opening routine, I was dreading going back to the dressing-room for the first quick change, but fortunately, when we returned, he was nowhere in sight.

Back at the hotel, after this latest episode, I sat down and composed a letter to the English agent in reply to hers:

'Dear Marion, I think you would also cry if you were constantly out of work and on the rare occasion that you did work, you were never paid by the agent. How would you like to live off one sandwich a day? How would you like to worry where your next meal was coming from? I did not come here to be sat in a hotel room, I came to work. This is not how you ´sold´ the idea of six months in Korea to us. . . '

I was so engrossed in the letter, it wasn't until Sharon informed us that she was going out, that I was even aware that she had been getting ready.

"She won't be back tonight!" Louise said, with a knowing nod as Sharon sauntered off down the corridor.

"What makes you say that?"

"I've just watched her pack an overnight bag: toothbrush, make-up, kimono, knickers - the lot."

"I wonder which one she's meeting tonight?"

"God only knows!" Louise replied.

* * *

Saturday the 29th of April, we followed our usual almost daily routine: a breakfast of salted crackers; a couple of hours' sunbathing on the roof; a potter about in the hotel room; and get ready for work. The only difference was that one person was conspicuous by her absence. Louise had been correct. Sharon had not come back last night.

As we were putting on our make-up and spraying our hair with water to keep it in place, (it was cheaper and more readily available than hairspray) and were discussing how we were going to do the show as a duet rather than a trio, the door opened with a crash, slamming into the wall.

"Sorry I'm late," Sharon said, breezing in. "I stayed on the army base last night. I slept in the barracks, which isn't officially allowed, but they all seem to have their own rooms, so he sneaked me in when nobody was looking."

"Who's 'he'?" I asked.

"Big Malc," she said. "He's African American and he's been here about a year."

"We thought you weren't going to come back for the show," Louise replied.

"Yeah, well, I would have been back sooner, but I convinced him to buy me dinner."

The silence was deadly. Louise and I had not eaten since breakfast and could just about afford an eggy-bread sandwich after work if we were lucky. The social distance between Sharon and us was widening considerably with each passing day.

Work that evening went fine at the Ambassador, but when we got to the Fishtank, we were stopped at the door and turned away.

"You go now. No show today!"

"Here we go again," I said.

It was exasperating never to be given an explanation as to why these things kept happening. At the same time, I immediately thought of the loss of money. This triggered my almost constant state of annoyance that Mr Lee held the purse strings and paid us as little and as infrequently as he desired.

The cancellation of the first show meant that we arrived at the New Seoul earlier than normal and could watch some of the acts which were on before us. As we slipped into some empty seats at the back of the venue, one of the bouncers sidled over and presented me with a red rose.

"I want be your friend," he said, a simple gesture which helped to brighten my mood.

The first act we witnessed was a lesbian act (surprise surprise), the second was a trio of three guys who did a martial arts act; they cut themselves with knives, walked on lit light bulbs and threw darts into each others' backs. The third act consisted of two tumblers who also worked at the Fishtank. Apart from acrobatics, they juggled with fire and footballs and finished each trick by shouting, "Hey hey!" I still found it hard to believe that our show, which seemed tame in comparison, was on the same bill as these acts.

* * *

On Monday, 1st May, the three of us went onto the roof to sunbathe again with the other girls, but this time, it was not the light-hearted, happy-go-lucky ambience as usual. The five girl group was far from content. Mr Lee had been unable to find them work for the past two weeks. Their carefree manner was slowly being replaced by anger, irritation and boredom, three feelings which I knew all too well.

The subject of money – or the lack of it - came up, and as they complained to their head girl, Louise and I joined in, aiming our comments at our head girl. It did not take long for Sharon to take the hint. She went down to reception to call Mr Lee and charged the call to the room. A few minutes later, she returned.

"Mr Lee said he is going to come tomorrow night," she said.

"And what did you say?" I asked.

"Nothing."

"What! Why the hell didn't you tell him that we need cash now?"

"Well, he said he was busy!"

"Yeah, busy spending our money!" I said.

Storming off to the reception, I decided to call him myself. I knew I was about to break an unwritten rule, as Lee only ever liked to address himself to Sharon on the phone – possibly as she gave him the least hassle – but I had had enough.

"Mr Lee, this is Michele. I'm not very happy, not very happy at all," I repeated as he tended to do. "You will have to bring some money because we haven't got any; no money at all and I'm not prepared to starve for anyone!"

"Oh, I busy tonight, but I come tomorrow at 10:00 am."

"Well, you make sure you do, Mr Lee, because I haven't eaten today and I'm starving!" Then I slammed the phone down for added effect.

I was surprised by my actions. I had never liked arguing and had always preferred to talk my way out of trouble, rather than stand up and fight. Granted, it was easier to be confrontational over the phone, rather than face to face and, although I knew I should have said more, I felt that it was a start towards a new, confident, arrogant me.

I also knew that I had Louise to thank for my transformation. From the beginning of the contract, I had admired her forthright approach. She spoke her mind and when she did, people listened. In our current situation, to survive in this male orientated world, a girl needed attitude! It was the only way to be heard and not be taken advantage of. Unaware I was doing so, I had started to model myself on Louise.

That night as we went to the Ambassador, who should be waiting for us, but Mr Lee. He smiled and held out a week's money in his hands.

"Here, girls. Salary."

"Oh, money!" Sharon smiled, taking the wad of dollars with a gracious smile and handing it out.

"Yes, because I phoned him!" I said.

"Well, Michele," said Louise. "At least you have got the right approach. It's about time someone put him in his place!"

"You had no right to phone him!" Sharon fumed.

"I have every right if you aren't doing your job!"

"But, I'm the head girl!"

"Then, bloody well act like it!" I replied.

Mr Lee stopped our bickering by telling us to be quiet, as he had something extremely important to divulge.

"From now on, whenever you are working here, in the Europe (Fishtank) you must pay attention."

"To what?" I asked.

"If the lights go out and the music changes, you must get off the stage immediately. Immediately, you understand? You must also leave the club as quickly as possible," he told us.

"Why?" we asked.

"It will be police. They are checking all the clubs. Here, many clubs no have license for foreign dancers. Europe no have license."

"You don't say!" Louise exclaimed sarcastically. "So, basically if the room is suddenly plunged into darkness and we can't see bugger all, we're supposed to get off the stage, grab all our costumes and leave in five seconds flat!"

Mr Lee nodded. "Exactly."

"Deep joy!" I muttered.

Chapter 7

A PARTY, A PRACTICE AND A PREGNANCY TEST

After work on Friday 5th May, I chose to stay in the hotel room, while Louise and Sharon went out to Itaewon. Subsequently, on Saturday morning, I was informed that two important events had occurred. Firstly, Louise had met an American whose name was Jim, and secondly, our trio and the quintet were having a joint party that evening.

It had been arranged to have the party in our room, as our quarters were much larger than the girls' two smaller rooms. I guessed that the group of five was trying to let off steam. They were still out of work; therefore drinking in the hotel room was a much more economical way of drowning their sorrows. That night, after we had finished work, the girls arrived, each with their respective boyfriends, making quite a crowd of us.

As the night wore on and everyone was a little drunk, three of the girls decided to play a trick on Sharon. They were aware of how many men she had been associated with since our arrival, and they wanted to prove a point to their boyfriends; basically that it appeared that she would go out with anybody! They persuaded one of the guys, Tommy, to ring Sharon from their room and arrange to meet her that night in Itaewon.

"Hi, is that Sharon?" Tommy asked as the three girls crowded around the phone to listen in.

"Yes, who's that?"

"My name is...er... Frank. I've seen you around Itaewon and I find you really attractive."

"Oh, yes ...?" Sharon replied, giggling.

"Yes. Listen, I'd like to meet you. Could you come to the Twilight zone now?"

"Now?"

"Yes, I'd like to get to know you better, if you know what I mean!"

"Okay!" she replied. "How will I recognize you?"

"Er... I'll be wearing a baseball cap of the Bulls and carrying a rose," he told her as the three girlfriends stifled their laughter.

Soon afterwards, she set off, on her own, to the centre of Itaewon at four o'clock in the morning, to meet a man she had never met. According to Louise, she also packed an overnight bag. It was a silly, dangerous trick to play, but the girls wanted to prove to their partners that she would do it. Two hours later, the joke sort of backfired when Sharon returned with a man. The guys were amazed, but the girls felt that they had more than proven their point.

Throughout the party, I felt quite detached, sad and disillusioned. Everyone seemed to be coupled up and I was the odd one out. My boyfriend was thousands of miles away and after Louise had received her 'Dear John´ letter, I was starting to wonder if I was wasting my time trying to remain faithful. I decided that I had two options. I could end up spoiling the party by sitting and crying, or I could find solace in alcohol. I stupidly did the latter.

To drown my sorrows, I concocted a lethal potion of 'punch´, which consisted of a bottle of Sodu, half a bottle of gin, a splash of Jim Beam and peach juice to top it all off. Then I wandered around the room offering it to everyone. There were no takers.

"I'd seriously reconsider drinking that if I were you!" One of the guys advised. "Or, at least, put some yoghurt in it, to line your stomach."

"Nah! It's fine!" I said in my drunken stupor and swigged another long draught of the lethal concoction.

Shortly afterwards, being the only person idiotic enough to drink my potent, miasmatic brew,

I crashed out on my bed, dead to the world while the party continued in full swing around me. During the next few hours, I woke up several times to drag myself to the toilet to be violently sick. The remaining members of the party who were still conscious sat and laughed at my self-inflicted predicament.

"Now, you can officially wear your 'I've had the sodu experience´ t-shirt!" They chortled. I, on the other hand, was far from laughing.

* * *

Due to the worst hangover I had ever experienced in my life, I missed most of the following day. I eventually returned to the land of the living (or just about alive) at around 6:30 pm. My head was throbbing, I could not see straight and I felt dreadful!

Mr Lee arrived, bringing more post. Seeing me lying prone on the bed, he grinned, finding it highly amusing that I was suffering from a hangover, as he had only ever seen me drink coke or screw my nose up at beer.

Fortunately, our contract at the Fishtank had finished on Saturday, so I only had to struggle through two shows. I was determined to work and I did. How I managed to do it though, without throwing up, I am not entirely sure!

* * *

Two days later, the three of us went to say a temporary goodbye to the quintet. After being out of work for over three weeks, Mr Lee had rung the day before to inform them that he had found them some work. The following day, they would be leaving for Cheongju, a distance of about 70 miles from Seoul, so that morning, they were busy packing. The excitement on their faces at the thought of finally working again was heart-warming.

Later, when we returned to our room, the telephone rang, it was our agent.

"Mr Lee said he can't pay us until Thursday because he has to find the money to send the quintet to Cheongju," Sharon said, putting the phone down.

"So, what did you say?" Louise asked.

"Nothing," Sharon's sullen reply prompted an immediate shake of Louise's head.

"Great!"

"That's not our problem," I complained. "I'm so sick of having to fight for our money all the time!"

"Too bloody right!" Louise concurred. "I'm fed up with it too."

Sharon shrugged her shoulders and sighed."Well, what do you expect me to do?"

"Ring him back and tell him it's not good enough!" I said.

Louise and I waited for a reply, which was not forthcoming.

"Right then, this merits a trip to his office," Louise stated. "I want my bloody money. Who's coming with me?"

"Me!" I replied.

Sharon remained mum. As we prepared to leave, she made no effort whatsoever to get off her bed and make the journey with us.

As previously stated, taking long bus journeys in the heat of the day, being stared at, pushed and jostled almost continuously did not help to put one in a good mood, so Louise and I were raring to go and ready for a confrontation by the time we entered Lee's office.

Our agent did not have time to hide away, as he was just leaving as we entered. Whether he felt outnumbered, or he could tell that we meant business, I'm not really sure, but he handed over a full week's money on the spot.

Consequently, we spent a pleasant afternoon shopping in Iteawon. I even ordered myself a leather trouser-suit with a strappy top and matching jacket with tassels down both arms. I struck up a deal with the tailor, which would allow me to pay in instalments – the only way it would have been possible when relying on Mr Lee for regular income.

When we returned to the hotel, we discovered that after the five girls had packed all their belongings, Mr Lee had phoned them again. He informed them that the contract had fallen through and that, unfortunately, they weren't going anywhere. I felt awful, as it made me wonder if this was because we had taken their bus fare by insisting on our wages. I wisely decided to keep my thoughts to myself!

* * *

A couple of days later, I woke up with a streaming cold. (I blamed the Sodu!) Deciding that my defence system must be bordering on virtually none existent, I took myself off to the chemist to ask for vitamin pills. Despite doing my impression of a weakling with a cough and no energy, the poor guy behind the counter did not have the slightest inkling as to what I was trying to say. I resorted to counting out the vitamins on my fingers.

"Vitamin 'A´, vitamin 'B´, vitamin 'C´, vitamin 'D´...."

"Ah!" He said raising his index finger aloft, signifying a moment of lucidity. Telling me to wait, he disappeared into the backroom and returned a few seconds later.

"Finger dressing!" He said.

I sighed, realising that I was getting nowhere but he looked so pleased with himself, I did not have the heart to argue. I left the chemist with a box of plasters and a roll of lint!

That evening, we prepared for work. We were still only doing two shows a night now, but we were consoled by the fact that at least the New Seoul was a decent venue. However, that night, when we started the opening number, all the members of the audience, who were usually quite well behaved, were intoxicated. We spent more time pushing people off the stage than dancing!

The finale of our show was no better. During my playback number, a man began imitating me by walking up and down in front of the stage, making the audience laugh. I, on the other hand, felt humiliated and more than a little angry, so I decided to take my revenge.

I had had enough of being ridiculed, so the next time he sauntered past, I leant forward and walloped him on the head with considerable force with my trusty microphone. In fact, I hit him so hard, that the top of the microphone broke into two pieces! He cried out and clutched his head, then he swung around to face me. His jovial expression had warped into a murderous one. He launched himself onto the stage. As I fled screaming to the back, bouncers had to step in to protect me while they removed him.

Unfortunately, after the show, things did not get any easier. I was standing against a wall, waiting to leave the club when a man walked past me, turned around and nipped my behind. He then just sauntered off as though nothing had happened and leant against the same wall but further down. As I was still fuming from being ridiculed on stage, this was the last straw! I charged up to him and nipped his backside so hard that he yelped in pain!

"You don't like it, do you?" I said, trying to look as intimidating as possible. "Then don't do it to me!"

As he scurried away, bowing and rubbing his bottom at the same time, I felt more than a little jubilant and smug that my actions had had the required effect. I also had to admit that the naïve young dancer who had arrived six weeks ago was beginning to toughen up. I was not sure if that was a positive attribute or not, but I had started to believe it was necessary.

* * *

Early the next morning, I announced to the girls that I was going out.

"Where are you going?" Louise asked. Up until this point in the contract, she had taken me under her wing and 'mothered´ me – something which I greatly appreciated, as she was much more street-smart and worldly-wise than me. She had also taken to accompanying me everywhere, as she was well aware that I had NO sense of direction what-soever. Unless I have repeated a route at least six times, I have little hope of finding my way anywhere!

"Just to the photoshop and the post office," I replied. "The same two places as always."

"Wait a minute, I'll get dressed and come with you. I think you had better not go alone," she said.

That particular morning, I got the impression that she was offering to accompany me more out of obligation than pleasure. I knew she was tired, as she had been out with GI Jim the night before. I did not want her to feel impelled to accompany me, and after all, this was the new confident 'me´, who felt much more prepared to face the world alone.

"Louise, I'm sure I'll be fine. I'm only going to the photoshop and the post office," I repeated. "I know my way there and back, we've done it so many times now. I'm quite capable of going on my own. – What could possibly go wrong?"

Off I went, feeling quite proud of the new self-assured me and my newfound independence. After collecting my photos, I tripped off to the post office, and it was there, that everything unexpectedly went awry!

I was standing at the counter after just buying some stamps when, without warning, a deafening air-raid siren reverberated outside. The moment it began to resonate around the city in a blaring cacophony of sound, it became immediate action stations within the post office. The postal workers pushed all the Koreans into a side room, but they chose to manhandle me to the main door, pushed me outside and locked it!

I stood there in shock. I had no idea what was happening. The noise was earsplitting and on top of that, the frantic scene unfolding before me did nothing to calm my nerves.

Everywhere I looked, people were running for shelter, so I started running too! Main roads with six lanes of traffic, which were usually impossible to cross, had come to a complete standstill. The occupants had abandoned their cars and were sheltering in shop doorways and subway entrances. All the little stalls which were always stationed up and down the street had been deserted or taken away.

At that point, I started to panic and continued to run. An old man grabbed my arm and pulling me to a stop, he gabbling in Korean, looked heavenwards and pointed to the sky. I looked up too, expecting to see aircraft fighters; but all I could see was a clear blue sky. Nevertheless, I was convinced the man was trying to tell me that fighter planes were on their way. Visions of war films flashed through my head and I was petrified!

This is it! I thought to myself. *I'm going to get bombed by North Korea. I'm going to die here!* My only lucid thought was to get back to the hotel and the girls as quickly as possible. I ran as fast as my legs could take me. Along the, by now, almost deserted streets, shaking off anyone who tried to drag me into subways and shop doorways. If I was going to die, I wanted to be with the girls!

When I managed to reach the hotel and ran inside, my heart was pounding, I was short of breath but even then, I did not stop running until I charged up the stairs, reached the seventh floor, burst open the room door and came to an abrupt stop.

"WE'RE GOING TO BE BOMBED!" I shouted.

Sharon and Louise, who were sitting quite calmly munching on tuna and mayonnaise sandwiches (complements of Jim), turned their heads and looked with amusement in my direction. I could not quite comprehend how they could sit there, so pleasantly relaxed while the air raid siren continued to ring out across Seoul.

"What?" I asked, confused by their lack of urgency.

"Michele, look at the television, it's just an air-raid practice!" Sharon said. "They do these every couple of months so that the South Koreans know what to do if ever they are attacked by the North."

Running along the bottom of the screen in English it read:

"This is an air-raid practice. Please stay inside. Do not go out."

I stood there, red-faced, with my hair all over the place, sweating buckets, and breathing like I'd just finished a marathon, with my letters and stamps still clutched in my hand. The realisation that we were safe came with mixed feelings. Relief, obviously, but I also felt utterly embarrassed. What a complete idiot I had made of myself! I had to admit that my naivety, which I had assumed I had banished forever, was still there after all.

My tough façade was not as strong as I thought it was either!

Louise continued to look me up and down with a bemused expression on her face as she continued to eat her sandwich.

"I told you not to go out on your own," she said.

* * *

Later that same day, we were surprised to learn that the quintet (who were still out of work), had had a massive argument. Three of the girls had told Mr Lee that they had had enough and wanted to go home, but the other two preferred to stay. This was causing a huge rift between them all, and it became commonplace to find two or three of them in our room at any given time of the day or night, in an attempt to escape the tension.

The realization that we were still working, even if we were only doing two shows a night, somehow did not seem too bad after all - despite still having to endure our weekly fight for wages with Mr Lee.

It was during this time that one of the girls, who shall remain nameless, asked me to do her a favour.

"I haven't started my period, and I think I might be pregnant!" she confided in me.

"What are you going to do?" I asked.

"I was wondering if you would go to the chemist for me and ask for a pregnancy kit?"

"Me?" Remembering my last attempt at trying to obtain vitamin pills, I surmised that I was probably not the best person for the job. Knowing my luck, I would end up with medicine for constipation or something worse.

She seemed to read my thoughts, (or my facial expression.)

"Don't worry, I know exactly where the tests are. All you'll have to do is point to it. I'd do it myself," she added. "I just don't want the others to find out. After all, it might be a false alarm."

Against my better judgement, I reluctantly agreed and we set off for the chemist's, whilst I was given instructions as to the exact location of the pregnancy test. I went inside while she chose to wait outside, trying not to look conspicuous. I was served by a woman pharmacist this time, who looked quite concerned for my welfare. She gave me the pregnancy kit, and as she handed me the change, she patted the back of my hand and gave me a reassuring smile.

Great! I thought. *Now she thinks I'm pregnant!*

Back at the hotel, the test was carried out in the bathroom. The results turned out to be negative and nobody was ever aware of the situation. However, it would be me who would suffer the repercussions.

For the next few months, I became aware that every time I passed the chemist, the woman would stare fixedly at my stomach. I guess she was looking for some signs of growth! After two months, her watchful eye was becoming tedious, so I decided to stagger past the premises, holding out my dress, as though I were heavily pregnant. She laughed (behind her hand of course) and never looked at my stomach area again.

* * *

The following evening, we went off to work to do our two shows. At the New Seoul club, every time Louise danced, a man stood up as though drawn to her magnetically and made his way to the front of the stage. He stood in front of her and stared in amazement at the size of her chest. It was hilarious. Even Louise saw the funny side. In the end, a bouncer had to move him away.

Later, in the same show when I performed the 'playback' routine, a different man stood in front of the stage transfixing me with lifeless black eyes full of hatred.

"YOU! YOU!" He repeated over and over again, pointing at me and eyeing me with malicious intent.

"What's his problem?" I muttered to the girls as we went through the routine.

"Maybe he's the guy you hit with the microphone the other day!" Louise quipped. We all started laughing.

After the show, Mr Lee made a surprise appearance.

"Come, come. You have show in other club. The Carnegie nightclub."

"Are we getting paid for this one, Mr Lee?" I asked.

"Audition, audition!" he said, walking away.

"No surprise there then!" Louise muttered as she stuffed her costumes into the case.

I was hoping that this would be another opportunity to earn a bit more money, but when we arrived at the venue, there had been a change of plan. It appeared that the manager had 'stepped out'. We hung around for a while but eventually left, never to return. Whatever dodgy deal Mr Lee had arranged, appeared to have fallen through.

* * *

The following night, all eight girls went into Itaewon to the usual haunts: Twilight zone, Kings, Seoul Train and the kettle house, which meant that we didn't get home until 7:45 am. We had been sleeping about an hour when our door crashed opened and in came one of the guys from reception whom we had nicknamed Stuart.

"Excuse me, excuse me," he said brightly, marching across the room and opening the curtains to allow the early morning sun to stream into the darkened room. As our eyes adjusted to the light, we realised that bringing up the rear was a little man dressed in a gas mask and overalls. He was carrying a big square container on his shoulders, with a thick rubber hose attached to it.

"Oh. Look! It's the Ghost-busters!" I quipped.

As we had not been given any time to do anything except sit up and watch the proceedings in a stupefied, befuddled manner, the little man began by walking towards Louise's bed and spraying some foul-smelling liquid all over the carpet.

"Hey! What the hell are you doing?" Louise shouted, rubbing her sleep-filled eyes and cupping a hand over her mouth so as not to breathe in the putrid, stinking concoction that was soaking into the carpet.

The Ghost-buster babbled something inaudible through his mask and continued spraying.

"Clean carpet," Stuart informed us – as if we had not already guessed that much.

"Well, bugger off, we're sleeping!" Louise said and narrowed her groggy eyes in his direction but to no avail.

The Ghost-buster moved over to Sharon's bed and then mine until the whole room reeked of rancid chemicals, and the carpet was decidedly soggy underfoot. Then, just as abruptly as they had appeared, they left.

"What the hell are we breathing in?" Louise complained putting her hand over her mouth again. "If he's got to wear a mask, I don't think we should stay in here."

Sharon and I agreed, so at 9:30 am after just one hour's sleep, we found ourselves back in Itaewon again.

We eventually returned to our hotel and a soggy, odorous carpet in the early afternoon. Ex-

hausted, we managed to cram in just four hours'
sleep before we had to go back to work.

* * *

The next day, we found out that three of the five
girl group would be going home that day. It was
quite a sad occasion and marked the end of an
era. The two remaining girls would start work as
a duo, adapting the show accordingly.

Mr Lee came to the hotel to collect the departing three, but he seemed unable to look at them. I
could not decide if this was because he felt guilty
for not fulfilling his part of the contract by provid-
ing them with constant work or if he was annoyed
with them for leaving and breaking the deal. Either way, I was upset to see them go. However,
intermingled in their leaving, was the flicker of
hope that, perhaps now, with fewer dancers, we
might get paid a little bit more regularly.

* * *

On Friday 18th May, in the late afternoon, as we
were preparing for work, our door opened and in
walked another guy from reception. This time he
had a team of men with him.

"Will you bloody knock before you come barging in here whenever you bleeding well feel like
it!" Louise shouted.

"You move room. Men clean carpet."

"Again? What the hell are they going to put on
it this time?" I complained.

"You cleaned it two days ago, Sharon told them.

"You change rooms. NOW!"

"Hang on a minute," said Louise, looking at us. "Let's think about this. If we change rooms, it will probably be permanent. I doubt we'll get this one back again."

"Good point," I replied. "The other rooms that we've seen are much smaller. And apart from that, I've grown quite accustomed to this room now - warts and all. You know, the cockroaches, brown dripping tap water and everything!"

Louise turned to face the intruders.

"We're not moving, you can clean the room around us."

"You move!"

"Nope!" We sat in silent protest on the beds and refused to budge.

After a few minutes of our non-verbal standoff, we won. The team entered with vacuum cleaners, steam cleaners, foam – the works and cleaned around us, as we decided to commandeer the mirrors and continued putting on our makeup. All the furniture was fumigated and placed on top of the beds, the carpet was, once again, washed and steam cleaned. We squelched out of the room to go to work, returning that night to a slightly less soggy carpet and smelly furniture which was still on the beds, its odorous concoction of chemicals slowly seeping into the bedclothes. Despite this, our morale was on a high. We had succeeded in keeping our big room and that felt like a huge victory.

* * *

On Saturday night, we did the shows and Louise's zip broke again. Sharon was angry and confronted her after the show.

"Go into Itaewon tomorrow and get it fixed," she ordered. "Take it to the same place where you got it repaired before."

This turned into an argument as Louise did not like being told what to do by anyone – and particularly not by Sharon.

"You do it. It's your job. You're the head girl."

"But it's your costume."

"I couldn't give a shit!"

The ride home in the Bongo van was tense, to say the least. Back at the hotel, after I could no longer stand the strained atmosphere, I forced myself to suggest that all three of us should go out for a drink and chill out. However, as soon as the taxi dropped us in Itaewon, I regretted it. I always felt uncomfortable there at night, and it certainly wasn't somewhere I could chill out.

As usual, we visited the same four clubs, this time ending up in the Twilight Zone rather than starting there. Apathy must have been etched on my face because a GI came over and sat down next to me.

"What's wrong? Why do you look so bored?"

"I look bored because I *am* bored!" I replied, wondering how I was going to get rid of him.

The guy looked at me in total shock.

"But...? That's just not possible! How can you possibly be bored when there are over a thousand GI's here?" he said, with a look of complete incredulity on his face.

"So what?" I replied. "I'm not interested in finding a man."

"But...we are American soldiers!" He replied, genuinely shocked.

"Just because you are a soldier in the army doesn't mean that I am obligated to go out with you," I replied.

He left, only to be replaced five minutes later by another GI, who came swaggering over to try his luck. This one presented me with a rose.

"I've been looking all around this place and your beauty is beyond description. You are by far the most beautiful girl in the joint," he said.

Yeah, yeah... I thought. *Here we go again. More corny chat up lines!*

There later followed more small talk and corny one-liners, but when he realised that he was getting absolutely nowhere, his demeanour changed.

"Why are you playing so hard to get?"

"Look," I said trying to let him down nicely. "I'm just not interested. I have a boyfriend in England, okay?"

"So?" He replied. "I've got a wife in the States, but it doesn't stop me!"

I felt so sorry for his wife! "Well, you see, the thing is that I've got morals, something that you obviously lack!" I replied.

"You can say what you want," he spat. "But I don't believe for one minute that you haven't slept with anyone since you got here!"

"I don't care whether you believe me or not!" I spat back. Throwing the rose back in his face, I told him to leave me alone.

Later, one of the girls from the five girl group who had stayed behind to form the duo came in, she also did not appear to be too happy. I asked her what was wrong, but in retrospect, I was the last person who should have enquired.

"I feel like shit!" she said.

"Why, what's happened?"

"I was in bed with my boyfriend, right?" she began. "And while we were doing it, do you know what he said?"

"No, what?"

"He said, 'you know that Michele? I think she's really lovely. She'll break a lot of hearts without even trying. All the guys find her attractive because she's like a little girl,'" she sniffed.

"Oh... I'm sorry about that!" I said, feeling extremely incommodious. Conversation from that point onwards ground to an uncomfortable halt. I searched my brain with frantic urgency, trying to find something to talk about in order to change the subject!

"So, what's it like working as a duo?" I said, cringing inside.

* * *

I woke up on Sunday morning to find Sharon in bed with another GI she had pulled the night before. As I contemplated getting up, the phone rang. It turned out to be her African American squeeze 'Big Malc', who seemed to be an on-again-off-again- regular in Sharon's life.

As he questioned her about her antics the previous night, she fiddled with the sheets.

"No, of course, nothing happened! We were just talking, that's all."

I shook my head in complete bewilderment. There was the guy she had 'only been talking to', strewn across the bed, as large as life, struggling to sit up.

Louise and I made a quick exit and spent most of the day outside, leaving Sharon with her latest conquest. Later that early evening, we returned to find that the GI had gone and Sharon was sitting on her bed, applying her make-up while eating a packet of crisps.

When the time came for us to check we had packed all the correct costumes and accessories, there was a heavy stand-off between Louise and Sharon when it became apparent that both of them had forgotten to mend Louise's zip which had broken the previous evening.

"I thought *you* were going to mend it," Sharon argued. "You've been out all day you could easily have done it."

"I did it last time. It's not my job. If you spent less time in bed, you could have done it!" Louise replied.

The arguing continued, but it was too late to do anything about it. We were scheduled to leave in fifteen minutes. In the end, we had to wear outfits borrowed from the second show's costumes, which we no longer performed. To further add fuel to the already enraging fire, Sharon then informed us that we would not be wearing the feather headdresses either, as she had mislaid the huge clips we used to keep them in place.

I felt like any hint of professionalism we still possessed was slowly waning away, to be replaced by complacency, coupled with a severe lack of interest from all members of the group.

Doing a show was now equated to a factory production line. We churned out the goods with little thought about the end product. In fact, the only time we made any real effort was when we were forced to do the unpaid auditions. At least then, we had to try and win a contract, but the lack of respect we received from agents and managers on a daily basis was what had made us into the disgruntled trio we had become.

After work, Big Malc turned up (probably looking for evidence of the other GI) and Sharon told him he could stay the night. It was less than twelve hours since another soldier had been sleeping in the exact same spot. However, at least the one from the previous night had not disturbed me. Unfortunately, with Big Malc, I didn't get a wink of sleep because of his snoring. In the end, tired and exasperated, I woke him up and politely asked him to leave.

* * *

Monday 22nd May was Louise's birthday. Sharon's boyfriend Big Malc returned with a birthday cake for Louise and a card for me. I was slightly confused as to why I was receiving a card, but when I opened it, I realised that it was to apologise for my lack of sleep the previous night. I thought this was a kind gesture, which made him rise in my estimation.

Shortly afterwards, Louise's boyfriend, Jim, arrived and took us all to Yongsan army base for lunch. The afternoon passed all too quickly and we had no choice but to return to the Central Hotel to get ready for the shows.

After work, we all headed to Itaewon. I was not in the mood to go again and to be honest, I felt like a gooseberry as I was the only one without a partner. At one point I ended up crying, as I felt so lonely. For this reason, when an Iranian named Mohammed approached me and said he was going home the following day, I decided that it would not do any harm to talk to him. He told me that he had seen me in the hotel as he was also staying there. It crossed my mind that he could actually be stalking me and had followed me to the club. However, as I did not want to ruin Louise's birthday any more than I already had by my outburst of tears, I played along.

Unfortunately, for me my plan backfired, as the following day, the Iranian rang my room (I had not given him my number), to inform me that he had changed his plans and was extending his visit to Seoul for another week.

Later that day, he knocked on the door and said he wanted to talk to me. I began to feel really uncomfortable. He seemed like a nice guy, but I did not want to encourage him. I had no intention of having anything more than a friendship with him, so I tried to make it quite obvious that his visit was inconvenient.

I continued washing my clothes in the bathtub and cleaning my part of the room assuming that he would get the message that he was wasting his time. His visit lasted an agonising five minutes and then he left. I hoped that that would be the end of it – but I was wrong.

* * *

Two days later, the three of us went to Mr Lee's office in search of our wages and then went shopping. We had been paid the full amount - probably due to the fact that the quintet had become a duet - so I treated myself to an amethyst gold ring which cost a mere £32- this made the thought of working that night, seem slightly more acceptable.

That evening, after we had finished the second show, we climbed into the Bongo van thinking that we were heading back to the hotel. However, our driver swung the van around, veered off our usual route and began weaving in and out of some of the back streets of Seoul.

"Where the hell is he taking us?" Sharon questioned.

"Perhaps we've got another audition that we don't know about," I said. My prediction turned out to be correct. The Bongo van pulled up outside the 'Diamond´ nightclub, where our agent was standing outside.

"This is audition. You do good show. You work here one month, maybe two," Mr Lee informed us with his usual false grin.

"Yeah, yeah, we know," I replied; my voice dripping with sarcasm. "Yet another free show."

After the audition, we were forced to sit at a table with the owner and Mr Lee as they haggled over prices and drank whiskey. I felt like a piece of merchandise and no longer a member of the human race as the owner of the club eyed the three of us up and down evaluating our worth.

We got back to the hotel, in the early hours of the morning, feeling both tired and irritable. To make matters worse, we had only been back in our room a few minutes when Mohammed appeared again. This time he bore gifts: some English tea and a handful of pistachio nuts! Louise read my facial expression and knew that I was uncomfortable about accepting these things. He was a nice guy, but by bringing gifts, he affirmed what I had previously dreaded. He wanted more from this friendship than I did.

"Sorry, Mohammed, but Michele and I are going out, so you can't stay very long," Louise informed him, helping to relieve him of his presents.

"Where are you going?" He asked, – a fair question seeing as how it was about two-thirty in the morning.

"There's an all-night indoor market that we've heard about," Louise explained. "And we want to go and see it."

"Great, I'll come too!" he replied.

This was not what we had hoped he would say but after taking off our make-up and changing into something more suitable, the three of us trooped off to find the market.

It was a large indoor building, with high ceilings and little stalls with merchandise which reached as high as the roof. We wove in and out of the multiple aisles, taking in the atmosphere. The place was bustling with customers even at that early hour of the morning. The stalls sold ready-made clothes or material, sequins, beads and accessories to make your own.

Mohammed offered to pay for anything I expressed an interest in, but I politely refused. I did not want to accept anything which could be misconstrued as encouraging his affection. An hour or so later, somehow, without purposely doing so, we lost Mohammed in the market and made our way back to the hotel.

* * *

On Thursday 25th Louise and I went shopping for food in a department store called Printemps. We were always limited to what we could buy, due to not having any cooking facilities in the hotel, but we stocked up on sandwich supplies, Ramen noodles, crackers, crisps, chocolate, cake, water and fizzy drinks. Within five minutes of our return, there was a knock on the door. Sharon peered through the spy hole then looked at me.

"It's Mohammed," she whispered.

"I'm not here!" I hissed back, shooting into the bathroom and silently castigating myself for ever having spoken to him in the first place.

"Sorry, but you've just missed her, she's gone to the shop."

"Oh, okay. I'll come back later," he said. The situation was becoming exceedingly more exasperating as the days went by.

That evening I managed to sneak out of the hotel without seeing Mohammed and we went to do our final show at the Ambassador. This meant that we would soon be down to one show a night which signified that our wages would decrease drastically and that was already starting to concern us all.

The only remaining venue, the New Seoul, was our one step away from unemployment and unfortunately, was no longer the most pleasant of places to work. The disco dancers there were no longer talking to us very much. The atmosphere in the dressing room had become uncomfortable, bordering on hostile - something to which Sharon seemed to be oblivious, which was surprising, considering that she was the cause of the contention.

The reason for this hostility was because Sharon had started flirting with one of the DJs who just so happened to be the boyfriend of one of the disco dancers. Consequently, every time the dancer saw Sharon hanging around him, it caused jealousy, uneasiness and confusion. The situation had become so intense, that it was almost a relief to leave there every night.

After work that evening, as the driver dropped us back at the hotel, he climbed out of the van and came towards us. With a solemn expression on his face, he held out his hand.

"See you again some time," he said. With a sombre expression on his face, he shook our hands. We looked at each other nervous expectation.

"That sounds ominous," I said.

"Tomorrow, no work?" Sharon asked him in Pidgin English.

He shook his head.

"Well," Louise sighed. "It looks like we're out of work again."

We trudged back to our room in a state of deep despondency.

A few minutes later, the telephone rang.

"I bet it's Mr Lee to tell us the bad news!" I said.

"Nope," Sharon whispered. "It's Mohammed for you. Are you in?"

"I'm not here!" I whispered.

"Sorry, she's gone to Iteawon with Louise!" she told him.

* * *

Early the next morning, Louise and I sat on our beds looking at Sharon as she rang Mr Lee to get the bad news.

"Last night our driver said he wasn't coming tomorrow. Does this mean we aren't working, Mr Lee?" Sharon asked.

"No. You work. He not work. He not work for me anymore."

"Ah, okay!" Sharon grinned, and we all breathed a sigh of relief.

"Manager from another club was in New Seoul last night," said Mr Lee. "He see your show. Maybe you have other contract."

That was much better news than we had been expecting! As we sat on our beds, relieved, smiling and chatting about the unexpected turn of events, a massive cockroach, about ten centimetres in length, ran out of the bathroom and stopped in the middle of the room.

"Shit!" I cried.

"That's a Fuck off cockroach!" Sharon exclaimed, making me immediately think of Jeffrey 'The big fat fucker' and his propensity for sex.

"What are we going to do?" I voiced aloud. The cockroach had stopped running and now stood motionless in the middle of the floor, glaring at each of us in turn as it plotted its next move. We knew from experience that cockroaches of this size were virtually impossible to kill when on a carpet. Stamping on them on the bathroom floor could usually finish them off, but then we had to wash our shoes, as the eggs could be spread across the carpet as we walked.

"Here," said Louise throwing me an empty coffee jar, "Trap it under there, then we can slide some paper underneath it and throw it out of the window."

After a couple of failed attempts – because I lost my nerve whenever it moved – it was finally trapped inside the upturned coffee jar. I then began the process of sliding a folded piece of paper underneath. I was hoping that the cockroach would facilitate the procedure and oblige by stepping onto the stationary, but this one had other ideas.

"Oh My God! It's eating the paper!" I screamed.

Sure enough, a sizeable chunk had gone from the folded piece of stationery, and we could actually hear it munching! This made the thought of picking it up decidedly more daunting!

"I vote that we just leave it where it is for now!" I said. "We can think about moving it later."

It was unanimously agreed that the cockroach was going nowhere, so we kept it in our room under the coffee jar and named him Clive. Even the cleaners seemed to respect his position on the carpet and hovered carefully around him. Maybe they thought that Europeans were decidedly weird to want to keep a cockroach as a pet, but they played along.

Clive lasted a full week before his welcomed demise when he was scooped up onto a piece of paper and unceremoniously dumped out of the window.

* * *

On Wednesday 31st May, another trip was made to Mr Lee's office to demand our money. He must have heard all three of us coming up the stairs, as he hid in his back office. The three receptionists tried – unsuccessfully - to convince us that he was out, but we were not so easily persuaded.

"We'll wait," Louise stated, adopting her authoritative, not to be messed with tone of voice and corresponding body language.

In an attempt to make the secretaries feel uncomfortable, I paced continually backwards and forwards across the office floor, while Louise decided to sit cross-legged on the top of one of the desks. Almost instantly becoming bored by just sitting there, she picked up various contents, held them aloft and examined them all one by one. This later progressed to the drawers when Mr Lee had still not put in an appearance. (Sharon stood outside in the corridor.)

After about fifteen minutes of my pacing and Louise's delving, one of the secretaries tried, unsuccessfully, to make a discreet phone call to Mr Lee. The shrill ringing of the phone within his closed, supposedly empty office seemed amplified to heightened proportions in contrast to the complete silence within the front office. When the ringing stopped, and the secretary began to mutter into the telephone, it only concurred with our original belief that our agent was hidden away in there, avoiding us.

A few seconds later, Mr Lee came sauntering out of his room. He feigned surprise and told us he had just returned. As his office had no other exit apart from the one he had just walked through, we knew he was lying, but we chose to ignore it.

"Where's our money?" Louise demanded, still sitting on top of the desk.

Our agent's hand went swiftly to his inside jacket pocket and pulled out a wad of notes. This time he gave us half our salary and some mail.

"Tonight you will do three shows," he said, surprising us all. Apart from the New Seoul, we would be working at a new venue; 'Cheer-girl' and returning to the 'Golden Star', where we had done an audition at the beginning of April.

We were not too impressed that we would be returning to the Golden Star, this was where the clientele had been much older than in the other clubs, they had also been intoxicated and had shown their dislike for the show by pouring milk on the stage. Nevertheless, money was money and we were hardly in a position to turn work down.

That night, as we performed at that venue, a group of men sitting at the front of the stage began waving their complimentary warm, white hand towels in the air, like a flag to catch our attention – which worked.

As we danced, one man began to fold his up in such a way that, as it was being wrapped and manipulated, it slowly rose up off the table to resemble an erect penis! They thought it was highly amusing, I, on the other hand, was more intrigued as to how it had been done.

After that show, we went onto The Cheer-girl which had a decent-sized stage and a pleasant atmosphere within the club, which made a change. However, after the first show, we were told that the management would prefer us to wear more than a bikini and feathers for the opening number. They did not specify as to what they preferred us to wear, and we were rather limited as to what we could offer because we only had four full sets of costumes. The following day, we replaced the bikini tops for the sequined butterfly tops. After the show, we were told that these tops were worse than the original bikinis and that we should revert to our original attire for the next show!

The subsequent day, our driver arrived an hour late. This meant that we didn't do the show at the Cheer-girl that night. The driver said it was due to a time change, but I had a sneaking suspicion it had something to do with the costume debacle. My intuition proved to be correct. We also did not work in the Golden Star, but we had no idea why. This meant that we only worked at one venue. Once again, our dream of three shows a night appeared to have evaporated into thin air.

As always, every time we were reduced to one show, I felt uneasy and constantly fretted as to how long we would continue before we were out of work again. We seemed to live in a vicious circle. First the constant fight for our money, then whenever we got paid, we would send some money home concealed within carbon paper in letters to our parents – at least I did! Or we would buy something frivolous on a mad shopping spree. The rest of the week would be spent limiting ourselves to more noodles and sandwiches until the fight for money began again.

We also had an ever-present predicament with debt in the hotel, in the form of our constantly rising telephone bill. Sharon was either phoning Mr Lee or one of her many boyfriends, and we had all rung home on occasion, to speak to our parents when we didn't have sufficient funds to buy telephone cards. As time passed and the account rose, the end result was being shouted at from reception, every time we entered or left the building.

"Telephone Chargee!" they would bellow at every available opportunity, flapping wads of paper in their hands as we scarpered, making a hasty retreat for the exit or the lift.

"Naeil" (tomorrow) – we usually replied, but sometimes we chose to ignore them completely.

The telephone was also a source of contention in our room. Sharon had first rights to it being head girl, and it had to be said, that the majority of the time whenever the phone rang, it was for her. However, nine times out of ten the person on the other end of the line was of American descent and not our agent. The phone calls at all hours of the day and night were becoming nothing less than infuriating.

One day, when Big Malc had phoned several times to speak to Sharon who was out with someone else, our patience was wearing exceedingly thin. The next time it rang, we both sighed.

"Right, I've had enough of this!" Louise grumbled. Then, she picked up the phone. From the devilment etched across her face, I knew she was up to something.

"Hello?"

"Hi, it's Malc, can I speak with Sharon? Is she back yet?"

"Hello?" Louise repeated, faking a bad connection. "Hello, is there anyone there?"

This amused me no end. It was something which would have never occurred to me to do, and I was trying my hardest to stifle my laughter.

"Hello? HELLO!" she yelled into the telephone. "Michele, can you hear anyone on the telephone?" Louise pushed the receiver towards me and shook her hand urging me to take it.

I wiggled a finger in her direction and shook my head, trying to curb my giggling behind a cupped hand. Louise, revelling in my predicament, insisted that I took the receiver.

"Hello. . . .? Mr Lee is that you?" I managed to say without cracking up. "No, Louise, I can't hear anything!" I said, pushing the receiver back to her.

"HELLO?" Louise yelled into the phone. "I do wish people would stop giving us silly phone calls and leave us in PEACE!" she slammed the phone down.

We burst out laughing. I could not remember the last time I'd laughed so much since my arrival in Korea. It helped to release so much pent up frustration. I vowed to try and see the funny side of life more – something which was much easier said than done.

Later that day, we went to the New Seoul to do our one and only show of the night. Sharon began to flirt with the DJ again and was oblivious to the mood in the dressing-room. I, on the other hand, was not. The atmosphere was electric with nervous, aggressive tension.

The Korean girls flashed angry glances at Sharon and then back towards each other. I looked across at Louise who gestured that she could also sense the unpleasantness. Without warning, the DJ's disco-dancer-girlfriend, who had been watching the proceedings through narrowed eyes, abruptly threw a fit. She stood up and charged forwards, screaming, yelling and pushing the DJ, who stood there in silence with a complacent, smug expression on his face.

Sharon withdrew to a safer distance, looked at us and shrugged.

"It's amazing that she has no idea of the tension she has been causing!" I whispered.

"Just keep your voice down and don't make eye contact with anyone," Louise said in lowered tones.

To be honest, on this occasion, I had not needed to be told. I was waiting for the dancer to pick up the proverbial chair and throw it across the room, so I was standing as far away from the action as was humanly possible. However, this did not happen, so I had to assume that it was only a trait practised by Korean men.

The girl continued screaming and yelling until she collapsed on the floor and started crying. At that conjuncture, the DJ turned on his heels and sauntered out of the dressing room with his hands in his pockets as though nothing out of the ordinary had occurred.

All eyes were on the distressed dancer, yet no-one dared to approach her. Eventually, she pushed herself up onto two arms and theatrically dragged herself out of the dressing-room, never to be seen again.

"Well! What the hell was that all about?" Sharon asked. She could not believe the incredulous scene we had just witnessed.

Louise and I shook our heads in disbelief.

"You must have known that was her boyfriend," Louise replied.

"Well, of course, I knew!" Sharon replied impatiently. "But, for God's sake, I was only talking!"

We were unable to establish if the dancer had quit her job or if she had been sacked. From that point onwards, the breach in the relationship between us and the remaining disco dancers widened significantly.

* * *

After the show, our driver told us that he was taking us to meet Mr Lee for a beer but after the antics in the dressing-room, none of us wanted to go. We were not in the mood. Louise and Sharon had both made previous plans for the evening anyway and spending free time with our agent was not on the itinerary.

Louise's significant other, Jim, was waiting for her in our room at the hotel, and Sharon was meeting Big Malc in Itaewon. As far as I was concerned, the less I saw of our agent, the better.

"Tell Mr Lee we don't want a beer," Louise told the driver. "I'm sick of being pushed around. We are all tired. Take us home."

The driver did our bidding, but the moment we stepped inside the Central Hotel, the telephone started to ring. It was an extremely peeved Mr Lee:

"You get back in van. You must do what driver say! You have audition. NOW!" he screamed down the phone.

Under much duress and more than a little moaning, we conformed and dragged the case back to the Bongo van.

Our audition was to be performed in the 'Pan Korea´ club, a large venue with tables laid out like a restaurant, with table cloths, cutlery, china and glassware. The guests could dine by candle-light whilst watching a show at the same time.

"Wow! This is quite a marked step up from all our previous venues!" I remarked as we were led through the club to the dressing-room.

The girls nodded in agreement.

The stage was enormous and behind each act, there was a complicated water display taking place. Our show would be no different.

As we stepped over sheeted plastic to our designated spots, there was a whirring of machinery and jets of water rocketed into the air. These were accompanied by a myriad of different lights that created a display of synchronized swirling, exploding patterns that, in all honesty, was probably more entertaining than our show!

I say this because, to be honest, our performance that night was atrocious! There was so much water leaking and spitting onto the stage where we were dancing that we were constantly splashed. These spattered drops of icy cold water which landed unexpectedly on our bare flesh caused us to jump and yell out. This and the ever-growing puddles created by dodgy plumbing caused us to slip, lose our balance and almost fall over innumerable times.

Not only that – but probably because of it- I made a complete mess of the opening number! We had been doing the same routines for so long now that it was possible to dance while thinking about other things entirely: what we were going to do after the show, where we were going to eat, contemplate on the day etcetera. However, on this occasion, when my mind returned to the present, I realised that I had been doing a different part of the dance to the other two!

To complicate matters even further, on top of this, Louise was constantly crying in between each number. She had developed a terrible pain in her side and could hardly stand up straight, never mind dance.

"Huh! Well, I doubt we'll be back there again!" Sharon sniffed as we left the club: me apologising and Louise crying. Fortunately, Sharon was wrong!

Chapter 8

TOWERS, STADIUMS AND APARTMENTS

On the morning of Sunday 4th June, Jim invited Louise and me to his army base, Camp Essayons, in Uijeongbu, which required us to travel by subway for almost an hour. When we arrived, Louise casually asked me if I had brought a form of identification.

"What? No! I didn't know I'd have to!" I said, immediately stressing out and believing that I would have to spend the entire day off base or make my own way back on the train and knowing I'd never find my way there.

"I never thought," Louise replied. "But, yeah, the guards won't let you in without I.D."

Just then, Jim arrived.

"Leave this to me," he said and approached the two young soldiers on the gate. I was unable to hear most of the conversation until he turned and pointed in my direction. "Well, just look at her, guys. She's hardly a threat to American security, is she?"

I flashed my sweetest smile in their direction and one guard sheepishly beckoned me towards him and let me sign in.

I was so glad he did, as I had a lovely day. At lunchtime, we had a barbeque at the communal BBQ area, a small patio zone with bricked structures or open grills to cook on – or as Jim called it, 'a cookout'. Later, we played pool and darts then Jim sneaked Louise and me into his room. I was intrigued to find a single room, not a communal bedroom. It was compact but complete with a bed, wardrobe and desk. We had some photos taken sitting on his bed, wearing his army jacket and holding a cushion with the American flag emblazoned on it.

In the early evening, we sneaked back out of his barracks and went to the canteen to get some takeaway food. I stopped to have my photo taken holding my dinner tray next to two huge tanks: A photo which I still love to this day.

All too soon, it was time to return to reality and go back to the Central Hotel to get ready for our two shows. As we rushed inside the hotel to echoes of "Telephone Chargee" I could not help but wish that I was living in Korea under different circumstances.

* * *

The following evening, when we arrived at the Diamond we found a new group commandeering the dressing room. They comprised of a male singer and his six backing dancers who had all just come off stage. As we said hello and started to prepare our costumes, the singer left us in no doubt as to his contempt in having to share a dressing-room with foreigners. His eyes narrowed to such an extent that they were barely visible, and he muttered constant expletives under his breath.

His dancers were decidedly edgy as they changed into their outdoor clothes and gathered up their belongings. It was more than evident that they had experienced his behaviour before and knew what to expect. We, on the other hand, did not.

Before we knew what was happening, he picked up a drum and threw it across the room. As soon as it landed, he turned around and slapped one of the girls hard across the face. She stood there in submission and lowered her eyes while he continued glaring at us with distaste. Without warning, he turned on Louise.

"You Motherfucker!"

"Don't you call me a Motherfucker you stupid Bastard!" she retorted, drawing herself up to her full height and thrusting out her chest.

The tyrant was so shocked that Louise had answered him back and had not immediately bowed into submission that he was momentarily unable to reply. For a few seconds, there was a nervous, jittery tenseness in the air, coupled with complete silence in the dressing-room. Nobody moved, nobody spoke, the distant tinkling of Korean music in the nightclub being the only audible sound. Everyone waited with bated breath, anxious to see what would happen next as Louise and the singer eyed each other with mutual loathing, both waiting for the other to back down.

Fortunately, for him, he chose to whip around and turn his back on his prospective aggressor and headed towards the mirror to check his reflection. However, I was already there, and I was annoyed too. He had shouted at Louise for no reason at all.

"Move!" I said. "You've finished. This is ours now!"

This prompted another tantrum. This time a chair was thrown, (surprise surprise). Then, a girl who had forgotten her hat became the innocent creature who received the backlash of his pent up fury.

The offending hat was thrown in her face. This was followed by a reprimand that required the singer to put his face as close as was humanly possible to hers without touching it, then assaulting her with a bombardment of rapid-fire Korean and spit. When he had exhausted his repertoire of expletives and condescending remarks, he turned on his heels and stormed out. A further barrage of Korean swearwords drifted down the corridor as his six minions scurried after him in single file.

"Well, what a lovely man!" Louise sniffed.

* * *

The sixth of June marked Memorial Day in South Korea. It is held every year to commemorate the men and women who have died in military service during the Korean War and other conflicts. The South Korea flag is flown half-mast and the National Cemetery in Seoul has a memorial service each year. At ten o'clock in the morning, an air-raid siren emanates across the city so that people can say silent prayers for those loved ones since departed.

Fortunately for me, when the siren rang this time - although I had no idea as to why it was doing so - I remained in bed and did not feel the need to panic.

Memorial Day meant that for us, we had a day off work - not that we needed one! So we three girls and Jim decided to visit 'Namsam Seoul Tower', a popular landmark and tourist spot in Seoul. It stands at 236.7 meters high and was originally constructed in 1969 as a broadcast tower to send radio and television signals.

We had learnt that at the top of the tower, there was a revolving restaurant, where diners could sit in comfort and survey the panoramic views of Seoul. This sounded like a good idea to while away the afternoon, so we took a bus to the tower and started to climb up a thin flight of enclosed spiral stairs to reach the top.

Unfortunately, three-quarters of the way up, we encountered a queue of Koreans, who had all had the same idea.

We established that the restaurant was full, and these people were waiting in line for the next available tables.

"Great! What shall we do now?" Sharon grumbled, attempting to plonk herself down on the nearest step.

"Well, we could leave but, let's be honest, we haven't got anything better to do," I replied.

"Michele's right," Louise said. "I vote we stay here."

We joined the queue and waited about forty minutes in ever-increasing temperatures in the enclosed spiral construction before we were pointed at by the head waiter and told to go inside.

"Great!" we grinned as we extricated ourselves from the staircase and tentatively stepped onto the slow-moving floor of the restaurant. We were still smiling as we were shown to a table, but our happy expressions soon evaporated when we saw the menu prices!

"Well, thanks to Mr Lee and our lack of salary this week, it looks like we are reduced to ordering a soft drink and a sandwich each," Louise sniffed.

We were further disappointed as it was an over-
cast day, so the promised panoramic views were
not particularly spectacular either! However, we
had travelled all that way and were determined to
get our money's worth, so we sat there nibbling
on our elegant sandwiches while the restaurant
completed a full revolution in forty-five minutes.
At least it gave us all a chance to cool down, and
we all agreed that it had made a nice change to
do something different from the norm.

* * *

The following day, we took yet another trip to Mr
Lee's office to try and get some money. This time,
he paid in full and presented us with our residence
cards. These were pink in colour, complete with
our photos on them. I felt that they would make
a good souvenir but, other than that, I doubted
we would be required to show them in any official capacity during our stay. We had been in
Korea for three months and had only had cause
to show some form of identification, on two occasions: once at the British Embassy and once at
the US army base.

Nevertheless, I felt almost certain that, after
our trip to the English Embassy, in case of war,
the Koreans would make more of an effort to find
us than our own countrymen probably would!

That evening after the show, Louise and Sharon
went to Itaewon. I chose to stay in our room,

which in retrospect, turned out to be a wise decision. When Louise came home, she was cut and bleeding. Her lip was burst and the beginnings of a black eye were already beginning to form. Her clothes were covered in blood. She was in a terrible mess.

"Oh my God! What's happened?"

"She got into a fight with an Arab in Kings," Sharon explained as Louise lay down gingerly on her bed.

"He kept pestering her all night. He just wouldn't leave her alone, and she finally lost it," she said. "She told him to go away and then she turned her back on him and walked off. The trouble was that he retaliated."

We cleaned her up and I sat with her until she fell asleep at 9:00 am asking me to phone Jim. When I managed to speak to him, it was not good news.

"I won't be able to come for a week," he told me.

"Why not?"

"Well, you see... I'm on report," he explained.

"What for?"

"The sergeant accused me of having girls in my room," he said. "I denied it, of course, but he didn't believe me."

"Why not?" I asked.

"Well, ..." he said sheepishly. "I think it had a lot to do with the fact that I'd put pictures of you and Louise on my wall wearing my jacket and sitting on my bed."

"Yeah, Jim, I guess that could have had a *lot* to do with it," I replied. "Idiot!"

The Iteawon occurrence with Louise really unnerved me and put a stop to my night-time visits to Itaewon for the following month. I had gone out of obligation most of the time anyway or because I did not relish the thought of sitting in the hotel room all alone. Consequently, I resorted to my usual homely self and sat watching American television, embroidering, reading or writing letters home.

* * *

The evening after her attack, Louise tried to cover her cuts and bruises with make-up and we went to work. She was feeling depressed and I could not blame her. Her body was covered in bruises and it hurt her to smile. However, something happened during the show, which made her break into painful laughter.

As we were performing the opening routine, I turned around to find that a morbidly obese, loping Korean had got onto the stage behind me. As I turned around and saw him, he jumped into the air and landed causing the whole stage to shake. With a swift kick, he threw his leg out to the side and slammed it down to assume the Sumo starting position. I became motionless with shock and did not know what to do. I had nowhere to go. His bulk and girth were occupying a third of the stage as he maintained his squat sumo position. I regained my equilibrium and attempted to dance, picking my way around him, but it was impossible. I certainly could not push him off as I had done with other intruders in the past, and visions of being slung over his shoulder and taken away into the audience were starting to freak me out!

My two partners did nothing to help and finding it amusing, they laughed at my unfortunate predicament. A bouncer approached and by speaking calmly to the man, the Sumo was persuaded to leave the stage and normal service was resumed.

* * *

Saturday 10th June turned out to be probably the most stressful day of the entire six months in Korea. After a brief shopping trip to Itaewon, Louise and I were on the bus back to Chong-gye-Chong, when I felt her go tense.

"Oh... My ... God!" She muttered, each word elongated for emphasis.

Her big eyes grew to twice their normal size as she lifted an arm aloft and slowly pointed ahead with a quivering hand. I looked out of the front windscreen of the bus to where Louise was staring. I saw hundreds of student demonstrators armed with fire torches, banners and firecrackers heading straight towards us, running and shouting. Their anger was more than evident as they charged forward, seemingly unstoppable, into the six lanes of traffic which had all come to an abrupt standstill.

The demonstrators ran in hoards, shouting and chanting, hitting cars and buses with angry fists as they charged past. Someone threw a petrol bomb and then another. Pavement slabs were ripped up, followed by any other readily available object which would double as a 'missile' and could be thrown into the throng.

"American go home! American go home!" they chanted, smashing shop windows and car windscreens.

Some of them ran alongside the bus, shouting and hollering, adrenalin surging through their bodies, totally enthused by the situation. Then, they spotted us. Our very existence further angered them, as they wrongly assumed that we were Americans, the very object of their ire. We were trapped. The bus could not move and we were like sitting targets waiting to be picked off at any moment.

"What the hell are we going to do?" I said, turning to Louise as the mob surged towards the bus.

"AMERICAN GO HOME! AMERICAN GO HOME!"

"I've no idea," she yelled over the banging and chanting. "But if they get in here, we've had it!"

We stared at one another, unable to move or think straight. For the third time since my arrival, I wondered if I was destined to die in Korea. The students were five lines deep around our vehicle, and the noise was deafening as they continued to hammer on the side of the bus and shout at the top of their voices.

The bus began to rock from side to side as the vigilantes pushed, ordering the bus driver to open the doors. Fortunately for us, he refused to obey, but they continued to try and gain access to the inside by forcing the doors apart.

One Korean lady passenger jumped to her feet and walked towards us. I cringed and fleetingly thought that perhaps she was going to attack us herself or at least insist that we were thrown off the bus into the angry throng. However, she motioned for us to squat down between the seats, something that, once she drew our attention to it, was obviously the most intelligent thing to do.

No sooner had we assumed the squatting position than we heard whistles being blown.

"Thank God! It's the riot police," Louise finally breathed. "We should be alright now."

I hoped she was right. Unfortunately, what we did not know was that the police were overpowered in number by the demonstrators, and they had no intention of staying for more than a few minutes.

All of a sudden, an awful, strong smell, resembling bleach permeated the air. Our eyes began to sting and tears coursed down our faces. Everyone on the bus instantly started coughing and wiping their eyes. They scrambled with blurred vision to secure the sunroofs and any other windows which had not already been closed.

"It's tear gas!" Louise said, covering her mouth and closing her eyes.

"Shit!" I said, totally freaking out, quivering under the seat and praying for a favourable outcome.

Risking a quick look out of the window, Louise bobbed back down again,

"The bloody police are running away! They've let off tear gas and they're bloody going!"

"Great!" I replied sarcastically from under the seat. The hope of being rescued by the only people who could possibly help us fled as quickly as the police had done!

The release of tear gas, coupled with not being in view of the demonstrators and cowering under the seats had definitely helped our situation. The rebellious crowd began to thin out, lose interest and slowly move on further down the street.

"How long do you reckon we'll have to stay here?" I asked.

"As long as it takes," Louise replied. "I don't fancy trying to get off the bus at the moment, do you?"

I shook my head vehemently.

The bus driver revved the engine into action and through an amalgam of intricate manoeuvres, he miraculously managed to turn the vehicle around. He swerved through six lanes of none moving traffic and headed off in the opposite direction, away from all the fighting. How he was able to do it will always remain a mystery to me, but I am pretty certain he saved us from a fate worse than death that afternoon.

We stayed on the bus as it travelled further and further away from where we needed to be. Our eyes were still in pain and streaming from the effects of the gas. Everyone, including the driver, was sneezing and coughing. Our throats were on fire and exposed skin was beginning to itch.

We eventually emerged from under the seats and took our places again, keeping our gaze lowered to avoid eye contact with the remaining passengers who were eyeing us with suspicion or with open contempt.

Little by little, the occupants of the bus started to get off at each designated stop, but we remained on board, partly because we had no idea where we were, but mainly because we were too afraid to get off!

Eventually, the bus pulled into the main terminal and everyone was obliged to exit. We were fortunate in that the staff there were very helpful. They escorted us to the correct bus and permitted us to enter before it was due to set off. We were unsure if this was an act of kindness as they had been made aware of our predicament or if they assumed that, under the circumstances, it was probably better to keep us out of sight. Whatever the reason, we were extremely grateful.

Around ten minutes later, the bus driver entered and drove to the first stop. When he opened the doors to let the passengers on, one Korean woman climbed aboard, then stopped dead when she saw us. Pointing and waggling her finger from side to side she started shouting, making it more than evident that she refused to travel on the bus with Americans.

"We're English, you stupid bitch!" I heard myself shouting. The frustration of the entire situation impelled me to release some of my pent up anger and exacerbation. The woman about turned and refused to board the bus. Others entered with tentative steps and attempted to sit as far away from us as possible.

It took two hours for us to get back to Cheong-gye-cheon and the devastation that the students had caused. The nearer we came to our stop, the more unnerved we became. We had no idea if the demonstration was still in progress and if we were unintentionally taking ourselves back to the battleground again.

All seemed quiet as we left the safety of the bus and headed on foot to the hotel. The smell of tear gas still permeated the air, causing us to cough and our eyes to run again. Avoiding eye contact, we scurried through the aftermath, encountering the stragglers of the demonstration and the walking wounded, who were staggering along the pavements nursing injuries. Some walked with tissues over their mouths, in an attempt to not breathe in the remnants of the tear gas. Their looks of animosity whenever they encountered two foreign girls were sufficiently nefarious, that we were scared to death.

Envisaging being beaten up, stabbed or even killed, we agreed to keep our eyes downcast, then almost immediately, we broke into a slight jog. This soon progressed to a run, and we sprinted all the way back to the hotel.

Later that evening, as we left in the Bongo van for work, we could see, in slightly safer surroundings, all the damage which had been done. Broken windows were in the process of being boarded up, the pavements had virtually disappeared; the ripped up paving slabs littered the roads. We even saw two Koreans lying face down on the remains of the sidewalk. They appeared to be dead, but we were not going to stop the van to find out.

As the Bongo van left our neighbourhood and we had finally begun to calm down, we became aware that our driver, Mr Lee, seemed to be more than a little agitated. He was sweating; his hands gripped the steering wheel in a vice-like grip and he shook his head, muttering to himself under his breath.

"What's wrong?" I asked.

"We late!" He informed us. We were scheduled to perform our final day's work at the New Seoul. He exhaled. A resigned sigh as though he had made a necessary but unlikeable decision, then he swung the van around, driving on the wrong side of the road into oncoming traffic!

"This quicker!" he informed us, craning his neck around to explain while we all pointed in horror at the plethora of vehicles heading straight towards us!

"Watch the road!"

As I contemplated getting on the floor under the seats for the second time that day, we all clasped each other's hands and watched, horror-struck as with a cacophony of honking horns, a lot of articulate swerving and the occasional banging on the side of the Bongo van with an angry fist or two, the vehicles miraculously drove past us!

"Bloody Hell!" I said when we came to a stop outside our venue. "If we have been given nine lives for this contract, then we must be down to about four now!"

For the rest of our time in Seoul, our driver repeated his hair-raising ride into oncoming traffic on several occasions whenever he thought we would not get to the next venue on time. We always arrived safely – and on time – fortunately, without a single scratch to the Bongo van or us.

* * *

The next day, I woke up to find myself alone. Both my dancing companions were at their respective army bases with their respective boyfriends. I had just resigned myself to a lonely day on my own, when there was a knock on the door. It was Amy.

"Hi Michele, I was thinking about going to the Olympic stadium, do you fancy coming with me?"

"Ooh, yeah, that would be great!" I said.

The Olympic Games had taken place in Seoul the year before, in 1988, and I had wanted to visit the site for a long time. We took a bus to Songpa-gu to see the Korean construction which had cost a whopping 491 billion won to build and could hold almost 70,000 people.

On arrival, we were given a little book which served as a passport. We had to present our 'I.D´ as we visited each venue, where it was stamped to prove that we had been there. We had our photos taken with 'Hodori´ the official tiger symbol of the Olympic Games and we discovered that the ribbon he held above his head created the letter "S" to signify Seoul.

Amy and I wandered around several stadiums, drinking in the sights and trying to imagine how exhilarating the atmosphere must have been during the games. After a while though, one stadium becomes very much like another, so we headed to the gift shop where I bought a book and a badge, before setting off back to the hotel.

Just outside the stadium, there was a tiny stall with a little man selling flags of all nations.

"Igŏsŏŭn ŏlmaimnikka?" (How much is this?) I asked him, pointing in general to all the flags on the stall, (I did not know how to ask for things in the plural!)

"3,000 won," he replied. (£2.40).

"Okay. Give me the flag of Great Britain," I said.

He obliged by putting it into a bag and handed it to me.

"6,000 won," he said.

"What?" I exclaimed. "You said three thousand won!"

"Ah, yes. Three thousand, Korean flag. Six thousand, English flag."

"What! You can't do that!" I complained. "Why is the English flag more expensive?"

"Ahh! Because yes. I have many Korean flag. Not many English flag." He explained.

I had to admire his cheek, but I decided against buying one.

On the bus ride back to the Central Hotel, Amy and I got talking about the difficulties of living in Korea. I told her that my main problem was loneliness. I had stayed faithful to my boyfriend in England, but it was hard to watch all the other girls with their partners. I felt like such a gooseberry most of the time. I complained about the clubs, the men treating us like second class citizens and I confessed that I constantly felt down, I cried a lot and I believed I had a weak character.

Amy surprised me with her reply. "Michele, you are one of the strongest people I know! It's amazing that you can remain faithful to a guy on the other side of the world. I don't know anyone here, man or woman who has managed to do that. I couldn't do it! That shows a great amount of strength."

Her words served to boost my confidence. She had forced me to view myself in a different vein and all at once, I felt empowered with the strength to carry on.

* * *

Two days later, in the early hours of Tuesday 13th June, 5:45 am to be precise, we were woken up by the never-ending sound of banging. As I looked out of the window to the dwellings below, I saw a group of Korean builders who had decided to construct a new roof. Despite shouting down and asking them to shut up, they merely laughed, continued hammering – and to infuriate us even more - they turned their radio on. The volume was turned up as high as it would go, then they laughed and shouted to each other.

"Stupid bloody Kimchi brains!" Louise complained. The name stuck. From then on, anyone who did something stupid was immediately christened a Kimchi brain.

Another expression we adopted was 'Kimchi squat´ this was because rather than form an orderly queue by standing up, Korean men would squat down in a line. Their feet would be slightly apart and flat on the floor and they would bend over in such a way with their behinds resting by their ankles. (Or as Louise so 'poetically' put it, they looked like they had been taken short and were bobbing down to go to the toilet!)

Later that afternoon, the remaining two girls from the quintet, Vicky and Amy came to visit. They told us that Mr Lee had taken them to see an apartment.

"He wants us to move out of the hotel," Amy explained.

"I suppose it's more economical for him than living in the hotel," Vicky added.

"But, it was awful! The whole place was filthy! There was an old mattress on the floor, no television or phone..." Amy continued. "And we would have had to share the kitchen and bathroom with a Korean woman with two fifteen-year-old teenage boys."

"The stairs up to the apartment were full of litter, and there were rats everywhere," Vicky said.

"So what did you say?" I asked.

"We refused point-blank."

"Christ! I hope Lee isn't thinking about moving us too," Louise replied.

I had to agree. The Central Hotel was hardly luxurious, it was full of cockroaches and we had often heard rats scurrying about behind the walls, but it still sounded a hell of a lot better than the apartment.

* * *

Two days later, as Mr Lee had conveniently not been available for the past couple of days, we took another trip to his office for money. He handed over two days' pay with a reluctant expression more than evident on his angry face, then surprised us all by asking us to take a walk with him. We looked in consternation at each other. He had never suggested anything like this before. None of us had a particularly good feeling about it, but we followed him with reluctance, not sure what to expect at all.

It was the middle of the day; much too hot to be walking about aimlessly, but walk we did. After about ten minutes, he stopped in front of a small shop.

"I buy you ice-cream," he said, fumbling in his pocket for some change.

As he ordered the refreshments, I could not hold my anticipation any longer.

"So, what do you want to talk to us about, Mr Lee?"

"Nothing! It is nice day. Nice day to take walk in city."

Why did I not believe him? The three of us made fleeting eye contact and shrugged. We were more confused than ever.

Unexpectedly, his arm bent inwards at the elbow towards his face in his weird manner of reading his watch.

"I am late. We go now."

I looked at the girls. They both shrugged. They were as bewildered as I was. There was nothing for it but to follow him back to his office.

As we reached his office building, he turned to us and told us not to bother going inside.

"Tonight you do three shows. You have new contracts in Pan Korea, New World and Diamond."

If that was all he wanted to tell us, then, for the time being, I was happy with that. Louise grabbed him by the lapels and pretended to beg.

"Oh, please, Mr Lee, I need the money. Can we do four shows?"

Our agent feigned a laugh, forcibly extricated her hands from his jacket lapels and, leaving us on the pavement, he marched inside.

Chapter 9

SHOOTING, MODELLING AND HOSTESSING

June 21st 1989

For the following few days, we worked at the three venues; Pan Korea, New World and Diamond, and the shows became relatively routine. However, this was Korea and we were accustomed to something unusual happening almost every day.

At the Pan Korea, we realised that the band had started finishing each set (their time slot to play) in an odd way. As the final song was coming to a close, they began walking casually off the stage while playing their instruments.

The drummer, who was sitting on a raised platform, was pushed off by two stagehands dressed in black while he continued to drum. For some reason, every time I saw him being shoved into the wings, I imagined a great big shepherd's crook coming round his neck and yanking him off the stage!

Once the band had gone, the stage opened up, a waterproof backcloth was dropped into place, then the water show started, the leaking began, and we paddled through our dance routines.

At the Diamond nightclub, Louise found that she had an avid admirer. Every time she went on stage, he seemed to be drawn by magnetic force to the front of the stage where he would watch her every move. Then one evening, he followed us off the stage and propositioned her by asking how much she charged!

"Get out of here!" Louise bellowed. As she turned him around and pushed him out of the room, she found Sharon and me chortling at her predicament, much to her consternation.

At the New World, we had finished the evening's show and were walking through the audience to leave the club, when a man grabbed me in a vice-like grip and proceeded to give me a wet, slobbery, beer tasting kiss! Once again, I felt that this was karma for laughing at Louise's prior predicament.

On Wednesday night (21st June,) when we arrived at the Diamond, we were only half-dressed for the opening routine, when the music began.

"Bloody Hell! Why does this keep happening to us?" I complained, frantically pulling on my feather backpack as fast as was humanly possible.

"God only knows," Louise replied, "But I'm getting more than a bit tired of it!"

I reached the stage first and danced about a third of the routine on my own. The DJ began talking over the soundtrack. I do not know what he said, but the audience abruptly started to applaud! It was nice to get some appreciation, even if I had no idea what it was for!

Later that same evening at the New World venue, Mr Lee arrived. Grinning from ear to ear he told us that, as of Thursday, we would be doing three disco spots at the Diamond nightclub. We had a sneaking suspicion that the reason for this extra work was because the manager fancied his chances with Sharon, but we welcomed the thought of some extra money, no matter how tedious podium dancing had become.

Unfortunately, our aspirations for extra money were short-lived. When we arrive at the Diamond on Thursday, we were stopped from entering.

"You no do more shows here. No more. You no do disco! Disco cancelled."

"Why?" Sharon asked.

"Go! Go!" The bouncer replied without making eye contact. He refused to give us any explanation for our dismissal. Instead, he brushed us away with his hands as though we were three annoying mosquitoes.

Confused, we got back into the Bongo van and drove to the Pan Korea. We sat in the vehicle, outside the venue, contemplating what had just happened. In the space of a few minutes, we had gone from expecting to earn extra money, to being one show down and earning less!

"It say on news that big problem for foreign dancers in Korea," our driver informed us. "It say Korean men are going to nightclubs and shooting dancers!"

"Jesus Christ!" I exclaimed.

"You girls careful, eh?" he warned us.

We walked into the Pan Korea, where we were unexpectedly met by three bouncers who chaperoned us throughout the bar and into the dressing-room which, after what we had just heard, was quite comforting yet eerily disconcerting at the same time.

"Huh! I could get used to this," Louise quipped, to lessen the stress that we were all beginning to feel.

Tension rose as we took our places for the start of the opening routine.

"I'm looking for guns," Sharon said, emitting a nervous laugh during the opening routine.

"Me too," I replied, thinking that we were definitely living on borrowed time.

"I'm looking for anyone who looks in the least bit shifty," Louise said, eyeing the audience through suspicious eyes.

We all tried to make light of our predicament yet we tensed whenever a member of the audience unexpectedly stood up. It was a deeply unnerving situation.

After the show, we were chaperoned once again until we boarded the Bongo van. Once inside, we were informed by Mr Lee that the show at the New World had also been cancelled. We were not sure if he meant we were not working there that evening, or if it would be a permanent arrangement but after hearing about the killing sprees, I was overcome with a sense of relief, tinged with apprehension. To know we were out of danger by not having to perform was obviously the main priority, yet at the same time, I worried this would be the end of our working career in Seoul.

Needless to say, we were all feeling pretty dejected by the time we got back to the hotel. We were further despondent as we had also been expecting Mr Lee to meet us with some money, but he never showed. Louise and I continued moaning about our lack of shows and shortage of cash, hoping that Sharon would take the hint and ring our agent, but it fell on deaf ears. In fact, she showed no intention of doing anything at all, except eat crisps, so Louise did the honours – something which Mr Lee took great offence to. Our agent quickly lost his patience and the conversation rapidly deteriorated into a shouting match as both tried to dominate the other. As Louise pushed and pushed, Mr Lee became exceedingly patronising. He told her that he had no intention of doing anything and ordered her to go to his office the next day. He then slammed the phone down. This confrontation coupled with the evening's events was the final straw for Louise; she started to cry.

"I've had enough. I want to go home!"

I knew how she felt. I looked around at my meagre rations of a few packets of crisps, some crackers and a tub of noodles. I felt as though we were being mentally abused by this man who kept us on the brink of poverty. We never seemed to have enough money to buy anything else to eat. I hated being reliant on Mr Lee. I loathed not being in control of my own money and I was sick of living like this.

"I know what you mean," I replied, "I'm fed up of being messed about and treated like shit! To be honest, I think that, when God created Korea, he must have been on a downer!"

This outburst unexpectedly lightened the atmosphere and we all found ourselves laughing at our ridiculously hopeless, precariously dangerous situation.

* * *

The next morning saw us at Mr Lee's office, where he paid us a meagre fifty dollars each. Our first stop was to Popeye's, to eat something other than crisps, crackers and eggy-bread sandwiches. Yet, we knew that as soon as we had finished eating, we would instantly feel guilty because we had no idea when we would be getting paid again.

We had arranged to meet up with Amy, who was talking to two Korean guys when we arrived.

As I tucked into my food, one of the men, Mr Woo, seemed to glance in my direction over and over again. I was ignoring his gaze and thinking that I would probably find myself having to fend off his advances when he pointed an impetuous finger towards me.

"You are just the girl I need," he said. "I'm looking for someone to model some fitness machines."

"Sorry, what?"

"Can you do some modelling for me?"

"Er...I'm not sure..." I dithered.

"He's alright, Michele," Amy quietly reassured me. "I know him. Vicky has worked for him in the past ... and the pay is really good!"

"I can offer you seven hundred American dollar."

"Okay!" I replied immediately.

"I will call you tomorrow," he promised.

My head was reeling. I could not believe my luck; seven hundred dollars. Great! I would probably never have to eat another bowl of noodles and crackers in my life!

"Louise smiled and elbowed me playfully in the side. "You go, girl," she said.

Sharon stabbed her pork chop with malice and refrained from comment.

* * *

That night we were doomed to work only one show again. It was true what our driver had told us the day before. There were literally thousands of police checks being carried out throughout Seoul, in the search for foreign dancers.

According to the Korean Government, all foreign dancers were the reason for the rise in crime rates. The number of reported rapes had risen significantly and the number of kidnappings was also said to have increased. It was conveniently not mentioned if these crimes had involved foreigners or had been committed amongst the Koreans themselves. Nevertheless, the residents of Seoul were asking for a new law to be put into place which would make it illegal for foreign dancers to work in Korea. Things were looking decidedly grim.

(What strikes me as odd today - being older and slightly wiser - is that I never once stopped to think what the consequences would have been if the police had found us dancing in a club without a license. I do not think any of us did. I had assumed the clubs would be fined and that would be that. We had our residency card but whether it allowed us to dance or if we were working there illegally, we never knew, and I guess we never even thought to ask.)

Later that night, back at the hotel, as we were sleeping, the door opened and in came two men from reception. They crept up to each bed and sprinkled breadcrumbs on the floor with liberal abandon.

"Here mousey-mousey! Here mousey-mousey!" they chanted.

"What the hell...?" Sharon said, opening her eyes and staring groggily at the scene.

"Is this some kind of joke?" Louise punched her pillow angrily.

"I don't believe this place!" I said. "Just do what you've got to do and get out!" Turning over, I ignored them and went back to sleep.

* * *

On Saturday morning, (24th), after just three hours of sleep, I was waiting in reception for Mr Woo. My contact into the lucrative world of Korean modelling. He arrived on time and we exchanged a few pleasantries before he escorted me outside.

I was nervous, to say the least as I got inside his car and he started to drive away. I had decided to go alone, as I felt that it was the correct thing to do. Yet I found myself reminiscing about my motorcycle incident in Kyongju and was not looking forward to finding myself in a similar situation. However, I need not have fretted. He eventually pulled up outside an impressive, highrise office building in the heart of Seoul.

"This modelling contract will be for very important Korean newspaper," Mr Woo explained. "This morning you meet with owner of newspaper. If he like you, you get contract."

"Oh... okay!" I said, trying to sound cheerful but starting to feel a little peeved. I had wrongly assumed that the decision had been Mr Woo's and that I already had the contract. It appeared that he was the photographer, but the final decision lay with the editor of the newspaper.

Mr Woo knocked on an office door and we went into a decent-sized room to find a corpulent, decidedly young-faced man sitting behind a capacious desk, almost hidden inside a cloud of hazy cigar smoke. Mr Woo and the owner made their introductions in Korean, then Mr Woo pointed in my direction and I was eyed up and down like a prize cow at a cattle market. The owner coughed and hacked up some phlegm, but he did not spit it out, (he was obviously a bit better educated!)

"This is Mr Kyong," Mr Woo said, presenting the owner to me.

"Hello," I said, holding out my hand to him.

He shook it. "So, you are a model?"

"Yes, sir, I am," I lied.

"Where have you worked before?"

"Oh, many places in my country. Many times, many places."

"Where is your country?"

"I'm from England."

"Where in England? I went to England one time."

"I'm from the North," I explained. "I come from Leeds, in the county of Yorkshire."

"Ah! Yes! Yorkshire in England is very famous. It is very famous for its pigs!" He said emphatically.

"I don't believe so. . . ?" I replied.

"Oh, yes. I know. I insist." he said.

I had never seen a pig in all my years in Leeds, but I decided to stay quiet. Adopting a pensive expression, I gave a slight shrug in a 'maybe you could be right' sort of way.

Whatever! I thought. *If you want to pay me seven hundred dollars, to ride an exercise bike, then yes, Yorkshire is VERY famous for its pigs!*[1]

"I think you will be the best girl for this contract," he said. Then he turned to Mr Woo and they chatted some more in Korean while I stood there trying to be inconspicuous.

"The modelling contract will be for the 14th of July, okay?" Mr Woo questioned, finally looking in my direction.

"Yeah. Fine."

"Good!" said the owner. "Now, I offer you a second contract to model mink coat, Okay?"

---

1. *(There is a Yorkshire breed of pig, which originates from York, in England. It's name was later changed to the "English Large White" but is known as 'The Yorkshire' throughout the rest of the world.)*

"Yes, that's fine with me."

"You do the photos on the same day. I pay you one thousand American dollars in total. Okay?"

"Okay!" I said, grinning uncontrollably from ear to ear. "Now I come to think of it," I said. "You know what? You're right. There *are* pigs in Yorkshire. They're absolutely everywhere!"

He grinned.

"You see," he said, extremely pleased with himself, "I am right!"

I was ecstatic. I could not believe I would be earning a thousand dollars for a few hours of work! *I think I'm in the wrong business,* I thought to myself as I was ushered out of the office.

Mr Woo was contented that the owner was pleased, so he invited me out for lunch. We dined in a top-class Japanese restaurant and later he took me to a bar for a coffee. For once, I finally felt human again. I could not remember the last time I had been treated with so much respect during my time in Korea. Mr Woo dropped me back at the hotel, handed me a yellow flower and told me he would be in touch.

* * *

Two days later, I was back in Itaewon with Louise. Her zip had broken again the night before, so we were returning to the dressmakers. While it was being repaired, we wandered around the shops and trying to think optimistically, we bought a couple more outfits for any future disco spots we may have to do.

Later that day, when we got back to the hotel, Sharon informed us from her prone position on her bed, that, all being well, we would be doing two venues that night; the Diamond for one show and a disco spot, then on to the Pan Korea to perform one show. Afterwards, we would return to the Diamond again to tread the boards a second time with a second show and finish off with two disco spots.

"Great! This means we can wear some of our new disco apparel and our shopping trip hasn't been a complete waste of time," Louise grinned.

As we tried on our new outfits and prepared for the show, Louise decided to put on her costume with the newly adjusted zip. Try as she might, the zip would not close. The dress no longer fit. The seamstress had taken it in too much. Louise sighed, a mixture of exasperation and oppression then promised to return to the dressmakers the following day. Consequently, we had to delve in the costumes in storage for the second show.

Sharon was causing a rumpus, but what surprised me was why the same thing was not happening to Sharon's attire. Her stomach now hung over her bikini bottoms and she constantly ate rubbish.

As we scurried across reception and headed for the Bongo van, conveniently ignoring the shouts of "Telephone chargee!", another receptionist came running up to me. With an inane smile, he pushed a letter into my hand, then bowed as I took the envelope and hurried outside. Confused, I settled myself in the Bongo van and opened it as we started to drive away:

To Miss Michl, my name is Han Su Mon.
English speak is just a beginner.
I would like to love friendship with you.
I will love you. Good night. Thank-you.
From Han Su Mon.

"Ooh! It looks like Michele's got another admirer!" Louise jested as she read the letter over my shoulder.

I rolled my eyes, but it appeared to be true.

"Ooh! He's infatuated by her!" Sharon crooned, snatching the letter and reading it herself.

"But I don't think I've ever even spoken to him," I said. "Now I've got an added reason to avoid the reception area."

"He's in luuurve!!" Sharon drawled.

"Or in lust!" Louise added.

After work, when we got back to the hotel and I purposely avoided the reception, the three of us headed out to a little restaurant behind the hotel which we had never visited before. As we perused the menu we found ourselves laughing out loud at the abundance of amusing spelling mistakes.

"Ha! Look at this! We can have an Agg sandwich and a Cock!" I giggled.

"Thank goodness you're vegetarian!" Sharon laughed.

I stuck to my usual and had Om-rice.

The following day, Thursday 29th June, I woke up with terrible pains in my stomach and blamed the Om rice from the night before. I felt dizzy and my hands had become so dry, that they were starting to crack open. I felt dreadful, but I could not afford to be off sick. There seemed to be more and more dance groups out of work, and I worried all the time that we would find ourselves in the same predicament, so I dragged myself off to reception to wait for the Bongo van.

In my dizzy, disorientated stupor, I had momentarily forgotten about my receptionist admirer. I was unable to move fast enough from the elevator to the front doors. Halfway across the floor, I heard the distinctive sound of someone scurrying behind me.

"Michele, Michele!" I stopped and turned around. There was the receptionist, Han Su Mon, waiting to give me a second love letter. Once again, I accepted it and opened it within the confines of the Bongo van. However, this time as I started reading it, I had more than a sneaking suspicion that my admirer had employed someone else to write it – someone with a sense of humour:

Dear Mitchelle,
Ever since I first saw you, I have been having strange feelings that are hard to explain.

Every sight of yours tends to increase those heartfelt sensations. Could it be love? I have been asking myself this question repeatedly. Finally, I have come to the conclusion that if it's not love then there is no other diagnosis as such. Sometimes, I really wish to cut open my heart to show you how much I care for you; and my desire to be as close to you as possible for the rest of my life and more. Mitchelle, what on earth could I do to bring you close to me? Handicapped with inexperience, all I could do is to write to beg you for your understanding. Please Mitchelle, please show this slave of yours some mercy so that we may open a new chapter on the greatest love story that has ever happened in this universe. I was actually only made for you. My existence doesn't carry any meaning without you by my side. Mitchelle, I am a house without walls without you. I fear I will break down one day if you do not come to my rescue. Since you came into my life, though it has always been a one-sided love story, I've found a meaning for my life. Mitchelle, please, for the sake of true love don't ever leave me; for I can't live without you for a single second. Our love shall stand all temptations. Mitchelle! Please! Please! Please! Oooh! I need you! Ooooh! I love you. Oooh! I am finished. . . with endless love, Han Su Mon.

"Bloody hell!" said Louise, laughing when I finished reading the letter aloud in the van. "He's got it bad!"

"I've only ever asked him for our room key!" I argued.

"It's him that wants the key. The key to your heart."

"Shut up, Louise!" I laughed, slapping her playfully. I put the letter in my bag and smiled to myself.

I was looking forward to working at the Diamond Club, as my mum had sent me a black leotard and I was determined to wear it that evening. She had spent hours decorating it with sequins, beads and droplets and I wanted to wear something different, something that she had taken the time to make for me.

That night, the costume made its debut appearance but despite receiving positive appraisal from Louise, Sharon and the rest of the disco dancers, when I came off the podium and entered the dressing-room, the manager was waiting for me.

"You look better yesterday. I no like costume today!"

The day before, I had worn a pair of Lycra bicycle shorts with a matching top! "Oh, come on!" I argued. "This is stylish. You can't possibly compare the two!"

"This black costume I no like!" he repeated.

"Well, I do, but okay," I replied. "Obviously, there's just no accounting for taste."

He sniffed and grunted, apparently pleased with the outcome, then he cupped his chin with one hand and narrowed his eyes.

"I think maybe tomorrow, you girls do consummation here too," he added with a casualness that unnerved me.

"WHAT?" we said in unison. Consummation was the Korean word for Hostessing, which meant that members of the audience could pay if they wanted particular disco dancers to go and sit with them to talk and drink. It was not something which we had done before, and I did not particularly relish the thought of starting it now. We had seen how some of these men constantly pushed the boundaries and were often trying to fondle the Korean girls.

"It bring more money for you," said the manager.

"Yeah, and more hassle too!" I replied.

The manager grinned and walked away, leaving us all in varying degrees of contemplation and dilemma – mine probably being the worst of the three!

"It's bad enough doing the disco spots," I complained. "I don't want to start doing Hostessing too."

"If I had to sum up disco dancing in one sentence," Louise said, absentmindedly, "I'd say it's like when your best friend asks you to dance with her at the disco; you do it, but you don't really want to. But Hostessing..." her voice tapering off as she ruminated on the idea. "Ha! Well, it might be a bit more interesting than dancing on those stupid podiums night after night."

"I did some consummation on my last contract in Japan," Sharon said. "It wasn't so bad, and the money was really good."

'It wasn't so bad´ did not bode well with me. Sharon's revelation of doing consummation did not surprise me. If she wanted to do it then fine, but I did not want to get involved. It felt more than a little sleazy to me. It appeared we were slumping to a new low, and I believed that, by doing so, I would be losing what little self-respect I still had left.

* * *

Friday 30th saw us taking yet another trip into town to Mr Lee's office, in the weekly battle for our salary. This time he paid up the full amount, so I decided to buy myself a ruby ring as an early birthday present. I would be twenty-one years old in three days and I felt like I had earned it.

After shopping, the three of us took ourselves off to Popeye's for lunch only to find Mr Kyong, the owner of the newspaper, sitting at the next table!

"Annyŏnghashimnikka" (Hello/ how are you?) he said in surprise.

"Annyŏnghaseyo" (Hello), I replied. "Ne, chossŭmnida, komapsŭmnida." (I'm fine, thank you). We chatted in English, and I introduced him to my dancing partners. He insisted on paying for our meal, which was a nice surprise and gratefully accepted by us all.

Later he admired my newly bought ruby ring.

"I decided to buy myself a present," I explained, "as it is my birthday on the second of July".

"Then tomorrow I will take you all out for lunch as a present for your birthday," he said.

"Great!" I answered, grinning broadly. Thinking for the second time that I was definitely in the wrong profession!

* * *

As promised, the following day, the newspaper owner, Mr Kyong, arrived at our hotel to take the three of us out for a meal. Louise changed her mind at the last minute, as Jim had rung, and she decided that she preferred to meet up with him.

Sharon and I clambered inside a long, white limo and grinned from ear to ear as we were driven in style through the streets of Seoul to the five star Hyatt hotel.

The interior of the Hyatt was stunning; so spacious and elegant, which made a stark contrast to our dingy Central Hotel digs. Greeted by so much opulence and glamour, we soon began to feel particularly underdressed as we walked through to the hotel restaurant and weaved in and out of the tables in our cheap summer clothes from Itaewon market. We were ogled and assessed by the upper classes in their tailored suits, gold jewellery and their overall air of self-importance. It was a relief for both of us to sit down and hide part of our clothing under the heavy tablecloths.

When the menu arrived, and we saw the prices, we exchanged secret glances, silently thanking our blessings that we were not expected to pay the bill! I ordered sea-food soup with croutons and garlic for a starter (4,000₩) followed by succulent grilled sole with a rich sauce of mushrooms, tomatoes and more garlic for the main course, (12,800₩). It made a fabulous change from noodles and crackers!

After the meal, to my surprise, a chocolate truffle birthday cake arrived with candles on it. (Sharon later discovered that it had cost 20,000₩) And the newspaper owner presented me with a Korean phrasebook.

"Happy birthday! This will help you," he said, handing me the book.

"Kamsahamnida," (Thank-you) I replied.

He raised his glass to propose a toast.

"May we have a good, long working relationship! Geon-bae!" (Cheers).

"Geon-bae!" we replied, toasting my birthday with glasses of champagne.

At the end of the meal, when Sharon and I both assumed that the fun was over, Mr Kyong escorted us to the hotel bar, for the first of three cocktails. Later still, he took us on to two other venues, both high-class bars around Seoul.

Once again, I could not help but notice how there was a completely different side to Korea which, up until that point, I had been totally unaware of. Sharon was thinking the same thing.

"Bloody hell, I wish we worked in venues like these," she whispered as we sipped our drinks and took in the palatial surroundings.

"Tell me about it," I replied. "This just makes most of the places we've worked in look like pigsties!"

Reminiscent of the picnic in Kyongju, once again I realised how a tourist's view of Korea and my view would be on extremely different planes. Staying in five-star hotels and visiting top class localities such as the bars and nightclubs we had frequented that day would paint a completely different picture of the country.

However, I also had to admit that, despite everything which had happened throughout my stay in Korea, taking the rough with the smooth, I was glad I had been exposed to everything which I had experienced. In my opinion, without a shadow of a doubt, I was having a truer, more realistic view of the country. I was seeing the real Seoul, (or the real soul) of the city and felt that living through the negative experiences was, in effect, shaping my personality and changing me as a person. I categorically believed that I was maturing, little by little, I was becoming stronger and certainly more astute.

Later that evening, however, after work, I was forced to change my views yet again. The three of us went to Iteawon with Jim, to celebrate my 21st birthday. As soon as we arrived, I remembered why I had not been out drinking in the evening in Itaewon for over a month. It reminded me of a cattle market and most of the time I felt uncomfortable and extremely vulnerable. Trying to fend off guys who were laced with alcohol was always a dodgy business!

We went drinking in East and West, where Sharon picked up a guy called Foster, then we went to Kings, where an African American tried to chat me up and would not leave me alone. I had just managed to get rid of him when another soldier tagged on as we walked to the Twilight zone for Om-rice.

"For God's sake!" I complained to the girls. "I'm started to feel like a bitch on heat!" There seemed to be males everywhere, just waiting for a chance to pounce. This latest guy hung around, despite being totally snubbed by me until we left and headed for a taxi. As we all clambered inside, he also tried to gain entry. He reminded me of a stray dog that would attach itself to anyone in the hope of finding solace.

"Sorry mate," Jim told him. "There just ain't enough room for you too."

In a last desperate attempt, the guy stuck his head through the window.

"Can I see you again?" he said, flashing his puppy-dog eyes.

"No, sorry," I said and breathed a sigh of relief as the taxi finally pulled away.

* * *

All things considered, my 21st birthday was a bit of a non-starter. After going out the night before, I did not wake up until three o'clock in the afternoon. I looked across at Sharon, Foster, Louise and Jim who were still crashed out on the two single beds. I felt a little guilty seeing them all squashed together while I had a double bed all to myself. I pottered around making noise on purpose, hoping to wake them up, but apart from the occasional grunt, I could not rouse them. In the end, I had to admit defeat. Feeling slightly downhearted, I decided to go out and phone home.

As I stepped outside the hotel, it was the smell that hit me rather than the heat. Over the past week, we had been experiencing the results of a refuse strike in Chong-y-chong. The amount of garbage that had been amassing up and down the streets was abhorrent. It towered over us; an abundance of decomposing mass, as high as small hills. A conglomerate of black, plastic refuse bags, all poised precariously to topple on an unsuspecting passerby at any given moment. It was both stifling and shocking! The smell was oppressive, rancid and totally overpowering.

Rats as big as felines ran helter-skelter up and down the refuse, rampantly searching through the rubbish for food, seemingly unnerved by the frequent passersby. I cupped my hand over my mouth in a vain attempt to avoid breathing in the waste as I edged past the vermin and went in search of a phone box - preferably one far enough away that I would not feel the need to gag while I was talking to my family.

Mum was disappointed that I had not received her card, but there was also a postal strike in Korea at that time, so it was not her fault. I chatted about various predicaments which I had found myself in, carefully editing any stories which I considered too unnerving for a mother to hear, then I took my time and wandered back to the hotel room.

My roommates were still in the land of nod, but I managed to make sufficient noise (accidentally on purpose) so that they would wake up this time. Giving them a five-minute reprieve, I tried a second time to convince them to leave their beds and finally succeeded to accomplish this fete by half-past five in the afternoon.

"Come on! Get up. I want to go out, it's my birthday," I said whining like a child.

"Alright, alright," they muttered.

"Where do you want to go on your special day?" Jim asked.

I only needed a second to think about it.

"The zoo!"

"THE ZOO?" They replied, screwing up their faces.

There were various grunts and groans and it was established that despite it being my birthday, the zoo was a no-no.

"Let's go to Pizza Hut!" someone suggested, so that's what we did. After eating, we came back to the hotel and I opened the few cards that had arrived before the postal strike had started. Louise and Sharon had bought me three lovely, Korean dolls dressed in national costume inside a glass display case. I was really please with it, but I had no idea how I was going to get it home.

Birthday or not, I still had to work, so a few hours later, off we went to do our two venues and disco spots. Ever since our talk with the manager of the Diamond, nothing else had been said about the hostess work, and I hoped that it had been forgotten. However, he had recently started lingering in the dressing-room every evening, watching us undress, and I was beginning to feel uncomfortable.

That night, as I was changing, he sidled closer to me and then his hand shot out to try and touch my breast. Fortunately, I saw what he was trying to do, and I reacted by fiercely batting his hand out of the way.

"Don't do that!" I warned, glaring at him.

He grinned like a miscreant and I had a desperate urge to hit him but remembering that he was the so-called manager, I restrained myself. I did not know if it was because it was my birthday, but his actions deeply upset me. I could not get the incident out of my mind.

After work, we had been back at the hotel for about an hour, when Jim appeared.

"Here," he said, handing me a big box.

"Thank-you, what is it?"

"Open it and see!"

Inside there was a slightly soggy looking birthday cake, covered in pink icing, with the form of a key decorating the top.

"Sorry!" he said as I eyed the melting icing. "I've brought it all the way from the base on the train!"

"It's lovely, thank-you!" I said, thinking that it was actually quite a feat to carry it on the crowded, hot, underground trains for an hour and get it here in one piece!

"Louise told me to put a key on it," he replied. "Apparently it's an English custom or something...?"

"Yes, that's right," I replied. "When you are twenty-one, you are entitled to the key of the front door, so people usually receive presents and cakes in the shape of keys."

"Weird!" he replied, with a puzzled expression on his face. "Whatever makes you happy!"

That night, as we all settled down to sleep, I thought about the events of the day. It had hardly been a great occasion, and I realised that nobody had sung 'twenty-one today' to me!

* * *

The morning after my birthday, the phone rang. Sharon answered it then passed it to me. It was the newspaper owner, Mr Kyong, again.

"Michele, I invite you and the girls to spend the day with me in Hyatt hotel. Would you like?"

I told the girls, who nodded with frantic acceptance.

"Oh, yes, that will be lovely, Mr Kyong, kamsahamnida," I replied, hoping that this might make up for my 'nonstarter' birthday the day before.

"Bring your swimming costumes and you can swim in the pool," he said.

An hour later, we were driving in style once more, in his posh car, heading for the Hyatt Hotel. I felt elated to be getting out again, away from our drab surroundings and mixing with a more affluent, eloquent group of people.

"Wow! This is the life, eh girls?" I said and broke into song.

"Somebody's happy!" Louise grinned as I continued warbling, and we all swayed from side to side, clicking our fingers in time with my singing.

On arrival at the Hyatt, Mr Kyong ushered us through reception towards the elevators.

"I have room upstairs for you," he told us. 'You change and we go to the pool."

The three of us glanced at each other with apprehension, wondering if the 'room upstairs' had different connotations to what we had been expecting. We followed him into the elevator in silence, each deep in thought. The reticence continued as the elevator began to rise; the three of us battling private scenarios in our minds. The energy inside the lift was electric, rising in intensity as fast as the elevator was ascending. As the huge contraption stopped, threw open the doors and spewed us out onto the seventh floor, we followed our guide, trudging down the corridor behind him, nervously awaiting our fate.

"Okay," he said as he opened the door to the room and swung around to face us. "I am at the pool." He sauntered off towards the elevator, leaving us to our own devices.

After discovering that nothing or no-one sinister was waiting for us within the confines of the spacious quarters, we all managed to breathe again and felt free to explore the room and its facilities. Peering out of the window, we could see the pool below, resplendent with yellow and white striped umbrellas dotted around it. We took in the panoramic views of most of Seoul, realising how high up the Hyatt hotel was positioned.

"Let's check out the mini bar," Louise suggested.

Once again we commented on how the other half lived, and it was great to be a part of it if only for a while. Later, we changed into our swimming costumes and donning large, white, fluffy bathrobes, compliments of the hotel, we headed down to the reception area. We felt a bit conspicuous in our pristine bathrobes and our dirty old flip-flops as we walked among the well-dressed clientele on the highly polished foyer floor, but there seemed to be no other, more discrete, way to reach the swimming pool area.

The pool itself looked inviting but was absolutely freezing! It took Sharon and me a long while to muster up the courage to gradually lower ourselves into the watery depths. (Louise dipped her big toe into the water, then refused outright and sat sunbathing on a lounger).

Fortunately, the only other person brave enough to have gone in before us was a Korean man.

At least we won't be subject to the usual comment banded about from the English when the water is bitterly cold I thought. *It's lovely once you're in!* The Korean swam up and down the pool with stoic resolve as though he were training for the next Olympics whilst we lowered ourselves slowly, inch by inch into the painful expanse of freezing water.

"Louise," Sharon shouted when we had succeeded in submerging ourselves. "Come on! It's really not so bad once you're in!"

I groaned!

After ten minutes, when every hair on my body was stood to rigid attention, my teeth were chattering uncontrollably, and I began to think that I could quite possibly die from Hyperthermia, I clambered out of the pool and ran to wrap myself in the fluffy bathrobe. Sharon followed a few minutes later then the three of us set off to explore the grounds of the hotel.

There was a low, stone wall around the property which overlooked Seoul city. Scattered around were perfectly manicured gardens, one with a waterfall which fell into a small natural pool. It was the most beautiful setting.

Throughout the day, Mr Kyong was as obliging as usual and money seemed to be no object, as he treated us to more than enough drinks, plates of smoked salmon and ice-cream. Sharon was obviously attracted to his money and was hovering around him like a child round a sweet jar, doing her best to flirt with him. Each time we sat down, she made a beeline to sit by his side. Louise caught my eye, and we discreetly expressed our non-surprise by her actions.

Unfortunately, all too soon, the time came round to leave Mr Kyong and the lap of luxury, to return to our reality of sleazy clubs, drunken men and hassle. It was time to go back to the Central Hotel and get ready for work again.

* * *

In retrospect, we could have stayed a little while longer at the Hyatt, as we found ourselves hanging around the hotel room, losing our patience, waiting for our driver, who arrived an hour late.

"Van no start!" he explained.

"Great!" Sharon replied. "That means we're out of pocket again. We've missed the first two disco spots at the Diamond."

I was not in the least bit bothered. I found the disco spots increasingly more tedious every time I had to do them.

We eventually arrived at the venue and we had just begun to change for the show when the manager snuck up behind me and this time succeeded in grabbing my breast. I was so shocked, that I turned around and slapped him hard across the face!

After giving him a barrage of swear words and calling him a 'kimchi brain', he stood before me, laughed, pushed his hands in his pockets and sauntered out of the dressing room with his head held high. I hung my head in shame, I felt totally demoralised and burst out crying. The stark contrast of the last few days compared to the dreaded nights had softened the faked, toughened exterior I had been working so hard to construct around myself. I hated my job. I wanted to go home.

After work, the girls and their boyfriends persuaded me to go out to Itaewon, in an effort to cheer me up, but, in retrospect, I should not have gone. I could not seem to stop crying but not just because of the incident in the club. A whole gamut of repressed turmoil seemed to overpower me as I uncontrollably replayed in my mind all the uncomfortable situations I had experienced over the past few months.

Almost immediately on arrival in Itaewon, an African American fell into step beside us and followed me around from the East to West bar, to Kings and the Twilight zone. This did not help my mood at all. I felt like I was being pursued by a big, black panther and I was the bait! Jim politely asked him to leave, but when that did not have the desired effect, there was a short scuffle as Jim was forced to manhandle the GI out of the club.

I decided that I hated Itaewon, but if I did not go out, then I was forced to stay in the hotel alone, night after night, and that could be soul-destroying. It gave me too much time to think, and I did not like it.

* * *

The next morning, feeling in a better frame of mind, the three of us went for a walk around our neighbourhood but almost immediately wished that we had not bothered. Within minutes of our departure, a young Korean mounted the pavement and rammed his motorbike between Sharon and me, missing our feet by millimetres.

"Americans go home!" he spat through snarled teeth before revving up the bike and screeching off into the throng.

"Get a life!" Louise shouted to the departing figure.

"That's a great start to the day!" Sharon remarked, brushing off the dust particles as I wafted the exhaust fumes away.

We continued walking, but everyone seemed to be on a mission of persecution. Several times that morning, the older generation - in particular the little old ladies - constantly rammed their shopping-trolleys into our ankles with a brute force which belied their stature. When we yelled out in pain, they feigned indifference or pretended that they had not realised what they had done. Two or three of them, however, had no intention of not claiming responsibility for their actions.

"Yongu! Urgh!" (English, urgh!) They said, looking us straight in the eyes then spitting at our feet as a final gesture of abhorrence.

"What's wrong with these people?" I asked nobody in particular.

"Maybe it's a full moon," Louise replied.

"Nope, it's just Korea!" Sharon stated.

* * *

The subsequent evening, after my run-in with the Diamond manager, I was not looking forward to going to work, but that night he stayed out of the dressing-room. I was secretly congratulating myself that perhaps he had finally got the message, rather than believe that he had completed his goal when Mr Lee appeared. His facial expression was one of anger and indifference. He did not mince his words.

"Tomorrow you finish show here!"

I was pretty convinced that my slapping the manager had had a lot to do with this sudden revelation, but I did not care. However, my happiness at the thought of leaving was to be short-lived.

"But you continue to do disco spots until July 26th," he added.

"Deep joy!" Louise muttered.

"Shit!" I said.

"Can't you find us any more clubs, Mr Lee?" Louise asked him.

"Very difficult, very difficult!" he replied. "You work here. No problem."

"I'm so fed up, it's untrue!" I let out a dejected sigh.

Sharon shook her head, sighed and shrugged. "Oh, well, such is life!" she said.

* * *

That night when we got back to the hotel, my admirer from reception, Han Su Mon, rang our room and asked me to go to the front desk. I travelled down in the lift, feeling nervous. I was unsure what to expect and half dreading what I was going to encounter. On arrival, I was presented with a third love letter and an accompanying present. The letter continued along the same vein as the last:

My dearest Mitchelle,

One thing that you will never understand is that where two hearts are involved, there is no language barrier. Words would just come out from the dumb and the deaf ones would hear the words of love. Regarding your claim that you have a boyfriend, I should add that my humble request is for you to give only slight consideration. Were I given only 0.01% chance, I am sure that I can win your heart as easily as one takes a hair from the butter. In three months' time, I shall go on my national army service. One thing I will miss the most will be you. For your information, the above is all original material and wasn't extracted from 'Romeo and Juliet' or any other novel. Caution: do not recite above or part of thereof at public places without prior written consent of the writer, failing which, you may be prosecuted under Korean Law of Love, Act 69. With greatest affection and ever hardening vigour. Han Su Mon.

I was more convinced than ever, that his friend who had written the letter was enjoying himself at poor Han Su Mon's expense! I fought to stifle my laughter as my admirer looked at me with such innocent expectation, that I felt quite sorry for him. The present, which he insisted I open in front of him, was a large clock with a flower display above it complete with optic lights. The clock ran off the electric, the flowers turned around and lit up, sparkling in different colours.

"Kamsahamnida," I said, bowing slightly. To be honest, I did not like it at all - but I knew my mum would love it – so now I had a double dilemma. How on earth was I going to get that and the Korean dolls home?

Chapter 10

FILLINGS, FIGHTS, FIRES AND FLASHERS!

On Wednesday 5th July, after a trip to Mr Lee's office for money, we had just got back to the hotel when the photographer Mr Woo, phoned. He wanted to invite us all to lunch. Sharon was going out on a date, but Louise and I cordially accepted.

I was rather expecting to be treated to another first-class gourmet experience similar to the first one but this time, we were taken to a traditional Korean restaurant with the obligatory low tables and cushions in place of chairs. This was a 'normal´, everyday restaurant, however, with not a Korean Geisha in sight.

As we could not understand the menu, Mr Woo said that he would order for us, which, in hindsight, was a big mistake! We found ourselves eating cold noodles which looked like worms and tasted like glue, all swilled down with watery, brown Ginseng tea. Louise and I exchanged glances and grimaced but managed to smile sweetly at Mr Woo as we toyed with the noodles, sipped the tea, thanked him for his hospitality and wandered back to the hotel.

"I'd have preferred Popeye's," I grumbled as I searched the side of my bed for something slightly more palatable to eat.

"Oh well, life is just a bowl of cherries!" Louise quipped. "Look on the bright side, at least it was free and better than crackers."

(I begged to differ!).

* * *

At the Diamond nightclub that evening, we were sitting with the Korean disco dancers in the dressing room after just finishing one of our disco spots, when a group of five Australian girls sauntered in. As we were no longer performing our show there, we correctly assumed that they were here to replace us.

"Hello," we said, smiling and trying to make them feel welcome.

"Annyŏnghashiminikka," said the Koreans in welcome.

We were met with a wall of silence. Each girl flashed looks of distaste in our direction and completely ignored us. The head girl began barking orders to the others, and then they talked amongst themselves and attempted to commandeer the entire dressing room. They began by pushing in between the Korean girls who were sitting in chairs in front of the mirrors and forcibly tried to get them to move out of the way.

The three of us looked at each other in disbelief. We had to assume that they had not been in the country very long, as it was apparent that they were not aware of the certain hierarchy which existed within the dressing-room. Each disco dancer had her own allocated spot, with the captain usually being at one end. The others were further positioned down the line depending on their status; in other words, how long they had been employed there. For example, we three foreigners did not even merit a place in the line. We were positioned on a bench behind them by the back wall.

Each Korean girl had worked hard for their current position and did not take lightly to being up-rooted from their spot. After all, they spent hours there every night waiting for one group of disco dancers to finish, so they could take over every fifteen minutes. As each girl went on the stage, her equivalent would take her place in the dressing room.

The Australian group seemed unaware that they were encroaching on Korean territory. The

Koreans deemed the girls' behaviour as a blatant act of invasion and that was not something they were ready to accept without retaliation.

Had the Australians been a bit more open and pleasant, we may have been more forthcoming towards them. We could have told them that if they were going to work there, they were committing a cardinal sin by trying to take over the dressing-room and seriously infuriating the Koreans. However, under the circumstances, we decided to remain tight-lipped.

The Disco dancers continued muttering to each other, they flashed deadly looks at the invaders and refused to move. There was a lot of pushing, shoving and elbowing in the ribs from both nationalities, but in the end, the Koreans found their voices. A barrage of swearing and gesticulating followed, which, even if you did not speak a word of Korean, you could immediately deduce that they were far from happy!

In the end, the Koreans won. The Australians laid out their costumes in any available space they could find – basically along our bench by the back wall - and had to resort to touching up their make-up by standing behind the seated Koreans and squinting towards the mirrors.

In between our disco spots, we donned our kimonos and snuck into the audience to watch the Australian group's show. We were far from impressed.

"Well there's a surprise!" said Louise, when the girls had packed up and left without saying goodbye. "With the way they were carrying on, I thought their show was going to be something spectacular when actually, it was a pile of shit!"

"I know, I thought our show was bad, but theirs was total rubbish! They danced as though they were all soloists, they weren't together at all," I said. "In fact, the only thing I liked about it was their feathers."

The Koreans realised that we were discussing the group, so they joined in. They thought the girls were loudmouthed, arrogant and looked stupid with their extraordinarily long, false eyelashes which made their eyes resemble cows' eyes.

Our days of false eye-lashes were well gone! It was impossible to keep them on with the amount of sweat we produced during each show. Furthermore, it was impossible to buy the glue needed to keep them in place. We had also resorted to spraying bottles of water instead of hairspray, chiefly because lacquer was almost impossible to find in the shops. Secondly, we did not have enough money to buy it and thirdly, because water was free – even if it came from the Central Hotel bathroom and was generously peppered with orange coloured rust particles.

* * *

The next day, Louise and I set off with Mr Lee for a trip to the dentist. Louise had broken a tooth, and I had lost a filling, so we had decided to go together.

Dentists seemed to be non-existent, but obviously, not being able to read Korean did not help the situation. Therefore, we had decided that having a Korean speaking chaperone would be a definite plus when it came to explaining what was wrong with our teeth – even if Mr Lee's English was far from perfect, it was still much better than our Korean.

We followed our agent as he wandered in and out of a maze of tiny, narrow back streets until we came to a halt outside a large building resembling a warehouse.

"Come on, come in here," Mr Lee said, waving us through the huge front doors.

When we got inside, Louise and I looked at each other in disbelief.

"What the hell is this?" Louise exclaimed.

We had both been expecting a similar set up to the UK: a reception, a waiting room off to the side and one or two surgeries where you would be called in one at a time. In contrast, this was one huge room, about the size of a primary school gymnasium, with a row of benches running all the way around it. These benches were fully occupied by people who were sitting shoulder to shoulder, waiting their turn.

In the middle of the room were two dentist chairs, occupied by two patients, while two dentists worked simultaneously on their clients' teeth.

"Bloody Hell! It's more like a circus ring than a dentist's," I remarked.

Just then, one of the patients yelped in pain and half of the impromptu 'audience´ stood up and inched forwards to get a better view.

"This can't be very hygienic with all those people breathing down on the patient!" I said, already finding excuses as to why I should not have any treatment done there.

"I'm past the point of caring," Louise replied. "I'm in so much pain, I've got to get this seen to."

Mr Lee hurried away to speak to someone, and I suppose we must have jumped the queue because a few minutes later, Louise was called to the chair. After a quick examination, the dentist told her that the tooth would have to come out, and he swiftly injected her.

Once again, we both wrongly assumed that the next stage of the proceedings would follow English protocol. We were expecting him to tell her to go and sit down while the anaesthetic took effect, but this was Korea! The dentist plunged straight in with his instruments, and Louise let out the most blood-curdling scream! Her feet turned upwards and started to curl, reminding me of the wicked witch from 'The Wizard of Oz´ whose feet curled up under the fallen house. Louise's hands gripped the armrests until

I thought she was going to rip them open with her nails.

The Koreans were exultant. The entire room edged forwards in shuffling steps for a better view. I inadvertently realised that Louise had received a standing ovation (more than we had every procured while doing the show.)

"Oh, you have very strong teeth!" The dentist proclaimed, when Louise had stopped screaming. He tried not to look panicked as he loaded a second syringe with more anaesthetic.

The performance was repeated again... and again... and again... and again! After five injections, I was the one panicking. I was convinced that Louise would never be able to talk normally or ever feel her mouth again.

Fortunately, the first injection must have finally taken effect, as Louise stopped gripping the armrest and the tooth was at long last extracted. As she walked gingerly towards us, cupping her face in her hands, Mr Lee turned to me.

"Come, now it's your turn." He pushed me towards the centre of the room, but I spun straight around and headed for the door.

"No, it's not! I've changed my mind!" I said.

"Mr Lee, I think we had better get Michele out of here," Louise garbled, dribbling blood down her t-shirt. "I think she's going to faint."

It was true. I was clinging on to consciousness by a thread. Despite Louise being the one who had undergone the procedure, I was the one who had to be escorted from the premises!

Mr Lee and Louise held me up under both elbows and marched me to the nearest café. I felt like such a fraud! Louise was nursing her jaw and was completely lucid and here I was wilting like a piece of wet lettuce!

Around twenty minutes later, when I'd returned to my normal weakling self, Mr Lee said casually:

"Oh, Louise, your passport is about to expire at the end of October. You need to renew it."

"No, Mr Lee, that won't be necessary. Our contract finishes in September. I can renew it when I get home."

"Ah yes, about that, well, no. I need you all to stay at least two months extra. I have plans for you."

"I can't stay," I said, thinking on my feet and fibbing. "I'm going on holiday in October and everything has been paid for."

"Yeah, and I've got a job on a cruise ship!" Louise fabricated.

If Lee knew that we were lying through our teeth – Louise with one less than usual – he did not let on.

"You should both have holiday here, in Korea. It is very beautiful country."

"I don't think my family would want to come all the way out here for a holiday," I replied. I had no intention of staying any longer than the six months. I was sick of fighting for my money and my dignity! I was bored with doing the same show night after night. I never felt particularly safe anywhere I went and on top of that, my health was starting to deteriorate. My digestive system was craving anything which did not re-semble noodles, eggy-bread sandwiches and om-rice. I frequently suffered from stomach cramps and had either diarrhoea or constipation, as did the other two girls. I felt light-headed all the time, my hands were cracked from the horrible water in the hotel, and I constantly felt like I was on the verge of cystitis.

"Er...I don't think so, Mr Lee." Louise replied.

"Me neither. We've had enough, to be honest."

Muttering under his breath, our embittered agent jumped up from the table. "It's time for you to go to hotel," he said, with a look of indignation more than evident on his face.

That evening, at work, Mr Lee turned up at the Diamond again to repeat the same conversation. He was probably hoping that Sharon, in her ca-pacity as head girl, would make the final decision or at least try to convince us to stay. However, as Louise had once said, Sharon was about as much use as a condom in a convent, so Lee was wasting his time.

"I want you to stay in Korea for longer time. You have work, I find you more work. It is better you stay."

"Look, Mr Lee, we all want to go home," I repeated.

Louise nodded, Sharon smiled, and Mr Lee sniffed. Then he dropped a bombshell.

"Well, good news, you have contract renewed here for another month. This time you make more money because now you do consummation too."

"WHAT? No!" I exclaimed.

"I spoke with Sharon the other day. She said no problem." Mr Lee replied. "Anyway, it's too late now, I've already signed the contract. You have to do it! The nightclub pay you every day for this. Okay?" Not waiting for an answer, he turned on his heels and marched determinedly away.

I spun around and glared at Sharon who had found something extremely important to do in her bag.

"Sharon, how the hell can you make that decision without talking to us first?"

"Well, we did discuss it. We talked about it in the dressing-room."

"Yeah, and I distinctly remember saying that I didn't want to do it!"

"Look, you're the one who's always saying that you're worried what will happen to us when these two contracts finish," Sharon argued. "I thought I was doing the best thing for the three of us. I'm the head girl and I've made the decision."

I swung round to look at Louise for support, but she had already resigned herself to the inevitable.

"Such is life!" she said and shrugged her shoulders.

* * *

Friday 7th of July we were woken up at 5:30 am by a deafening explosion from outside. We sleepily dragged ourselves to the nearest window and looked out.

Peering down to the rabbit warren of narrow, winding streets below us, we could see a significantly large blaze coming from one of the alleyways, dangerously close to the hotel. Flames were licking up the sides of a building and on the roof of that same dwelling were a couple of elderly Koreans, who were frantically throwing buckets of water down to the source of the fire but to no avail. The air reverberated with the sound of approaching sirens, as fire-engines approached from all directions. It immediately became apparent that the labyrinth of narrow streets was impossible for the dimensions of a fire-truck to enter.

"The alleyway isn't wide enough for a fire engine!" I said.

"That's a great example of Korean mentality, that is. Stupid Kimchi brains! Louise exclaimed.

We watched the scene as firemen donned axes, ran through the Central Hotel, out to the other side and hacked their way through doors and gateways. Dragging fire hoses behind them and blowing whistles until they reached the source of the blaze, they managed to extinguish the fire.

As the firemen began to disperse, we came away from the window.

"Okay, the show's over. Let's go back to sleep," Sharon said. "Now we know that we aren't going to be burnt alive in our beds."

"Actually, it does make you think," I said. "If there were a fire here, how the hell would we be supposed to get out?"

"Well, there's a rope there on the wall," said Sharon. "We could use that."

"Yeah, but we're on the seventh floor," I protested. "Look at the length of the rope. After we have tied it to something in here and lowered ourselves down, according to my reckoning, we would be dangling in mid-air about five stories up!"

"Fuck me!" said Louise.

"No thanks!" I replied.

"Then we'll just have to hope that there isn't a fire while we're here," Sharon remarked.

"Great!" I replied and mentally started to compile a 'Nine ways to die in Korea´ list: 1. Being abducted on a motorbike, 2. North Korean attack, 3.Student uprisings, 4. Being shot on stage, 5. Driving into oncoming traffic, 6.Fire. . .

* * *

That night at the Diamond, the dreaded time had come for our first night of Consummation. I was in a foul mood, partly from nerves but mostly due to the frustration of not being in control of the situation. Louise looked nervous too. Neither of us knew what to expect. Sharon, on the other hand, did not seem in the slightest bit phased.

Mr Lee had shown up, supposedly to escort us through it.

"Okay. You will be paid 20,000 won (about £16) for every five minutes you sit with the customers. You can become very rich girls!" he said, laughing.

I glared at him. I had never felt so like punching someone in the face as at that moment.

"I don't want to be rich and I don't want to do this!" My voice rose in exasperation. "I want the money I'm owed for dancing and that's it."

Our agent chose to ignore me.

"Yeah, now there's a thought," Louise said. "Have you brought our salary?"

"No. Not possible today. I bring tomorrow!"

"NO! Today Mr Lee!" I shouted, stamping my foot in frustration.

"Leave it, Michele, you are wasting your breath. Some people have just got no consideration." Louise sniffed, looked in Mr Lee's direction and narrowed her eyes in contempt.

After the disco spot, the three of us were called to our first table. Feeling half ashamed and half terrified as to what was about to happen, I walked resigned acceptance behind the other two, feeling lower than I ever had since my arrival in Korea.

We sat down and were introduced to three men. I do not know if the gentlemen were specifically chosen to break us in gently or not, but for the first time, they were a good choice. The men in question were more or less sober, and they bought each of us a drink. It became immediately obvious that, unlike the Korean hostesses, we were unable to hold a conversation with them, so everyone resorted to an amalgam of gesturing and laughing. The time passed in no time and before we knew it, we were back in the dressing-room.

"You see, I told you there's nothing to it," Sharon said, smiling.

I chose to ignore her. Although I was forced to admit that the experience had not been as daunting as I had originally expected, just the word Consummation made me cringe. As it was not a word I was familiar with, I had looked it up in the dictionary. Depending on how it was used it made reference to perfection, fulfilment, realization and achievement - positive words that, under normal circumstances would make a person feel quite self-assured. On the contrary, references to climax, orgasm, copulation and sex had quite the opposing effect!

Unfortunately, I was prone to believe that in our present situation, the latter four words were the most appropriate and I was NOT happy. I knew that there were bound to be times where we would be called to sit with drunken louts who would not be as gentlemanly as our first table of clients had been. Fortunately for me, it did not take me long to realise that if I danced on the podium and looked as miserable as sin, there was a lot less chance of being called to a table. For the first time ever on a stage, I danced without a smile on my face.

* * *

On the morning of Wednesday 12th July, the phone rang. I thought it would be Mr Lee, but I deduced that it wasn't, as Sharon was not doing her usual 'Yes, Mr Lee, no, Mr Lee' repertoire of phrases and short answers. I, therefore, deduced that it had to be one of her endless stream of boyfriends, as she was almost whispering into the phone whilst glancing sheepishly in my direction to see if I was listening.

"No, I can't... because I can't!" she was saying. "Oh, okay then. Yes, at two o'clock. Yes, okay, at two o'clock."

Her behaviour struck me as slightly odd and seemed out of character to me. Sharon was usually quite forthcoming with any boyfriend on the phone, regardless of whoever was listening. However, I thought no more about it.

As she put the phone down, it rang again. This time it was our agent. He was ringing to inform us that we had been extended at the Pan Korea for another month. This meant that we could all stop worrying about being out of work again for a while.

That night, at the Diamond, I danced with a sulky expression on my face once again and was not asked to go to any tables. I reckoned that I had got this consummation lark all figured out! Although it felt alien to me to dance without a smile, if it meant that I would not have to go and sit at tables, I was prepared to do it.

During the second disco spot, a fight broke out between two male customers who were heavily intoxicated. Usually, we ignored this kind of behaviour but, this time, they were situated at the very front of the stage and a little too close for comfort.

The fracas began when they jumped to their feet and eyed each other with malicious intent; this progressed to spitting and shouting; which further advanced to finger prodding and pushing and finally hitting each other in a deadly brawl. In the midst of the fight, one of them grabbed a beer bottle, smashed it on the edge of the stage and fiercely stabbed his opponent.

As blood flowed, more bottles were smashed, enticing more drunken men to join in the affray. The three of us maintained our positions on the stage and carried on dancing, cautiously looking from the men to each other and then to the Korean disco dancers, afraid that we were about to become embroiled in the situation.

As yet more bottles were shattered against the tables, a piece of glass flew up and embedded itself in the arm of one of the Korean girls. At that point, we all decided, Koreans and English alike, that enough was enough. We turned in unison and left the bar area, abandoning the men to their drunken skirmish.

* * *

Friday the fourteenth of July was the long-awaited modelling day. After only three hours of sleep, I got ready and went down to reception at ten o'clock to meet Mr Woo. After waiting twenty long minutes, he still had not arrived and I was more than a little concerned. This seemed to be out of character for him.

A few minutes later, when I was about to forget the entire thing, one of the receptionists on the front desk shouted my name and held out a telephone receiver.

"You have telephone call."

It was Mr Woo.

"Michele. I meet you at Hyatt Hotel at two o'clock. Okay?"

I said it was fine, but I was a little surprised that he was not coming to pick me up. However, surmising that a taxi fare would hardly make a huge dent in my one thousand dollars, I readily agreed.

At two o'clock, I made my prompt arrival at the Hyatt and found Mr Woo and Mr Kyong sitting in the coffee shop. Mr Woo flashed me a weak smile and beckoned me towards them. Mr Kyong refrained from even look in my direction.

"Hello," I said cheerfully, immediately sensing the tension between the two men. Mr Woo was decidedly jittery, whereas Mr Kyong was agitated and in a foul mood. He refused to look at me and proceeded to bang utensils down on the table over and over again. I started to feel more than a little uncomfortable. I had no idea what had upset him, but he certainly did not want to look me in the face.

After about five minutes of his table banging tantrum, he pushed back his chair, slammed his hands down on the table and marched away from the table without even speaking to me.

"What's the matter with Mr Kyong?" I asked.

"Oh. He is very angry! VERY angry!"

"Why?"

Mr- Woo looked rather embarrassed. "Er, sorry, but the newspaper no want to take your photo anymore."

"But, why?" I asked, more than a bit confused. "What have I done?"

"Oh, no, nothing! It's not your fault." Mr Woo patted my hand. "Mr Kyong is very angry because he arranged to meet Sharon two days ago. She promised to meet him at two o'clock, but she not come."

Visions of her secretive phone call two days ago flashed before me. I was fuming!

"Now, Mr Kyong is very offended and also he is embarrassed to be in your company."

"Well, that's just great!"

"I am sorry for you."

"Not as sorry as I am!" I said, thinking of my one thousand dollars which had just followed Mr Kyong out of the coffee shop.

"Don't worry. We go out for lunch," Mr Woo said, trying to console me as visions of a Hyatt Hotel meal also fell by the wayside.

Lunch turned into a full afternoon's activities in way of compensation, not that I was really in the mood to do anything. After eating, I was taken bowling. Later still, I was driven to two office buildings where Mr Woo's cousins worked. But, to be honest, I was feeling so miserable, I just wanted to go back to the Central Hotel. I was totally discouraged and could not stop thinking about the money I had lost, through no fault of my own.

On top of that, Mr Woo was starting to irritate me. As he walked me from one office block to another and introduced me to various cousins and friends, I realised that there was no real motive for visiting the offices at all. I began to feel like I was on parade. He was showing me off, and it was doing wonders for his credibility to be seen with a foreign girl.

Mr Woo's cousins presented me with two fans each depicting Hodori, the Olympic mascot. I bowed and thanked them, then turned to Mr Woo and asked if I could go back to the hotel. I was still livid with Sharon and did not want to see her, but I needed to go back to familiar surroundings and brood for a while. Although I was well aware that my host was trying his best to help me have a pleasant day, the loss of a thousand dollars was a bitter pill to swallow.

Eventually, when he drove me back to the Central Hotel - back to my reality - he walked me to the entrance and held out his hand.

"Here take this," he said, handing me a wad of money. "I'm sorry it not happen for you."

"Not as sorry as I am, believe me, Mr Woo," I replied.

He had given me 50,000₩ (£40) for my trouble. It was better than nothing, but nowhere near as much money as Sharon had caused me to lose.

It was fortunate for her that she was out when I returned, as I am pretty certain there would have been an argument or maybe even a fight. Louise was livid when she heard the news. She was really annoyed for me and called our head girl all the names under the sun.

When 'the temptress´ returned, it was Louise who confronted her and told her how she had lost me the modelling job.

Sharon did not even have the decency to apologise. She looked in my direction, shrugged and continued getting ready for work.

"I can't believe it!" Louise yelled. "You should at the very least say you're sorry! She's lost a thousand dollars and the chance of more work because of you!"

Sharon turned her head, refrained from making eye contact and mumbled a half-hearted: "Sorry."

"That's it?" Louise said incredulously. "I can't believe it!"

I found myself gripping the sides of my bed with angry fists. All my life I had avoided confrontations, preferring to talk rather than fight, but at that moment, I desperately wanted to scratch her eyes out. I needed to find a release for some of my pent up frustration, after months of working in Korea. Fortunately, common sense told me that we still had to work together and I should keep the peace. Besides, she may have been smaller in stature but I reckoned she had much more bulk and muscle than me. I doubted I'd come out of the altercation as the victor, so I decided to keep quiet, swallow my bubbling rage and seethe inside.

* * *

On Saturday evening, we were sitting in the dressing room of the Pan Korea when, without warning, one of the girls, who we had nicknamed Big Feet, came off the stage and stomped into the dressing room. She immediately confronted one of the other girls, whom we had christened Karma, (short for Karma-sutra.) A shouting and gesticulating match began between the two as the rest of us stood around watching.

The shouting turned into a physical altercation which augmented into a squabbling match on the floor. Akin to amateur wrestlers, they scratched each other and pulled each others' hair. Big feet picked up a bottle from a crate of grape juice, which was always readily available for all the Korean dancers in the dressing-room. She smashed it on the side of the dressing table and cracked Karma-sutra over the head with it.

Karma retaliated by throwing the ice bucket and making contact with Big feet's head. As Big feet swooned with dizziness and tried to remain conscious, Karma caught her off guard and counterattacked by landing a punch and bursting her opponent's lip. Within seconds, there was blood everywhere. Both of them seemed to be covered in it but they carried on fighting regardless. (This altercation made me feel more than justified that I had decided to contain my emotions and refrain from getting into an affray with Sharon the day before.)

Sharon ran off to find help and returned various times with several different men who seemed quite happy to observe the course of the brawl but had no intention of separating the girls. They watched with amused expressions on their faces for a few minutes before losing interest and sauntering out as casually as they had wandered in.

Eventually, some of the other disco dancers - realising that no males were going to intervene - managed to separate the two brawlers. I decided to try and help, so I picked up a cloth, wet it under the tap and went to mop up Karma's sanguine fluid. As she pulled her hair back, I gasped. Her neck was covered in thick, clotting blood which was oozing from a massive gash in her forehead, caused by the broken bottle.

"My God, there's so much blood!" I said. Then all hell broke loose!

Big feet collapsed onto the floor and began convulsing and retching like she was going to vomit.

"Oh, my God, I'm going to faint!" Louise slumped onto a chair. "I can't feel my hands!"

I grabbed another dancer's arm and pulling her over to me, Pushing the bloody cloth into her hands and showing her how to keep the pressure on the wound, I ran over to Louise and escorted her outside to get some fresh air.

Several minutes later, when we returned to the scene, we found two dancers attempting to tidy up the dressing-room by picking up the discarded ice-bucket, ice-cubes and broken glass. Karma was being escorted out of the dressing-room by two bouncers. I assumed that she would be taken to hospital, but we were unable to ever find out what happened to her and she never returned to the Pan Korea. Big feet came back later that same evening, with a huge gash and long scratches down her face that were still oozing pus. I doubted she would be called to hostess at any tables that night looking so rough and dishevelled.

Louise was unable to perform the show or the next scheduled disco spot. She was deathly pale and still had no feeling in her hands. Sharon and I re-blocked the show and worked as a duet.

Later, back at the hotel as I thought about the events of the day, I was quite proud of myself. Under normal circumstances, I would have been close to fainting at the sight of blood. I felt that I had worked pretty well in a crisis and had perhaps redeemed myself a little after the debacle I had made of myself at the dentists'.

* * *

On Sunday morning, I woke up to find Sharon sleeping with Foster in her single bed and Louise and Jim squashed together in the other. I swung my legs out of my enormous, double bed and headed for the window. As I pulled back the curtain to let in some light, I heard Foster complaining.

"Mind my retinas. Close the curtains!"

Mind my retinas? I thought. *Where's he got that expression from?*

"Say what?" I replied in my best impression of an American twang.

"It's too bright for my eyes. Close the curtains!"

"Er, just hang on a minute," I retorted. I had had enough of Korean men bossing me about and I was not about to let an American GI start doing it too, not in here! "This is my room. I want to get up and I'm not going to sit in the dark for you!"

He acquiesced, remained silent and pulled the sheet over his head in a weak attempt to block out the bright Korean sunshine. Once again, I felt I had won and gained a small victory in my male orientated world.

That evening, when we arrived at the Diamond nightclub, the manager paid us a visit. Since we had stopped doing the show, we had been told to dance together during the disco spots and to take centre stage. However, the manager had now decided that he no longer wanted the three of us to dance on the main stage, he wanted us to spread out.

"One in centre, two at sides," he said, meaning the two smaller podiums, one behind glass and the other open, which were situated at either side of the main stage, almost in the corners of the venue.

"Right," said Sharon. "Michele you go in the fish tank, (the one behind glass, obviously,) and Louise you take the other side."

This, of course, meant that Sharon had given herself centre stage, which at this point in the proceedings was no longer a surprise.

I flounced off, installed myself behind glass and started dancing to the music. To be honest, I was in a world of my own again. There were no clients over at my side of the club, so I was thinking about other things. Eventually, I became aware of a waiter standing in front of me, grinning. Other waiters were loitering in the background laughing and it took me a moment to establish as to why they were giggling.

The waiter put his hands on his hips and looked from me to his crotch and back again. Then everything became clear. He had extracted his penis from his trousers and was trying to get me to look at it. I was not sure if he expected me to show an element of astonishment or shock but nothing surprised me anymore about the antics of the men in this country so I decided to play along. I looked down at his dangling appendage and then looked back up at him. I held my hands up and out to the sides, looking confused, then I shrugging in a 'where is it?' type gesture.

Even from inside the fish tank, I could hear the guffaws of the other waiters. Marking time in expectance for the laughing to subside a little, I then looked down again, squinted, mimed a look of recognition as I pretended to see it for the first time and then took a step backwards in mock surprise. Holding up my finger and thumb to indicate about three centimetres, I shook my head.

The waiters were chortling so much, that the manager heard the peals of laughter from the other side of the club and was soon heading over in our direction. The waiter received a brutal cuff behind the ear and quickly attempted to put his prized possession away while the other waiters abruptly stopped laughing and scattered in all directions.

Rather than be embarrassed, I had actually found it amusing. However, if I had not been a vegetarian, perhaps I would have been put off cocktail sausages for life!

When we had finished the first disco spot, the manager came marching into the dressing room again. He looked maddened. I thought that perhaps I was going to get a telling off for fraternizing with the waiters instead of dancing, but the manager headed towards Sharon.

"Change position," he barked. Then he walked out.

Sharon looked at us and shrugged.

"Okay, Louise, you go centre stage, Michele you go to the other podium and I'll take yours," she said. "God knows what his problem is!"

After the second spot, the manager was back again. It was more than evident from his facial expression that he was incensed with the situation.

"No, no, NO! You change!" he said. He told me to go centre stage and the others to work the podiums. Sharon's piqued expression showed that she was not impressed by that at all.

* * *

Monday 17th July is Korean Constitution day. The first republic of Korea was formally launched on that day. It came into effect three years after the Second World War in 1948, during which, allied forces had defeated Japan and put an end to Japanese rule. A dominance which had been in existence since Japan had invaded Korea in the 16th century.

Constitution day is also a reminder to the Koreans of the North and South divide so, for many people, this is not a day to celebrate, as it reminds them of their loved ones who have been separated by the demarcation.

Regardless of whether each individual celebrated it or not, for the Koreans, Constitution day meant a day off work. However, for the Collier trio, this meant working as usual.

We had heard that there was going to be a marathon run through the streets of Seoul, in the morning but it must have been cancelled due to the weather. This was hardly surprising, as we had gone out for a walk and got caught in a monsoon. We came back soaked to the skin but still feeling warm. It was an odd sensation.

That night, at work at the Diamond, Sharon became annoyed again and began throwing things around the dressing-room. Not in so grand a style as the Korean males but not doing a bad impression. She was seething, hurling costumes and accessories into the costume case. This was because she had changed the positions on the podiums yet again, putting herself centre stage. After the first spot, she had been told by the chief disco dancer that she had to change back to the original position. In other words, she had to stay on a side podium.

Louise and I found the situation nothing short of hilarious. We could not care less which position we were allocated but for Sharon, centre stage was the prime position and she was not about to give it up lightly – hence her bad mood.

After work, to try and change her humour, we decided to take her into Itaewon again. The three of us and two boyfriends were sitting in the Twilight zone having a drink and a chat, when one of the waitresses walked passed, tripped and spilt a whole tray full of drinks all over me!

"Oh, I sorry, very solly," she said, bowing and picking up the glasses at the same time.

"Look at me. I'm drenched!" I said as my companions guffawed in various stages of amusement.

I stood up and a stream of alcohol dripped off me, puddling at my feet, like that morning's monsoon rain.

"Come, come!" the waitress beckoned me towards her. I followed her, dripping on the carpet and leaving a distinct trail of spilt alcohol all the way to the ladies' toilets. Once inside, she ushered me into a cubicle.

"You give me t-shirt, I wash for you!"

I handed over my top and stood there in the cubicle stark naked from the waist up. I heard the tap running in the sink, and then I became aware of an ominous stillness, which immediately caused me to panic. I could hear the music in the other room, but it was blatantly obvious that the toilets were now deserted.

"Hello?" I voiced into an empty ladies' room. "Hello?"

Nothing. I stood there with my hands clasped over my chest thinking, *Now what do I do?* I could not go back into the club topless, I was trapped inside the cubicle!

A few minutes later, a couple of Korean girls wandered in to use the facilities, so I tentatively poked my head out of the door and tried to explain my predicament, but I was not successful. They had either decided not to help me, or they had not understood me but as they laughed sarcastically behind their hands and eyed me up and down, it infuriated me and did nothing to help my frustrating predicament.

I wonder how long I'll have to stay in here until Sharon and Louise miss me?" I asked myself. That was a sobering thought, considering they were both making eyes at their boyfriends!

After ten minutes, I decided to sit down on the lavatory, still with my hands over my breasts waiting and hoping desperately to be rescued. I had visions of someone looking over the cubicle partition out of curiosity. They would surely contemplate as to what on earth I was doing and what strange fetish I must have, to sit half-naked on a public convenience!

After about twenty minutes, I heard, a hesitant: "Michele?"

"Louise, I'm in here!" I shouted. "The bloody waitress has buggered off with my t-shirt and I've got nothing on underneath!"

I heard her laugh.

"Okay," she said. "I'll go and find out what's happened to your clothes. Wait there!"

"Well, I've got no bloody choice! I can't go anywhere, can I?"

A few minutes later, she returned and swung my soaking wet t-shirt over the top of the cubicle door.

"What the hell is this?" I exclaimed. "I can't bloody wear this!"

"The waitress said she hasn't got anything to dry it with," Louise explained.

"Go and tell that stupid bitch that I can't wear a wet t-shirt that stinks of alcohol! She'll have to give me a Twilight zone t-shirt!" I snapped.

"Okay." Louise left and I resigned myself to sitting on the toilet again until her return a few minutes later.

"Michele? She said you can have a t-shirt . . . er, they cost four thousand won."

"WHAT! Is that stupid Kimchi brain really expecting me to pay for a bloody t-shirt when she's ruined mine!"

"Er. . . Yep!"

The management knew they had me over a barrel. . . .excuse the pun! I had two choices; wear a soggy t-shirt all night or buy one from the Twilight zone and spend the rest of the night advertising the very club, that at that moment in time, I had no intention of returning to. I had no choice but to pay up!

* * *

For the next few days, the only amusing event
for me was watching Sharon becoming more and
more irate every time the manager or the disco
captain of the Diamond, asked her to change
places on the podiums. In other words, remove
herself from centre stage.

The final straw came on Thursday 20th when
Sharon, once again, placed herself in the centre
during the first disco spot. When we returned
to the dressing–room, the captain was muttering
and sighing, shaking her head and waving her index finger in Sharon's direction.

"No, no, NO! You change. You podium!"

"This is RIDICULOUS!" Sharon sulked and
turned her back on the Korean.

The captain, seething at being ignored, walked
out in a huff and returned a minute later with the
manager who stomped over to Sharon and poked
her in the shoulder.

"You, no centre. You right podium," he said,
making it blatantly clear.

He turned and looked at Louise. "You left
podium. And you..." he finished, looking in my
direction, "You centre!"

"But, why?" asked Sharon. "I don't get it! Why
do I have to go to the podium?" she complained.
"Why is Michele always in the centre and us on
the podiums?"

"Because she small size you big size!" he replied.

* * *

On Sunday 23rd Jim invited the three of us to the army base again in Uijeonbu. This time I remembered to take some I.D and we spent the day sunbathing around the pool and swimming.

At five o'clock they have what is called the five o'clock salute. This was something which we, as non-military civilians, were not aware existed, nor what it signified. Basically at the beginning of the day, a tune called 'Reveille' is played at 7:00 am and the American flag is raised. In contrast, at five o'clock a bugler plays 'The Taps', a tune which is also known as 'Butterfield's Lullaby' or 'Day is Done', which comes from the first line of the lyrics. During this tune, the American flag is lowered and folded.

At both times of the day, servicemen in uniform are required to stop, face headquarters and salute. If they are in their civvies, they can stand to attention or at parade rest.

Civilians on base, including the Collier Trio, were expected to stop, stand respectfully still and place their right hand over their hearts. As the bugling began, everyone clambered out of the swimming pool and assumed their corresponding positions. We, not being au fait with the situation, merely shrugged and carried on swimming! By doing so, we attracted the scorn of a soldier, who was stood to attention. He spun his head in our direction and barked,

"Get out of the pool you idiots! Show some respect!"

"We're not idiots, we're British," Sharon replied - as I cringed!

A civilian explained in subdued tones what we were required to do and we begrudgingly left the pool, feeling more than a little embarrassed by our impropriety.

* * *

The following day I went to the post office to send the first of two parcels home. I decided to send the fibre optic clock and various other things in a big parcel which was available to buy in the post office. The staff packed everything up and sealed the package for a set fee of 3,000₩ (approx £2.40) and charged me 9,200₩ (less than £8) for postage and packaging. I had chosen the cheapest option, which meant that my parcel would go by ship and take up to three months to arrive in England. However, I figured that I would be due home around the same time so it made good economic sense to me.

Once knowing the process and how simple it all was, I further decided to return within the next few days, with the Korean dolls in the display case - as soon as Lee got around to paying us again.

That night when we arrived at the Pan Korea, we found several of the disco dancers standing outside the dressing-room. It appeared that the door was locked from the inside and they could not get in. As the wall did not reach the ceiling and wasn't overly high, I turned to Louise.

"I can open that," I said. "Give me a leg up."

She cupped her hands and I scaled the wall, dropped to the other side and opened the door. The disco dancers looked quite shocked yet impressed at the same time, which surprised me. Maybe in their culture, it was not something a female should do but to me, it was the most obvious and logical solution to a minor problem.

During the show, as we finished one routine and Sharon was leaving the stage, she fell off the catwalk, landing headfirst in the middle of a table full of Koreans! I am sure she must have hurt herself but Louise and I found it extremely amusing! One second she was there and the next she had disappeared. She sort of flopped over the side, reminding me of a sea lion in the way she seemed to undulate from the catwalk edge to the tabletop.

Later that evening, we were informed that it would be our last day. I do not know if Sharon's fall had anything to do with the decision but we were told that they no longer required the show or the disco spots. As usual, we all started to worry. We were now reduced to working the podium in the Diamond. The thought of another spell of unemployment was not a pleasant one.

Two days later, Mr Lee informed us that we had another audition at a club called 'The Academy'. At this stage in the contract, we did not need to ask if we would be paid for the performance and to be honest, we were all relieved that we could possibly have the chance of working for another month. So, we gratefully packed the costume case and headed off. We also asked for money, but again, at this stage, we were not surprised when the answer was in the negative.

"Don't worry!" Mr Lee reassured us. "On Monday, (in four days) I am going to pay you two weeks wages and the three hundred dollars for the disco spots."

"Yeah, right!" I scoffed.

"I'll believe that when I see it!" Louise said.

"Yes, okay Mr Lee," Sharon smiled.

"Oh, by the way," Mr Lee said pointing at me. "Your sister is coming out on the fifth."

"God help her!" I replied.

* * *

We worked in the Academy for the grand total of three days - (including the audition). During this time, Louise drew my attention to the fact that during the opening number, Sharon had started to move her arms differently so that her feather boa was in a different position to ours and in other parts, she had decided not to move the boa at all. Maybe this was her way of compensating for not taking centre stage in the disco spots but, whatever the reason, Louise, in particular, found it extremely annoying.

"What's happening with the boas?" she asked, confronting our head girl when we finished the show.

"How do you mean?" Sharon replied.

"Well, you've started doing different moves to me and Michele."

"It doesn't matter because I'm in the middle."

"We are supposed to be a trio," I chipped in. "So, we should all do the same!"

"That's not strictly true because if you are in the centre, it doesn't matter!"

"Oh for crying out loud!" I replied. "Of course it matters!"

"Leave it," Louise said to me. "With a mentality like that, you're wasting your breath, Michele!"

After more than three months in Sharon's company, the thought of having to put up with her for another three was a daunting prospect. She was slowly driving me crazy with her endless boyfriends, inability to do her job correctly and her incessant need to be centre stage and in the limelight all the time.

Our last show at the Academy was the 28th. We witnessed Mr Lee being paid off to take us out of the joint! This meant we were down to a few disco spots at the Diamond again and with Sharon's attitude towards her relegation to the side podium, I predicted that our days there were also numbered!

* * *

Sunday 30th found Louise and me back by invitation to the army base in Uijeonbu. It made a welcome respite from our boring, monotonous lifestyle. This time, knowing what was expected, we respected the five o'clock salute!

We spent the day in the mess hall, hanging out and watching videos. I was in my element when one of my favourite films, 'Charlie and the Chocolate Factory,' starring Gene Wilder came on. Jim had never seen it, and I insisted on telling him every time someone was going to sing. Two guys on the next table, who were obviously big fans like me, started singing along to the music. Later still, another six-foot-tall, African-American soldier began walking up and down the room singing with the Umpa Lumpas. It was surreal!

As usual, when we left the base, my spirits plummeted at the thought of going back to reality.

* * *

The following few days were pretty humdrum: working, eating, ringing Mr Lee for money, not receiving it and sleeping. But as always, at the back of our minds was the inevitable threat of unemployment if the Diamond contract finished in a few more days.

During this time, we regularly frequented 'Wendy's', an American franchise restaurant, which had empty plastic containers and a salad

261

buffet. The idea was that customers filled a container with as much food as possible and, as long as you could close the lid, you paid a set price at the till. We became rather skilled at stuffing food into these containers, eating some for lunch and taking the rest back to the hotel to eat later with our snacks and nibbles. We were already unconsciously starting to economize, in case of forced starvation in a few days time.

The following afternoon, Jim dropped round to see Louise. I was pottering around at my side of the room, minding my own business, when I realised that they were both wishing that I would disappear, as they obviously wanted a bit of time alone.

"Listen, you two," I said, decisively. "I'm going onto the hotel's roof, I'll be there for an hour, okay?" I did not wait for a reply. Gathering up a book, a drink and my writing materials I left them alone and headed for the roof.

I enjoyed my hour of solitude up there and stayed longer than I had intended to. It was a fantastic feeling to be isolated from everyone. After more than three months constantly in the company of others, having a little privacy for once was an exhilarating experience. However, when I decided to return to my room, I was forced to stay even longer on the roof through no fault of my own.

As I meandered down the stairs of the hotel, I inadvertently disturbed a rather large rat which must have been sniffing around, minding its own business. It instantly tensed, adopted a defensive stance, then it shot off into the darkness of the stairwell. Once there, it hissed its existence, scurried backwards and forwards in the shadows and got ready to lunge.

I froze! If I ran down, I assumed it would think I was attacking it and retaliate, but if I ran up, would it follow me? I turned around with painful slowness - not something I did lightly, as it felt so wrong to turn my back on my adversary, a trapped rodent which could spring on me and attack from behind. Then, with adrenalin coursing through my veins like a runaway train, I sprinted up the stairs again as fast as I could go, back to the roof, silently praying that I was not being followed.

Half an hour later, I dared myself to start my decent for the second time; ears peeled for the slightest sound and eyes darting from left to right for the slightest movement. Fortunately, the rat had gone, but I did not breathe a sigh of relief until I was back inside my room. I knew there were vermin behind the walls but I had stupidly assumed that they stayed there!

* * *

On the fifth of August, a Saturday, the date of my sister's supposed arrival, Mr Lee came to the hotel. We were naively expecting the promised 1,500 dollars he owed us.

"Here. I can't pay it all," he said. He had the nerve to hand us one hundred dollars each.

"Is this a fucking joke?" Louise vehemently crumpling the single banknote into her fist which she then shook menacingly at our agent.

"Where's the rest of it?" I shouted.

"We need our money, Mr Lee," Sharon said in a much more subdued tone.

"This week, it's impossible!" He replied, walking up and down the room like a caged circus animal. "Impossible!"

"Give up, you're wearing the carpet out!" I snapped. As I watched him pacing up and down, I could feel my anger rising.

"I give you all the money next week," he said.

"That's what you said last week!" I shouted. "You are nothing but a liar! I don't know how you have the nerve to ask us to extend the contract for two more months. What incentives are you giving us to stay here? Bugger all! You have gone from paying us on a Monday, to paying us on a Friday. Somewhere along the way, we've lost a whole week's money!" Every week's the same routine; we have to beg our salary out of you and I'm sick of it!"

As I finally released my pent up anger and gave Lee a piece of my mind, I felt quite liberated. It was good to be the front-man for a change, rather than hanging on Louise's coat-tails, letting her do all the talking and me backing her up.

Louise, on the other hand, looked at me in complete astonishment then burst out laughing. For some reason, she saw the funny side of my outburst.

"Ooh! Go for it, Michele!" she said, barely controlling herself.

"I don't find it funny!" I snapped. I was livid with stupid Mr Lee. "I'm not working again until I get my money!"

"Oh, do what you want!" Mr Lee replied.

"Okay, give us our tickets home, then."

He ignored me and turned to Sharon.

"You do last disco spots tomorrow at Diamond nightclub. On Monday you all move to Taejon for two-week contract.

"Oh, okay, Mr Lee," Sharon replied, smiling.

Louise's face changed and she immediately stopped laughing.

"Well, hang on just a minute there, Lee. I'm not moving to some other province with less than one hundred dollars in my pocket," she said.

"Me neither!" I confirmed.

"We'll go IF and WHEN you pay us ALL the money you owe us!" Louise yelled.

Mr Lee walked to the door in a huff, clenching his fists and shaking his head. As he was leaving he turned around and pointed at me.

"And, by the way, your sister's not coming today!"

"Good! It would be better for her if she didn't come at all!" I replied.

Chapter 11

TWO WEEKS IN TAEJON

Monday morning, the seventh of August, we were sitting in the hotel room, packed and ready to go to Taejon but on tenterhooks as to whether Mr Lee would pay up or not. We were adamant - and for once all in agreement - that we would make a stand and refuse to leave unless we got our money. Fortunately, Mr Lee not only paid everything we were owed, but he also settled the outstanding telephone bill in reception, which was a great relief.

We spent the day travelling to the province of Taejon and stopped in a little town called Young Song. Rather than a hotel, the Bongo van pulled up outside a two-story building, which looked like a small youth hostel in the middle of the countryside. As we contemplated our fate from inside the bus, Mr Lee went inside to negotiate a fee.

"You girls wait here," he ordered.

Ten minutes later he beckoned us inside. We dragged all our belongings down the corridor. Memories of our arrival in Korea inadvertently flashing through my mind as we followed an aged, Korean woman who shuffled down the gloomy hallway and opened two doors. The rooms were so minuscule, that we were forced to split up. Louise and I took one, and Sharon dumped her bags in the other.

"Well, this is just great!" said Louise, looking around with an expression of displeasure. "There isn't even enough room to fart!"

I burst into laughter, but her statement was completely accurate.

The rooms were extremely basic. A double bed occupied most of the floor space, plus a chair and a small rickety table. There was no wardrobe or chest of drawers. Our room sported a hole in the roof, about a meter and a half square, which looked suspiciously as though a toilet on the upper floor must have dropped through to our room at one time, and the ceiling had never been repaired!

"I hope nobody can get through that hole in the middle of the night!" I said.

"They might be spying on us from above," Louise replied as she squinted up into the dusty darkness. We both scanned our surroundings and sighed. "Great! It looks like we'll be living out of our suitcases," Louise complained.

"I know, it's a bit odd, isn't it? I mean, what type of hotel doesn't have wardrobes?" I replied.

"Humm, very odd," Louise replied pensively.

As we continued to look around our sparse surroundings, Mr Lee called us all together in the corridor.

"Ok, you start work tonight. Here, you need to work both shows. Here not like Seoul. Here, you do two different shows. Also, you do three disco spots. These are included in cost of show."

"Okay, Mr Lee," Sharon replied.

"Nope!" Louise attested. "No way! We get extra money for the disco spots! You told us that disco spots were always extra money."

"Yes, you did," I confirmed.

"Yes. . . but here is different. Different to Seoul." Our agent sighed.

"What a surprise!" I replied.

"This just isn't on!" Louise grumbled.

"Don't worry, don't worry. I speak to manager at nightclub," he said. (If he ever did, we never got any extra money.) "Now, come, we go for walk."

As we set off, aimlessly meandering through quiet country lanes, past a forest, and through a rural little town, we assumed this was a repeat of our agent's strange behaviour that day in Seoul, when he had taken us all out for a walk and an ice-cream. We put it down to another of Mr Lee's peculiarities, believing that there was no actual point to it whatsoever.

We came to a stop outside a nightclub called 'Casanova´.

"This is where you work," Mr Lee informed us. "And..."

"And what?" I prompted.

"Here, you no have driver. He go back to Seoul."

"So, who is going to drive us to work, Mr Lee?" Sharon asked.

"You walk. We walk now, you walk later!"

"Brilliant!" Louise said, her voice laced with sarcasm.

I was already panicking, as I had not been paying attention to the route. I had no idea how we had got there, and I was certain that I'd never find my way back!

"It only ten minutes walking," Mr Lee continued. "No problem."

"Yeah, right, more like twenty," I replied. "And walking back in darkness at two o'clock in the morning will be a totally different story!"

It was a frightening prospect for all three of us.

"We'll all have to walk back together," Louise said. "I don't fancy going past that forest in the dead of night. It'll be pitch black!"

* * *

Those few hours before our first performance in Taejon, we rehearsed the second show which we had not performed for months. Due to lack of

269

space, we were forced to practice in the corridor of the strange little 'hostel'. We had all forgotten different parts of the routines, but what one had consigned to oblivion, another had remembered.

I could not recall all of the 007 routine and had to choreograph parts of it again. I was quite looking forward to working, purely as we would be doing the second show. It would be a change from the normal boring routine.

While we practised, we found ourselves being interrupted by a steady flow of couples who entered (or exited) the corridor. They all appeared slightly caught off guard when they saw us. Each couple came to an abrupt stop and seemed unsure where to go or what to do; rather like novices under a spotlight on a stage for the first time.

Their facial expressions showed their obvious surprise at finding three foreigners dressed in bicycle shorts and tops rehearsing dance routines in the corridor. After the initial shock of realising they were not alone, those who were arriving immediately became more than a little embarrassed and jittery. Fumbling with their keys, they rushed to enter the little bedrooms.

"Hmm! Interesting..." Louise said, deep in thought after the procedure had occurred various times.

I looked at her and shrugged. I was more concerned with the thought of doing the second show, remembering the routines, and packing all the right costumes and accessories.

Despite being told by Mr Lee that we would have to walk to the venue, that first night, we had the privilege´ of being driven to the nightclub in a Bongo van.

The entrance to the club was small, with a flashing red, neon sign outside and a flight of red-carpeted steps leading down to the club. More red flashing lights on the ceiling which blinked incessantly on and off made me wonder what den of iniquity we were doomed to be working in this time.

Once inside, we were escorted through the venue to the incorrectly named 'dressing-room´ which appeared to be more of a storeroom than anything else. Stacks of chairs and old wooden podiums were occupying most of the floor space while the remainder seemed to house scattered pieces of litter: old crisp packets, empty noodle pots and chopsticks. Everywhere was thick with dust and smelt fusty, as though vermin had curled up and died in there. We swiped dust clouds from three of the chairs and feeling completely disillusioned, organized our costumes the best way we could.

Mr Lee appeared to tell us that we would be expected to do a disco spot before the first show, then, later on, another one (or two) followed by the second show.

"Don't forget to tell the manager that we get paid extra for the disco spots," Louise warned him.

"Yeah, yeah!" Our agent flapped her away with his hands. "Sharon, I will see you all after the first show." Turning around, he promptly left the room.

A few minutes later, the manager appeared and asked Sharon to accompany him to the stage for a moment. When she returned a few minutes later, she had her 'Dance-Captain' head on.

"Okay, here, there are only two podiums," she informed us. "So, you two can do the first disco spot."

"Surprise-surprise," Louise muttered as she fumbled with her costumes.

My annoyance level was slowly rising as I finished getting ready. Thinking that I was probably going to be working for free whilst Sharon sat on her backside doing nothing made me fume. I glared at her and felt like screaming. She was sitting in her kimono, fanning herself and eating chocolate. Her stomach hung over her bikini top in the opening routines, and it annoyed me every time she stuffed her face with more rubbish.

Louise and I wandered out into the venue to get our first view of where we would be spending the next fifteen minutes. The tables were covered with orange table cloths which clashed severely with the red carpet and blue lighting. We located the two black, wooden podiums which also seemed to be a little odd. Firstly, they were positioned in weird places inside the club. They seemed to be in the middle of the clientele, rather than set to one side of the stage as was the custom in Seoul. Furthermore, they were exceedingly low down, which was a daunting prospect. This inferred that we would be more vulnerable and easy targets for drunken men with wandering hands.

That first night was uneventful. The club was only about half-full and the majority of the clientele were considerably well behaved.

Mr Lee disappeared decisively quickly after the first show so that he could avoid having to talk to us or the manager. He left us to face that predicament alone. Trying to track down the nightclub boss and state our case about the money discrepancy regarding the disco spots fell on deaf ears – as we knew it would.

"No understand!" he repeated over and over again.

"Come on, let's go," Louise said, resigning herself to the inevitable truth that we would not be getting the money. "We're just wasting our time."

After we finished work at 02:00 am we were ravenously hungry, so we took our second walk of the day; this time in search of food. Since the beginning of our journey to Taejon, I had only eaten two dried crackers and four pieces of kimbap, the Korean equivalent of Japanese sushi, (seaweed roll with rice).

"I'm so hungry at this point in time, I could eat a scabby horse," Louise stated as we trudged down the street. Her eyes immediately lit up as she pointed to a little café. "Look! They've got pork chops. I've been craving pork chops for a while, now."

". . . Sounds good to me," Sharon replied, so we all trouped inside.

As usual, I was severely limited as to what I could order that did not contain meat, so I ordered a 'Mexican salad´, not knowing what to expect. I assumed it would be a basic lettuce and tomato base, with a few extras thrown in for good measure. We waited impatiently for our food, but when it arrived, we were unpleasantly surprised.

"What the hell is this?" Louise complained, staring at her plate of 'pork chops´.

Sharon lifted a sliver of meat with the tip of her knife and screwed her nose up in disgust.

"This looks like no pork chop I've ever eaten," she said. The meat was totally flat and, in appearance, looked more like fish in breadcrumbs.

The salad was no better. It bore no resemblance to any salad I had ever eaten in my life. Around the edges of the plate were several pieces of rice paper, overlapping each other and sticking out over the sides. In the middle was a splodge of something which did not look in the least bit appetizing.

"Look at this. It looks like someone has puked on my plate!" I complained. Then I tried it. "Urgh! - It tastes like it too. It looks like I'll be living off kimchi and plain rice for the next fortnight," I sighed.

"Believe me, this isn't much better," Sharon replied.

Louise agreed by nodding and pulling a face.

"What the hell are these for?" I said flicking the rice paper.

"That's for the Continental touch," Louise joked.

"And, these are not Seoul prices," Sharon remarked. "It's going to cost us a fortune to stay here."

After our disastrous meal, we set out on the twenty-minute walk in pitch blackness to our hostel. As we finally approached the establishment, we were surprised to see it completely lit up like a Christmas tree.

"Now, it all makes sense," Louise said, pointing to the sign. "You see that word there, 'Yeogwan´?" (It was written in English script.)

"...Yeah...?"

"Well, I was talking to Amy and she told me that these are like mini-hotels that are used by young couples. The rooms are rented out on an hourly rate!"

"What're you talking about?"

"Bloody hell, Michele! Do I have to spell it out for you?" Louise gave an exasperated sigh. "This is a love hotel. The rooms are rented out for an hour at a time so that people can come here and have sex!"

"Oh!" I said as the penny dropped. "That makes sense why there are no wardrobes and drawers."

"Precisely!" Louise replied, making me equate her deduction skills to those of Sherlock Holmes.

"Now we know why everyone was shocked to see us in the corridor rehearsing!" I said, starting to giggle. "They've probably been planning some secret rendezvous, trying to be inconspicuous and undiscovered, and there's us dancing down the passageway, ruining everything."

We all laughed.

"Well, that puts our latest accommodation at an all-time low," Sharon groaned.

"Urgh!" I said. "Can you imagine how many different bodily fluids will be on the mattresses...?"

"Oh, Michele, shut up!" Sharon replied. "How gross! That's disgusting!"

"...And we will be sleeping on top of them all tonight!" I added.

A sobering thought!

* * *

After sleeping on a heavily stained mattress for what felt like five minutes, Louise and I were awoken by a constant banging on the door.

"Michele! Louise! Come on. Open up. Get up, quick!"

"It's Sharon...?" I yawned. "What does she want?"

As Louise opened the door, we were surprised to see our head girl dressed for work. Sporting full stage makeup, with her fishnets over her arm and carrying her makeup case, she seemed extremely agitated and stressed out.

"What the hell are you doing?" Louise questioned, rubbing the sleep out of her eyes.

"Come on! Get up! Get dressed, we're going to be late for work!" Sharon said, urging us to get a move on.

Louise and I looked at our watches, then at each other and shrugged.

Louise started laughing. "Sharon, it's nine o'clock in the morning."

"No, it's nine at night. We've all slept in!

"Sharon. Look at the sky, it's light!" Louise replied.

"No, that's the sky before it starts to get dark!" Sharon argued. "Come on!"

"I think she means dusk," I said as an aside. "Stop a minute, Sharon, and just listen..." I continued, holding my finger up for effect. "You can hear the birds! It's nine o'clock in the morning!"

Finally, realization dawned. She believed us.

"Go back to sleep, Sharon. And don't wake us up again!" Louise said as she turned Sharon around by the shoulders and pushed her lightly in the direction of her own room.

"Silly cow!" Louise muttered as she got back into bed.

Later in the afternoon, while Sharon was still sleeping, Louise and I went for a walk around the town. It did not take long, as it seemed to be a very quiet area with very little to do or see. We passed paddy fields and a ginseng nursery, the woods, and then we reached the town centre.

We wandered through the streets and somehow strayed off the beaten path, where, much to our dismay, we found six dogs squashed together in a tiny cage. When we realised that they were situated behind a restaurant, we soon put two and two together and knew that they were destined to be someone's dinner. As we hung around trying to devise a plan with the intention of trying to free the dogs, several Koreans came out of the restaurant —one brandishing a meat cleaver- and told us to move away. Not relishing the thought of meeting a gruesome end like the dogs were destined to do, we were forced to leave. We both vowed not to eat in that establishment, but it broke my heart to see the dogs' little faces and knowing that there was nothing we could do. To this day I can still see that image as clearly as though it were yesterday.

That evening, after the first show, one of the staff came to the 'dressing-room´ to inform us that a gentleman in the audience wished to speak to us and that we should go sit at his table.

"I'm NOT doing anymore consummation!" I sulked. Crossing my arms, I threw myself onto the nearest chair. "I refuse to do it! I'm not going to sit at anyone's table!"

"Yeah, this will be another freebie!" Louise replied. "Like the bloody disco spots. I'm not doing it either."

Sighing, Sharon cast her eyes heavenwards, threw on a kimono and followed the waiter outside. She had only been gone a few minutes when she returned smiling.

"Ha! You'll never guess who it is! It's Mr Sol from Kyongju!" she said.

"Ah, well, that's a different story!" Louise said. I nodded in agreement.

We were elated that he had taken the time and effort to try and see us. Louise and I donned our kimonos and went out to meet him. He seemed genuinely pleased to see us all again. He invited the three of us to a platter of tropical fruit and a couple of drinks before we had to go and prepare for the second show. It was nice to see him and made me feel better that we had had the chance to say goodbye properly.

After work, we went in search of food again. This time we tried a different establishment called 'NOB Café'. I ordered a cheese sandwich that cost 2,000₩. Compared with Seoul prices it was expensive, particularly because, when it arrived, it consisted of two small triangles of bread, with the thinnest slices of cheese I had ever seen and a couple of slivers of rice paper in between.

"What is it with these people here and the need to put rice paper with everything?" I complained.

Sharon shrugged and tucked into her sandwich which was the same size as mine: one slice of bread cut in half. The three of us were still hungry when we had finished but were reluctant to spend another 2,000₩ on such tiny portions.

"This place costs a fortune!" I remonstrated.

"We'll have to buy some snacks and keep them in the yeogwan," Louise replied. "We have no idea how long we will be here, I mean;' the contract could be extended. We also don't know when we can expect to see Lee again, so we need to economize."

Sharon and I sniffed and nodded in agreement, not relishing the fact that, in truth, we had been dumped here, stranded in Taejon, conveniently forgotten about and left to fend for ourselves.

* * *

On Wednesday 9th August, the three of us went for another walk around town and decided to try a hotel restaurant for lunch, rather than the cafés and bars we had frequented without much success. Our chosen location was the Yu-Soung Hotel. We sat down and waited for a member of staff to approach the table, but all the waiters seemed to be more than a little uncomfortable by our arrival. Rather than try to serve us, they clumped together like a frightened flock of sheep, muttering to each other and casting scared glances over in our direction. As more minutes ticked away I finally lost my patience.

"Adashee!" (Young man), I shouted beckoning one of them − any one of them- to approach the table. I was hungry and not prepared to put up with their recalcitrant behaviour any longer.

The girls found this highly amusing but it did the trick, as one of them came over scurrying over in our direction.

Once again, the food was a minuscule amount on a huge round plate. My salad resembled a side salad and cost the earth.

"We may have been paid all that we were owed but two weeks here will make short work of it," I said.

* * *

On the third evening, while I was heading for the dressing-room, I passed a group of men, one of whom decided to slap my behind.

"Hey! what do you think you are doing?" I shouted, turning around and confronting him.

When I got no response whatsoever, and he stood giggling with his friends like a pubescent teenager, I retaliated, slapping him hard on his backside. At least that forced him to acknowledge my existence. He made eye contact and looked more than a little peeved by my actions.

Feeling pleased with myself, I glared at him and started to walk away, but he reached out and slapped me again, much harder this time. Immediately swinging around to judge his friends' reactions, he laughed again. I counter-attacked once more, hitting him back even harder than the first time.

"STOP doing that!" I yelled.

By that point, he was more than a little frustrated. He glared at me, obviously annoyed that his actions had not gone to plan and knowing that he now looked rather stupid in front of his friends. He lifted his hand as though he was contemplating slapping me across the face then he seemed to think better of it and lowered his arm.

As I turned to walk away for the final time, believing the confrontation to be over, he thumped me so hard in the back that I fell into one of the tables, knocking bottles of beer all over the place.

"Ha!" He said as I lay prone on the tabletop. He spat at my feet, laughed again more arrogantly and then sauntered away, grinning and joking with his applauding friends.

Later that same evening, as we were heading back to the dressing-room to change, a man sauntered over.

"Hello. Where are you from?" he asked, standing with his hands on both hips, blocking our path.

"Hi, we are from England," Sharon replied, smiling.

"Ha!" he fixed us with a menacing stare. Then, pointing two fingers towards us, in an attempt at resembling a pistol, he narrowed his eyes. "I shoot English people," he said, eyeing us with an ominous glare.

"Oh, do you now?" she replied. We stood our ground until the man shrugged and begrudgingly had to step aside, allowing us to pass.

"You don't think he's going to shoot us while we work, do you?" I asked, remembering the news bulletins we had been aware of in Seoul, where Koreans were shooting foreign dancers.

"I doubt it," said Sharon – not so convincingly.

"No, not here," Louise replied, also not sounding so assertive.

I began to wish that my plastic 007 gun was a real one, completely loaded just in case of an emergency!

After the show, during which we had been scanning the audience for shifty characters and anything resembling a weapon, we retired to a little café across the road, where we could calm down and treat ourselves to a soft drink until it was time to return to work.

This became a regular habit over the next two weeks. However, we very rarely managed to sit outside the café without being approached by someone or another. The encounters with Koreans at the café were in a lighter vein than in the club. Some of them were genuinely surprised to see foreigners in their town and just wanted to chat to us. Sometimes, we did not mind but other times when we were having a bad day, we would have preferred to have been left alone.

On one such occasion, a guy approached us and in an attempt to get him to move on, Louise adopted a French accent.

"You, are from France? You no speak English?" the man asked her.

"Very little," she replied with her perfect French twang.

"And you?" He said, looking in my direction.

"Very little; hello, how are you?" I said – in the worst impression of a French accent ever!

The man remained during the entire break period and we were forced to speak to him in English in the end. He was harmless enough, but we had wanted a bit of time to ourselves.

Another time, two guys asked for our address. I found it highly amusing to write:

> Michele E. Northwood,
> Nutcase,
> Kimchi's are thick,
> England
> 701994

They seemed quite happy and off they went, giving us a present of a face-cloth each with a picture of a lighthouse on it and made me feel exceedingly guilty for my silly antics.

* * *

One evening, one of the band members at the nightclub, a Korean who constantly wore a trilby hat and insisted that he was from California, approached me.

"I have to say, that you are very beautiful," he said.

"Er... thanks!" I replied.

Sharon immediately started throwing things in the suitcase again; she was not happy that I was getting a compliment, and she was not the centre of attention.

"Would you like to go out on a date with me?" he asked in perfect English.

"I'm sorry, but I can't. I have a boyfriend in England," I told him.

"Oh, well, I respect that," he replied. "Would you go out with me for a meal anyway, just as friends?"

I reluctantly agreed, but later, I told Louise that I was regretting it.

"Don't be silly!" she replied. "You have told him that you only want to be friends so there is no harm in meeting him. Besides, if you get a free meal out of it, that's a definite plus 'cause you know how expensive everything is here."

I had to admit that she had a point, but the following day, I was a nervous wreck as the hour for the 'date' approached.

He arrived on time and I left with him, feeling more than a little awkward. However as time passed, and he seemed more than content just to be in my company, I chilled out a little. I was taken to eat sushi in a Japanese restaurant, and

I also got to try Saki, the Japanese rice wine for the first time. The conversation between us both flowed quite easily and I found myself enjoying my time with him. Afterwards, he dropped me back at the yeogwan.

"Thank you for a nice afternoon," I said.

As I turned away and started to leave, he took my hand and brought it up to his lips. I acquiesced, believing that he was going to kiss it, but he pinched my skin between his teeth and bit me!

"ARGH! What did you do that for?" I snapped, rubbing the back of my hand, now complete with a distinct set of his teeth marks.

"Goodbye!" He replied, with a forced, almost sarcastic smile on his face. He spun around on his heels and walked away!

"Stupid Californian Kimchi brain!" I muttered after him. The men in this country certainly had some weird customs. I did not know what to make of it! Was he 'marking me´ as his property or what?

The girls were as confused as I was, so I decided to confront him that evening and ask him why he had done such a strange thing. However, stranger still was the fact that the band did not appear that evening. In fact, we never saw them again. They all simply disappeared. His teeth marks, however, remained on my hand for a whole three days, a lasting reminder of my weird date!

* * *

That same evening after work, Louise and I found Sharon packing her overnight bag.

"And where are you going?" Louise asked.

"I'm going to Seoul this evening. I'm going to meet Big Malc," she replied. "Don't worry, I'll be back in time for tomorrow's shows."

"How are you going to get there?" I asked. I could not help but admire her nerve at travelling to another town, on her own, in the middle of the night.

"By train. Malc's given me all the train times."

"Do you want us to walk with you to the station?" I asked.

"No, it's okay. I'll be fine."

Off she went at three o'clock in the morning, walking through the countryside in total obscurity to reach the town and the train station.

The following day (12th Aug) as showtime approached and there was no sign of Sharon, we were starting to worry.

"Maybe she never even made it to Seoul last night!" I said. "I mean; anything could have happened to her."

"Well, in my opinion, it's a bit stupid travelling all that way on your own," Louise replied. "Let's face it, we stand out like sore thumbs as foreigners. Anyone could have picked her up."

"I know. She could be anywhere, what are we going to do?"

"Let's wait until after the first show. If she hasn't appeared by then, we'll have to phone the police or something."

Louise offered to do Sharon's solo, and we re-positioned the dance routines in the yeogwan corridor again - much to the consternation of the clandestine couples who happened to come across us on their way to an illicit hour of sexual activities. Then later, we walked to work wondering where on earth she could be!

On arrival at the club, we informed the manager of Sharon's absence, but after the first show and two disco spots, when there was still no sign of her, we decided that we had better find the manager again and ask him to call the police. As we were leaving the dressing-room, our extremely flustered head girl finally appeared.

"What the hell happened to you?" Louise said.

"I'm sorry, I'm sorry! I couldn't get a train! The time table was all wrong. I've had to pay 65,000₩ (£52) to get back here!"

"Well, you'd better go and talk to the manager, because he's not a happy Hector!" Louise informed her.

As Sharon scurried away in a frantic search for the boss, Louise turned to me.

"65,000₩ for a shag! I hope it was worth it!" she quipped.

Later that evening, at the designated time of yet another disco spot, Sharon disappeared yet again! This time she had gone back to the yeogwan to have a shower. Consequently, she returned fifteen minutes late for the next session on the podium. This meant that, once again, one of us had to cover for her.

Both Louise and I gave her a piece of our minds and told her that she needed to start taking some responsibility. After all, she was supposed to be in charge. She was hardly setting a good example. For once, Sharon did not reply. She knew we were correct, and she reluctantly bore the brunt of our outburst.

* * *

On Sunday, mid-morning, Jim made a surprise appearance. As I guessed that Louise and her man would, in all likelihood, want to leave a fresh deposit on the severely semen-stained mattress, I thought I had better make myself scarce! I was still not really speaking to Sharon, so I decided to go to the bank to change some money and have a walk around the town.

At lunchtime, I decided to try the hotel around the corner from the yeogwan. I ordered 'curry rice´, which, as the name suggests, was a plate of plain boiled rice, served with a gravy-boat of curry sauce and vegetables. It was reasonably priced (for Taegon) and was delicious! I could not wait to tell the girls about my discovery.

Curry rice became my staple food during our stay in Taejon, (much to Louise's chagrin, as she said the smell of curry made her feel sick). We had all cut down to one meal a day and just snacked on fruit, crackers or crisps in an attempt to try and eke out our money. We estimated that here in Taejon, on food alone, we were spending as much money in three days than a whole week in Seoul. The ever evasive Mr Lee was being just that, evasive, so we had no idea when, or even if he was going to come back to pay us.

Another problem in regards to food was that in the yeogwan, it was crawling with ants, so any opened packets of food would be teaming with insects within minutes. One day, I had hung half a watermelon in a bag on the wall, naively assuming that the ants would be unable to climb up there. When I went back to it later in the day, there were two distinct black lines of ants, about a centimetre thick, walking up or down the wall carrying tiny pieces of my fruit! The bag itself was writhing with thousands of insects, making it fruitless (*ha ha!*) to even consider eating. Trying to conserve any food which was not hermetically sealed was an impossibility. One morning, I woke up and, still half asleep, fumbled around in a packet of biscuits. I was seconds away from taking a bite when something took a bite out of me. Through bleary eyes, I realised my biscuit was crawling with little brown ants, the exact same colour as the biscuit!

That evening, we walked to work accompanied by Jim, who had decided to come in and watch.

He stayed to see the first disco spot and show, then left – probably out of boredom!

After work when we all returned to the Yeogwan, I realised that Jim intended staying the night with Louise. This meant that I was relegated to Sharon's room for the night. As she and I were not on the best of speaking terms, due to her trip to Seoul and late appearance the previous day, it was not something which I particularly wanted to do. The atmosphere was strained to say the least, but I could hardly insist on remaining in my room and sharing a bed with Louise and Jim! – Well, I could have done, but it might have got a bit awkward!

The next morning, after a restless night's sleep and waking up covered in mosquito bites; including one above my right eye, which looked suspiciously like Sharon had punched me. I went with Louise and Jim to the train station, to see Jim board the train back to base camp. Later Louise and I wandered around the shops and town, trying to kill time.

On the way back to the yeogwan, we saw a farmer place a white sheet on the pavement and cover it with red peppers. (They would normally be left there for two or three days to dry out in the sun). I insisted on having my photo taken next to the peppers, as it was the most interesting thing I had seen since I had arrived in the little town.

Boredom was really setting in. During the day, we were reduced to sunbathing- but even that was proving to be rather difficult. Our original idea of using the roof terrace was quashed, as there was a large dog up there. We were not sure if it was someone's pet or someone's dinner - and we did not want to know - but it severely restricted our sunbathing activities. The yeogwan did not seem to have any outside space, so trying to find an alternative location where we could top up our tans without being interrupted was proving to be taxing.

There was absolutely nothing to do or see in Young Soung. At this late stage in the contract, we had read each other's books at least twice, and there were only so many letters home one could write. The yeogwan was surrounded by fields of corn, rice or peppers and the inhabitants of Young Soung seemed to dedicate themselves to agricultural activities, which again was not something that we could become involved in.

The evenings in the club had also become quite mundane. After that first night, the clienteles' behaviour resembled that of their Seoul counterparts, and we were usually accosted in one form or another whenever we entered the nightclub. Due to the enforced boredom, we came to the conclusion that our only feasible option was to start amusing ourselves during the show.

"In my opinion," Sharon said one evening, "the male population of Young Seoung would have preferred to watch a video about chicken farming rather than watch us three prancing around in feathers!"

"Ha! I agree," I replied. "I think I would get a better reaction if I wore a pair of green wellies for the James Bond routine, instead of my black, knee-high, 007 boots."

"Yeah, we should change the words of the songs too," Louise joined in. "Instead of 'Finger on the Trigger´ it should be: 'Finger on the *tractor*´.

"Yeah!" I laughed. "And instead of 'All right now´, we could sing 'All *rice* now´."

To prove our point, we decided to 'redesign´ our costumes. One outfit which was composed of a red leotard with a shiny black and silver skirt and a matching hat was the first to be given a different perspective. We borrowed the pink feather boas from the opening number and stuffed part of them inside our hats. We draped the rest across our faces so that we could just about see, then wrapped them around our waists and let them hang like a tail behind us. We looked ridiculous!

The strange thing was that the few members of the audience who actually bothered to watch did not bat an eyelid. I do not think they thought it was anything unusual – or maybe in their eyes, it was an improvement! Anyway, it made us giggle! Sharon – trying to show that she could, on occasion, act responsibly – refused to take part. Her only response when we came off stage was:

"I don't believe you just did that!" Then she laughed.

* * *

The Taejon girls had the same pastimes as the Seoul disco dancers. Every night, in the various clubs where we had worked, the Korean girls would sit and eat tiny slivers of dried octopus. They would flick on their lighters and gently heat the dried flesh for a few seconds before biting into the salty snack and chewing ... and chewing ... and chewing on it.

Their other pastime was sewing. Many of the girls had elaborate tapestries and embroideries depicting typical Korean scenes: Pagodas, tigers, landscapes etcetera. I had always loved that sort of thing and I was desperate to find them.

In Seoul, I had tried on several occasions to establish where I could buy one but had never seemed to make myself understood. Each time I had gone shopping in Iteawon, I would look for haberdasheries but to no avail. It was a mystery to me. Not being able to read Korean did not help, but now I was more desperate than ever to buy a couple. I knew they would help pass the time, relieve my boredom and also, I thought they would be great memories of my time in Korea.

That night, I sidled towards one of the girls and pointed to the complementary piece of paper which seemed to be inside each kit. It depicted various other tapestry kits which were available. The girl handed me the paper before I even had to ask! I was thrilled to bits, like a child with a new toy. Finally, I had my first clue as to the whereabouts of the elusive tapestries.

"We'll have to go out and try and find the kits here in Taejon before we leave," Louise said.

"Yeah, that would be great," I replied. "At least it will give us a mission, something to try and achieve whilst we're here."

* * *

That night after the show, we started the twenty-minute walk home. As we were passing by the edge of the forest, Sharon grabbed our arms.

"Don't look now," she whispered through clenched teeth, "but, I think we are being followed!" So, of course, we all immediately turned around.

"Shit!" Louise exclaimed. "I think I just saw someone jump behind that tree!"

"Which tree?" I asked as we all peered into the gloom.

"That one," She replied, pointing in the general direction of around one hundred pines!

"I can't see anything," I said, squinting into the dead of night.

"Yeah, but you're as blind as a bat!" Louise replied.

"Let's keep walking....but faster!" Sharon suggested.

We linked arms and quickened our pace. Not speaking, our ears were tuned for the slightest sound.

Within seconds, we all heard twigs snapping underfoot, as though a single heavy footstep had caused the noise."

"Did you hear that?" Sharon's harsh whisper seemed to echo around us.

"We know you're there. Bugger off!" Louise shouted into the misty darkness.

The responding silence seemed augmented by the still night air. I felt as though I was involuntarily taking part in a predictable horror film, where the outcome was always the same, the girls were gradually killed off one by one!

Then another twig snapped.

"RUN!" Sharon yelled. We did not need telling twice. We sprinted along the country road as fast as was humanly possible when carrying make-up bags, dress bags and wearing fishnet tights and flip-flops. We neither looked back nor stopped running until we were inside the yeogwan, and the door was closed firmly behind us.

"That's it, no-one should go out alone again," Louise stated.

The following evening, the same thing happened again. As soon as we reached the forest, Louise thought she saw someone lurking in the trees and then we heard twigs snapping underfoot.

"Do you think there's anyone there or do you think we are just hyped up, nervous and imagining it?" I asked. "It could be an animal..."

"I don't know and I don't care!" Louise replied. "Just keep your eyes and ears open and let's get a move on!"

The next evening, after the shows, Louise and I were hungry, so we went out on a search for cheap wholesome food – an impossible quest! Rather than wait for us, for some unknown reason, Sharon decided to walk back to the yeogwan alone. When we eventually returned to the digs and sauntered past Sharon's door, we found it open and it's occupant waiting for us, sitting on her bed rocking backwards and forwards, with her legs drawn up to her chest.

"Are you alright? What's the matter?" I asked.

"I saw the man!" she said. "The man in the forest! He followed me all the way back to the Yeogwan!"

"Really? What did you do?" I asked.

"I just ran! There was nothing else I could do!"

"Are you okay?"

"More or less, but it was mega frightening! I ran away screaming."

"What did he look like? Was it anyone we know?" Louise inquired.

Sharon appeared to think for a second before replying: "... It was too dark to see him clearly."

Back in our room, Louise sat pondering on our conversation. "Do you know what? I think she's making it all up for a bit of attention. I don't believe it happened.

The more I dwelled on the subject, the more I was inclined to agree. Why would she leave the door to her room open when the establishment was open to the public? The man could have entered at any time. If that had happened to me, I would have shut the door and built a barricade behind it!

Whether the incident did occur or not, the mysterious man was never seen or heard from again.

* * *

On Friday the eighteenth we encountered a group of five Australian dancers who were staying in Taejon and working in another nightclub called 'Kiss´. Unlike the three girls we had encountered at the airport and the group of five we had met briefly in the Diamond, these girls were really friendly. We began hanging out together after work.

Although they were staying in Taejon, unlike us, they were driven all around the surrounding area each evening, to do several shows each night.

As usual, I was quite envious of the number of clubs they were performing in compared to us. They had been in Korea longer than us, and I learnt that they had never been asked to dance disco spots or do consummation.

One evening, one of the girls, Fiona, managed to speak to me on my own.

"I don't know how to tell you this, but... we had all heard about your group before we even met you," she said in subdued tones.

"Oh, yes...? How is that possible?" I ask, puzzled. "What have you heard?"

"Well, you are the talk of Seoul!"

"What do you mean?"

"Well, you've got a nickname..."

"Go on..."

"Well," she said lowering her gaze. "They call you the 'Travelling Elephant show´ because of the size of your two friends," she said looking down. "I mean, obviously, it doesn't refer to you, but still..."

"Huh! Er... well, thanks for telling me... I suppose!"

"Sorry, I just thought you should know," she said.

"Okay, yeah, well, thanks," I replied, feeling embarrassed and more than a little bit angry. Talk about put a downer on your day! I was left with mixed emotions. Part of me was glad that Fiona had told me because up until that point I had constantly lived in hope that things would eventually change. This revelation was the eye-opener I needed to face up to reality. I had been fooling myself. Things were never going to get any better. The time when we had been working three shows and disco spots for three months in Seoul was the best it was ever going to be.

"Come on cheer up!" Fiona nudged me playfully with her elbow. "... Although, to be honest, if we were in your shoes, I'd feel the same way!" she said, patting me gently on my shoulder.

At that point, we all went into one of the 'workmen's tents´ located on the road. This one was bigger than the ones in Seoul and also served food as well as alcohol. Once we had received our OB beer, which I felt I really needed at that point, we became aware of three Korean men who were already installed at a long table. One of them pointed to an aquarium in which two octopuses languished idly at the bottom and told the waitress that they wanted one. The woman approached their table with a plate of equally sized lettuce leaves and a bowl of peeled garlic cloves. In my opinion, I thought she was being a bit precipitous, as I assumed that the octopus would take quite a while to cook. However, I had momentarily forgotten that this was Korea.

The waitress lifted one of the poor creatures out of the tank with a pair of tongs, laid it down on a wooden board, raised her cleaver and BANG, removed all eight tentacles in one chop!

"URGH!"

"OH MY GOD!"

"ARRRGH!"

"GROSS!" ... were just a few of the interjections we emitted as the wiggling tentacles were plated and taken to the table.

We watched agog as the men picked up a lettuce leaf, placed a clove of garlic inside it, dribbled a bit of oil then picked up a (still wriggling) tentacle and placed it inside the leaf. The lettuce was then rolled up, bent in half and eaten whole.

The above vociferations were repeated - and some expletives were voiced aloud as the men either shrugged or laughed at our reactions.

"How can the legs still be moving?" Sharon asked.

"Because, the nerves haven't died yet," one of the Australians explained.

"That's so gross!" Several of us replied.

The men found our facial expressions more than a little amusing and decided to present us with a writhing tentacle. We didn't eat it but spent the remainder of the time it wriggled dissecting it into smaller pieces to see when it would eventually stop moving.

* * *

The following day I went out alone to eat and wander around the shops. Fiona's words were constantly playing in the back of my mind and making me feel both irritable and annoyed. I needed some time on my own.

I had not told my dance partners what had been said. Firstly, as they would not have liked to have heard it and secondly, at the end of the day, it would not change anything.

Later that afternoon, we had an unexpected visit from Mr Lee. He said that he had remembered to bring the mail, but not the money - no surprises there, then!

"You finish at Casanova on Monday night and then you go to Seoul for few days holiday," he informed us.

We all knew what that meant; several days minimum without work ... if we were lucky!

"I don't want a holiday, Mr Lee. I came here to work!" I snapped.

"No work and no money! Deep joy!" Louise replied.

"Okay, Mr Lee," Sharon smiled.

"You work, you work but holiday first." Mr Lee said, ignoring Sharon and looking straight at Louise.

"Yeah, right!" I replied.

That evening, my mood was pretty black as I played over the events of the past two days. I had had enough and was ready to go home. The thought of returning to Seoul, to the grubby Central Hotel and on top of that, not working was exasperating. I hated being pushed from pillar to post on someone else's whim, but at the same time, I knew that I was in a helpless situation and unable to do anything about it.

At work that night, my mood had not improved, so when Sharon and I went out to do the final disco spot of the evening, to an audience of one, I was about ready to explode. Our only customer in the entire club was so drunk he had passed out, his head rested on the tabletop and his arms hung down slightly swinging, reminding me of a languishing chimpanzee.

Sharon jumped onto her podium regardless and immediately started bopping away to the music. Meanwhile, I reluctantly climbed onto mine and just stood there. My mind was racing. I was so infuriated. How had I let myself get into this predicament? We were doing these disco spots and not even being paid extra money for them! I was annoyed with myself, the girls, Korea, everything.

Right! I thought to myself. *I'm off!* I jumped down and stomped past a stunned Sharon.

"What are you doing?" she whispered.

"I am NOT standing on that podium for fifteen minutes and dancing for free to an empty room! This is ridiculous!"

Sharon did not think twice, she jumped down beside me.

"I was just about to say the same thing!" she said.

Yes, I'm sure you were! I thought to myself. "Come on, let's go!" I said.

* * *

By Monday morning I had calmed down and was on a mission. This was my final chance to go into Taejon on the elusive search for tapestries. Armed with my sheet of paper depicting the kits, Louise and I approached an unsuspecting man who was walking towards us and I shoved the paper in his face.

"Ah!" he said and turning on his heel, he beckoned us to follow him, so we did.

"This looks promising," said Louise as the man scurried up the street.

"Or not," I replied as he stopped in front of a florist's shop.

"No!" I said to him, instantly starting to become annoyed, "Tapestries, to sew!" I mimed a sewing action.

"Ne, ne!" (Yes, yes!) He insisted, ushering us towards the door.

"Stupid kimchi-brain!" Louise muttered, but we stood there as he opened the shop door and all my hopes began to fade away fast.

"In here?" I asked him again. "Are you sure?"

"Ne, kŭrŏssŭmnida!" (Yes it is!).

Louise and I shrugged and walked inside.

"This doesn't look good!" Louise sang as we looked around at all the flowers, vases, wrapping paper and other flower associated accessories.

A woman emerged from the back of the shop and approached us cautiously, eyeing us up and down. She looked as dubious about our visit as we did.

"Ne?"

"Erm....this?" I said holding out the paper.

"Ahh!" she exclaimed and beckoned us to follow her to the back of the shop.

Still convinced that we were in the wrong place, we shrugged but decided to follow her.

At the back of the shop was a small cubby-hole packed from floor to ceiling with tapestry kits. She pointed to my paper and asked me which one I wanted. I could not believe my luck. I was in seventh heaven! It was an Aladdin's cave of needlepoint! I tentatively pointed to a huge tapestry rug depicting a group of Korean dancers and a pagoda, which was my favourite design of all. She nodded and took it down from a shelf. I showed her another rug depicting tigers in the forest, followed by a tapestry with deer in the mountains, another of a sunset and a fifth of two women planting seeds in the countryside.

When I asked the price of each one, I was shocked. Each rug kit, complete with material and all the necessary wool was only 22,000₩, (approx £17.60). The smaller ones were about £5.50.

"Which one are you going to get?" Louise asked.

"All of them!" I replied. "I can post them back home. These will keep me busy for ages!"

"Are they expensive, compared to England?" Louise inquired.

"Ha! Are you kidding? I wouldn't even be able to buy one rug for the total price I'll pay for all of these," I replied.

The woman looked slightly surprised when she realised that I wanted to make a bulk purchase but was extremely happy when I handed over 67,000₩ (approximately £53). My quest was over and, even if it meant living off Ramen noodles for the next fortnight, at least now I had something to fill my time while we were out of work in Seoul.

Chapter 12

BACK TO SEOUL

On Tuesday morning, August 22nd, we were sitting in the yeogwan becoming increasingly irritated and disillusioned as the minutes slowly ticked away. Surrounded by all our belongings, which were packed and ready, we waited in a state of complete ignorance in respect to our driver's tardiness.

An hour and a half later than the scheduled arrival time, he made an appearance. He made no apology nor gave any explanation for the delay. He did, however, help us to load the van with all our belongings before driving us back to Seoul.

The three of us hardly spoke on the journey back. Each of us silently contemplating what the next chapter of our story in Korea would possibly hold. I had a distinct sinking feeling as the Bongo van pulled up outside the Central Hotel again. I looked across at the others; they looked as demoralised as me.

This time, our allocated room was 701, which was a tiny habitation. By the time we had dropped all our belongings and the costume cases in any available free corner, we were forced to clamber over the beds to get to the bathroom- or even get out of the room!

"This is a nightmare!" Sharon threw a bag down onto her chosen bed. "There isn't even enough room to turn around!"

"Yeah, and the air-conditioning is pathetic. It's on, but it isn't blowing cold air. This room is going to be murder to sleep in!" I said as I stood on my bed and fiddled with the air-con buttons.

"And listen to that scratching..." Louise added, as we heard distinct scurrying and squeaking noises coming from within the walls. "You can hear the rats inside the walls now, and it's only day time. God help us tonight!"

"As long as they stay behind the walls that's fine with me," I replied, remembering my confrontation with the rat in the stairwell.

"This is Lee's way of trying to cut down on costs," Louise replied. "He can't find us any work and he can't afford to get us a bigger room!" We nodded in agreement, knowing that she was correct.

The next morning, our agent knocked on our door. He was the last person I wanted to see. We had had a terrible night's sleep -or rather a complete lack of one would be a more apt description. We had been plagued by hoards of mosquitoes, overpowering heat and scratching noises inside the walls.

Ignoring our complaints and waggling money under our noses in an attempt to placate us, he handed over two week's money from our time in Taejon and told us to enjoy our non-volitional holiday´.

It was not as though we had been given a choice so armed with some cash, we headed to Popeye's in Itaewon to meet up with Amy and her new boyfriend Mr Kyong.

Our planned short visit turned into a marathon five-hour session, as Mr Lee was also there when we arrived. He was in good spirits – or rather, he had drunk several spirits before we showed up – and he seemed to be in an extremely jovial mood. He told us that he was there to meet a client, but he invited us to his table and, as he appeared to be paying, we readily accepted.

As the afternoon progressed and the members of our impromptu party all steadily became more inebriated, Mr Lee swung around to face me.

"Oh, I remember now. Your sister is coming tomorrow!"

As this was the third time he had told me she was arriving and she had yet to appear, I took it with a pinch of salt.

"Yeah, right, Mr Lee."

He performed his German salute to look at his watch. "Actually, she's flying to Korea right now!"

"What!"

"Yeah. She is on the plane now. Tomorrow you see your sister."

"Poor Bugger!" I found myself muttering under my breath.

* * *

The following morning, determined to try and keep positive and think of our days of forced unemployment as a holiday, we decided to go sightseeing to Seoul Grand Park; a theme park, occupying 157,000 square metres and located inside the natural forest of Cheonnggyesan Mountain.

The park comprised of different zones, designated towards nature, amusement and education. At that time, however, we were only aware of the theme park and that is where we assumed we would be taken. Our driver, on the other hand, must have wrongly assumed that we were much more culturally inclined than we were at that time and dropped us in the nature reserve called Green family land.

We wandered around for a while, searching in vain for anything resembling a roller-coaster or a poor, unfortunate Korean dressed as a cartoon character in boiling hot sunshine. But all we could find were trees; 470 different species to be precise and a variety of flora and fauna including 35 species of birds, surrounding rivers and Cheon-nggyesan mountain.

Calling the taxi driver various derogative names as soon as we realised that he had left us in a totally different place than where we had intended to go, we set off walking. Eventually, we managed to flag down another taxi and arrived at the amusement park in the early afternoon.

The park was loosely based on a Disney park, with parades and rides. Sharon and I almost instantly began to enjoy ourselves, but Louise was not in the best of moods. This was because whilst we were walking, the new camera she had bought in Taejon a few days before had unexpectedly blown up inside her backpack and set on fire!

"Stupid kimchi piece of shit!" she had remarked, throwing the offending camera in the nearest bin.

It must have been galling as I passed her my camera (an exact duplicate of hers) and asked her to take a photo of Sharon and me on what appeared to be a primitive see-saw. There was a pedestal in the centre, with a plank of wood on top. Underneath the wood, at both ends, were sacks of rice. Unlike the British see-saw where children sit on either end, in Korea, the apparatus was originally designed for women who had to stand on either end. The game was devised so that each woman jumped onto the end of the plank of wood, catapulting her partner high up into the sky. This originated from ancient times when Korean aristocratic women were not allowed to leave their walled premises during the day. It is believed that if they jumped high enough, the women could see over the compound wall and catch a quick glimpse of another world.

Sharon and I tried several times but never got more than a few feet into the air, partly because we were laughing too much and partly because both of us were frightened of breaking an ankle!

There were plenty of other photo opportunities, as there were several dragon sculptures and a huge lion statue at the entrance. We included Louise in our photos of course so that she would be able to get copies when we did our almost weekly trip to the photoshop.

Later, we decided to visit the zoo, something which I had wanted to do since my birthday. However, at that particular moment, now that the opportunity had arisen, I was having serious doubts about going in. Seeing how they seemed to treat most of the dogs in Korea, plus the state of other animals we had come across during our stay, I was afraid that I would become upset if the creatures were in poor condition.

Nevertheless, we went inside and I was pleasantly surprised as to their status quo and the environments which had been created for the various animals.

When we came across the elephant enclosure, I could not hold my tongue. "Look a travelling elephant show!" I blurted out.

Both girls looked at me in confusion, with vexed expressions on their faces, but I could not help myself.

That evening back at the hotel, I was informed that my sister had arrived. As expected the three-girl-group was installed in the Central Hotel, so the three of us went to see the new arrivals.

All three girls were tall and slim, and I hoped they would have better luck than we had had. We arranged to take them out that night, and the three of us took the new trio into Itaewon, the 'nucleus´ of Seoul, to show them the sights and sounds of the nightlife there.

It seemed like we had come full circle; the veteran dancers showing the 'newbies´ around. History was repeating itself. Our time in South Korea was coming to an end. Theirs was just about to begin.

As much as I enjoyed showing the girls the sights, I felt strangely overprotective of my little sister. I found myself showing her Hooker Hill and telling her to be careful with whom she became involved. My sister nodded and gave a condescending sigh, not appreciating being spoken to like a child. However, towards the end of the evening, I realised that my sister and I were definitely not cut from the same cloth. I got the distinct impression that she was more prepared for Itaewon than I would ever be, and I felt that I was probably cramping her style!

Later, in the Twilight zone I introduced them to Korean kimchi, but I accidentally (on purpose) forgot to mention how spicy it was. The Collier trio laughed as the three girls each took a big bite and screwed up their faces in disgust.

"Welcome to Korea!" I laughed.

* * *

Three days after my sister's arrival, they were working four shows a night and were housed in a very nice apartment, with air-conditioning, satellite television, a washing machine and a sun terrace. We, on the other hand, were living in an oxo box with faulty air-conditioning, clambering over beds to move, and still out of work!

We learnt that Mr Lee had sold my sister's group to a different agent. Our agent informed us in a 'matter of fact´ fashion that he did not want the trio.

"The choreography is almost the same as your two shows, and the girls dance like something out of kindergarten," he had said. Personally, I think he needed money and selling the trio was his best option. I also doubt that selling us had crossed his mind. I do not believe that we would not have brought such a lucrative price!

According to my sister's group, their agent visited them every day and met them after work to check that everything was okay. He had taken them out to eat every night since they had arrived. He made sure they had at least one soft drink between each show and also gave them food allowance on top of their salary. (How the other half lived!)

Although I was pleased that my sister appeared to have fallen on her feet, it did little to better my mood. By Monday 28th, we had been out of work for five days, and the 'holiday´ was starting to become more than a little bit tedious.

"Phone Lee again," Louise said to Sharon. "I've just about had enough! This room is the pits, I can't bear to stay in here any longer!"

She had a point. The air-con was so bad that the room became overpoweringly stuffy within minutes of our arrival. We had resorted to keeping the door and windows open to allow some flow of air. Unfortunately, an open window was taken as a free invitation for the entire mosquito population of Korea to enter for a free drink of blood. The open door apparently implied that any waif or stray who wandered past had automatic entry to our oxo box whenever they felt like it.

"Tell Lee we need to work and that our money is running out. That might make him pull his finger out!" Louise suggested to our head girl.

Sharon dialled the number with a sigh.

"Hello, Mr Lee, it's Sharon. Are we working today? ... No? ... Oh!... Okay, thank-you."

"Let's hear it," Louise sighed.

"He said that we're not working today but we might be going to Cheju-do island, which means 'The island of triple abundance'."

"Yeah, right!" Louise replied sarcastically.

"He's just fobbing you off, to keep us quiet!" I replied. "He can't find us any work. I don't know why he doesn't just send us home."

"Well, if we're not working, we might as well go back into Itaewon," Louise replied.

"Anything is better than staying in this room!" I answered.

* * *

Tuesday was another forced holiday. We were dubious to go anywhere as we were hoping to receive good news from Mr Lee. As we had no idea if or when we would be working or paid again, taking extravagant trips were out of the question. However, we were soon to discover that even staying in the hotel could bring some form of entertainment – even if it was not of the most pleasant variety!

That evening, Louise went to the army base to be with Jim. Sharon and I were just settling down to sleep, - or were trying to - with the heat and the scratching behind the walls when, without warning, Sharon bolted upright and screamed.

"ARRGH! A rat has just run under my bed!"

"What! Are you sure?" I immediately sat up and, on instinct, drew my legs up to my chest.

"YES! I thought I heard something in my bag because I've got some packets of crisps and chocolate things in there, and I thought I heard something creeping about. I turned on the light and it just shot under my bed!"

Without warning, the rat darted out from under Sharon's bed and ran under mine!

Now, it was my turn to scream.

"ARRGH!!" In a flash, I had leapt across onto Sharon's bed in fright. "Oh my God!" I exclaimed, clutching my chest. "Call reception, we can't stay in here!"

Sharon reached for the phone and explained the situation. "Come quickly! There is a rat in our room!" she gabbled into the phone. She spun around to face me. "He said he'll come tomorrow. And then he just hung up!" she said incredulously.

For a second, I was dumbfounded. *Where they really not going to do anything about the situation? Were they seriously expecting us to sleep in this room?*

"Right, come on, let's go down to reception," I said.

"Okay, but how are we going to get out of the room without the bloody rat following and biting us?" Sharon asked.

"Like this." I leaned across from her bed and managed to open the door without putting a foot on the carpet. "Right, I'll count to three and then we'll make a run for it."

"Okay."

"Ready? ... One... Two... THREE!" We shot off the beds and out into the corridor at breakneck speed. Closing the door behind us, we headed directly for the reception.

When we told the reception staff that we wanted to change rooms and why, we were met with hysterical laughter, which, under the circumstances, we both found completely inconsiderate and frustrating.

"Then, I want to speak to the manager," I said, standing my ground.

One of them picked up the phone but made no effort to dial a number. The three receptionists just stood there grinning, muttering to each other and laughing. It was so exasperating.

"Will, you come on! Phone the manager!" I yelled.

Another receptionist pointed a finger in our direction.

"You go your room, I come get rat," he said. "Five minutes."

We made our way back upstairs and sat in the corridor for about ten minutes feeling so dejected and waited for someone to come and resolve the problem. We had gullibly assumed that he would arrive with the necessary equipment to catch the rat – whatever that would be - but as he sauntered up the corridor towards us, he appeared to be empty-handed. Under his arm, he had two pieces of flypaper. He opened the door, sauntered into the room and casually stuck the pieces of sticky paper under the beds.

"There. Tomorrow, no rat!" he said.

Dusting his hands together, he walked away, apparently pleased with his handy-work. We, on the other hand, were rather less impressed! We stood, mouths agape, unable to comprehend the puerile attempt at rat-catching we had just witnessed.

"That's it?" I shouted after him as he wandered off down the corridor.

"This has got to be a joke!" Sharon exclaimed but regrettably, it was not.

"That flypaper is 'neither use nor ornament´!" I said. "It would be lucky to catch a mouse but certainly not a bloody big rat! Did you see the size of that thing?"

"Yeah, it looked more like a cat than a rat!" Sharon replied. "One thing's for certain, we can't sleep in here!"

"Right then," I said, squaring my shoulders. "Back to the reception, I think!"

As we went down in the elevator, I was seething and as we approached the reception for the second time, my bad mood was further enhanced when we were met with more laughter from the receptionists.

I slammed my hands down onto the reception desk.

"Give us another room!" I hissed through clenched teeth.

As they persisted with their annoying giggling, I lunged across the reception desk, attempting to grab hold of one of them by the lapels of their uniform and shake them into submission. I was so full of antagonism that, at that point, I would have quite easily thumped them if they had not taken several steps backwards, abruptly stopped laughing and reached for the phone.

In my naivety, I believed that my actions, tone of voice and facial expression were the reason for their sudden change in demeanour, I was completely unaware that they had already made further plans to entertain themselves.

"Okay, you go six floor. You ask for room 619," the receptionist said.

We stomped off to the elevator, knowing full well that the sixth floor was rented out by the hour. It even had its own reception desk. However, we both agreed that anything would be better than sleeping in a room with a great big rat! I mean, it was not as though we had never slept on semen-stained mattresses before!

As we stepped out of the elevator we were met by a grinning receptionist who, on seeing us, smirked even more. I knew immediately that we had been duped.

"No rooms, no rooms! Ha ha ha!" he said.

"Reception said room 619," Sharon informed him. This sent him into guffaws of laughter.

"What's so fucking funny?" I said, in a tone so deadly threatening, I frightened myself!

"Ha ha! 619 is my room!" he replied.

When he saw my thunderous expression, he managed to contain his laughter but continued to grin inanely. "You can sleep there, but I sleep with you! Ha ha ha!"

I had had all that I was prepared to take from this stupid little man and I completely lost control.

"GIVE US A FUCKING ROOM!" I screamed into his face. Venting all my pent up frustration on the poor guy's desk, I went berserk! I pushed the telephone onto the floor, then the lamp, the register and everything else which was not glued down.

Unfortunately, this did not help to solve matters in the slightest!

"CRAZY GIRL, CRAZY!" he shouted repeatedly as he picked up the items from the floor one by one and tried to put his desk back into some semblance of order.

"Right, we're getting absolutely nowhere. Come on, let's phone Mr Lee!" I said, marching off down the corridor.

"We can't phone him now," Sharon said, tripping down the passageway in my wake. "He'll be asleep!"

"Lucky him!" I replied.

Back in our room, stood on the bed, ready to make a hasty retreat at the first sight or sound of a rodent, I punched in the telephone number of our agent and waited. The phone rang several times, during which time I started to doubt that I should be ringing him in the early hours of the morning.

A groggy, half-asleep Mr Lee eventually picked up the phone. He was about as much use as the reception staff but at least he listened and did not laugh as I ranted and raved.

"Okay, I'll sort it out in the morning," he said.

The more I insisted, the more he repeated the same phrase.

"Tomorrow alright?"

"No, it ISN'T bloody alright!" I screamed and slammed the phone down. Then I burst into tears. I had tried to stand up for myself, but it had got me absolutely nowhere. Sharon tried to console me by putting her arm across my shoulders. We looked at one another, both totally lost for words and too tired and broken to do or say anything more.

A few minutes later, we left the room. Closing the bedroom door behind us, we flopped down into a sitting position in the corridor. We could not sleep, we were numb, debilitated and defeated. We sat in silence contemplating our situation, both too exhausted to speak. We must have been sitting there for about half an hour, not daring - or wanting - to venture inside the rat-infested room when we heard the telephone ring. Sharon braced herself, opened the door then sprang from the doorway to the bed to answer it. I followed close behind her.

"That was Mr Lee," she said as we jumped back into the safety of the corridor and closed our door behind us. "He has spoken to the manager and we have got another room."

Once again we headed off to reception via the elevator. Unfortunately, the lift stopped midway and the doors opened onto the sixth floor. As soon as the stressed-out receptionist saw us, he pointed at me.

"YOU! What is your name? You are very bad, Fuck you!"

"Charming!" Sharon replied.

"Fuck you too!" I added as the doors to the lift slowly closed.

* * *

Early the next morning, we returned to our 'rat room´ to inspect it with caution. The flypaper was still there. It had been moved from its original position and was now embellished with several, large, rat footprints, but, as expected, the rat itself had disappeared. We prodded bags with tentative fingers, secretly praying that there were no more rodents inside them as we started to remove our belongings.

It was during this process of removal that Louise appeared.

"What the hell is going on?" she asked. "One of the guys on reception is in a foul mood. He was cursing me out. You've seriously pissed him off, Michele. What the hell happened?"

We told her the events of the previous night and she helped to gather up her belongings and move rooms to 722. As a last-minute task, I took down the calendar.

"I don't want anyone else to go through what we've been through," I said. "I'm going to warn them."

Written in Black felt-tip pen was my warning to all future English speaking clientele. It said:

"Beware, this room has got rats!
Don't stay in here!
Ask for another room!"

In the afternoon, as Mr Lee was no longer answering the phone and we were entering our ninth day without working, we took the long bus ride to his office. He saw us coming and froze. He was cornered, he could not escape. Despite his forced entrapment, he kept his wallet tightly closed and told us that if he could not find us work within the next couple of days, we could go home.

I could not bring myself to feel the least bit elated by this news. The problem was that, at this late stage of the game, I no longer believed a single word he said.

The three of us went out for a drink, to drown our sorrows. On our return to the hotel, our agent rang.

"Mr Lee said that on Friday we are going to Chuncheon," Sharon informed us.

"God help us!" I replied, my voice seeped in sarcasm.

"Where will we be working?" Louise asked.

"I don't know, he didn't say, but it's work, right?"

We didn't reply, all three of us were lost in thought, contemplating our fate.

That night, Sharon went out on a date and Louise and I settled down to sleep in our new room. I was more than ready for a good night's sleep after the antics of the night before, but it was not to be. Unfortunately, another rat decided to make an appearance in our new room.

We charged down to reception, where Louise only had to lean across the reception desk and say:

"Give us another room or I'll rip your head off and shit down your neck!" and a set of keys were miraculously handed to her in seconds!

I would like to believe that the receptionists did not want me to repeat my performance of the night before, by pushing everything off the counter but, to be perfectly honest, I think Louise had perfected her truculent, feisty, countenance over the years and had it down to a tee. Nobody was going to mess with her! Nevertheless, I was just happy that the situation was resolved so quickly.

We walked back to our room with the new key but were so exhausted that we decided not to move all our belongings until the next day.

"I'm going to leave a note on the door to warn Sharon," Louise scribbling on a piece of card and stuck it to the outside of the door:

Sharon,
The rat came back!
We are now in room 618.

We ambled to the new room and fell into a fitful slumber. The following morning when we awoke, we immediately discovered that Sharon was not with us.

"Maybe she stayed with one of her boyfriends," I said.

"Maybe," Louise replied, but she didn't pack an overnight bag. Anyway, come on, let's go and move all our stuff again into this room."

We headed off to our previous quarters and were surprised to find Sharon fast asleep in her bed!

"What are you doing here?" I asked her. "Didn't you read the note?"

"Yeah, I read it..." she said groggily. "And...?"

"Well, I'm surprised you stayed in here when you knew there was a rat!"

"Oh! Was there a real rat?" she said. "I thought you meant that Mr Lee had come back!"

The three of us fell about laughing!

Chapter 13

TWO WEEKS IN CHUNCHEON

Friday the first of September marked our journey from Seoul to Chuncheon, a distance of about 46 kilometres which took about an hour and a half.

"Oh, surprise, surprise!" I muttered as we pulled up outside another yeogwan.

Sharon looked across at me and let out a dejected sigh.

"Deep joy!" Louise interjected.

Like the previous yeogwan, an elderly, disgruntled woman shuffled along the corridor and showed us to the rooms. In comparison to the first lodgings, these rooms were slightly bigger than the last ones but still as basic and certainly not as clean! Once again, Louise and I had to share, while Sharon commandeered the other room.

"Right, I go now," Mr Lee informed us, pushing fifty dollars each into our hands. He could not get away quickly enough.

"Wait a minute! What about work?" Louise asked, standing in front of the doorway and temporarily blocking his exit. "Where's the venue? How do we get there?"

"Yeah, what time are the shows?" I joined in.

"First show eleven o'clock. Second show twelve o'clock. Manager will come at ten o'clock. He'll tell you everything." With that, he waved goodbye and scurried off down the corridor.

"I don't like the sound of that," Sharon remarked.

"Nope, neither do I," I confirmed. "It all sounds a little fishy to me. There's definitely something going on here that he isn't telling us."

Later that evening as we approached our latest venue, chaperoned by the smiling manager, we heard the most hideous attempts at singing coming from inside.

"What the hell is that?" I asked, referring to the dreadful caterwauling.

"Oh, no! I don't believe it," Louise groaned. "We're going to work in a karaoke bar!"

Sharon broke into nervous laughter.

First impressions of our latest dancing location were not good. The exterior walls were caked with dirt, crumbling and badly in need of re-plastering and painting. However, if we thought the outside was in ill repair, it was nothing compared to the 'dressing room'. I use the word lightly, as, in actual fact, it was a corridor. It was thinner than the one we had traversed in the Diamond nightclub in Seoul. This one also had sloping walls but with added 'features' such as huge dangling cobwebs with corresponding giant size arachnids; litter all over the floor; rusty water-pipes on the ceiling which dripped constantly onto the wet carpet underfoot and the whole place was filthy! It smelt of a musty concoction of mould, old beer, rotting food and soggy, old carpet!

After the depressing dressing-room, we were shown the equally depressing stage. Firstly, we realised that it would be impossible to dance on, as the band's instruments occupied most of it. All that remained was a thin strip of wooden planks, about a metre and a half wide. There was an additional tiny piece which jutted out and was used as a podium for disco dancers. I very much doubted that the venue had ever had dance groups treading the boards there before. Drunken bums slurring songs into a microphone, definitely, but dancers – I did not think so!

The lack of stage meant that we were relegated to the dance floor, an area which was ill-equipped for a floor show, as the only lighting was set up for the stage. For our first performance, we were accompanied by the light of two disco balls, so we were almost dancing in the dark and occasionally speckled with revolving crystal droplets of coloured light. The floor was so slippery, it resembled an ice-rink and our first show resembled a rehearsal. It was such a mess as we stumbled, lost our footing and slid across the floor in a vain attempt to keep our balance and maintain upright.

Back in the dressing-room, after the first show, the mood was not a happy one.

"All those years of dance training and exams we've all been through, and for what? To work in this shit hole? It's just depressing!" Louise complained as we tried to change our costumes without being splashed by dripping rusty pipes.

"The floor is soaking," Sharon complained as she lost her balance and stepped on the water-logged carpet. "Don't step on it with your fishnets on or you'll have wet feet all night!"

"That's easier said than done when the workers keep manhandling us into the sides of these filthy walls so that they can get passed!" I grumbled.

The manager, who seemed to have been constantly in the background and always within our periphery, casually wandered towards us. He smiled as we started to get dressed for the second show.

"No! You no do show now. Now you do disco spot!" he said, pointing towards the stage.

"What?" Sharon yelled, sinking onto the long bench that ran the whole length of the corridor.

"You've got to be joking!" Louise groaned.

"Here we go again!" I said. "This will be another freebie, courtesy of Mr stupid Lee! We've done it once, so now he's taking it for granted."

The girls hung their heads dejectedly. They knew I was right.

Sharon played her "I'm the head girl" card and decided that Louise and I should do the first spot (like we didn't see that coming!) As we had not brought any other costumes other than the show, we found ourselves rummaging through the costume case again, improvising.

Ten minutes later, Louise and I were heading out to the club area.

The manager pointed to the little podium, which jutted out from the stage. "You go there," he said to me. "You, "he said to Louise, "Follow me."

As I took my position on the tiny jutting out podium, I watched as Louise found herself having to walk through the customers to a podium, which was behind the main bar, in the middle of the room.

From the moment she took her position, she was 'attacked´. She found herself bombarded with projectiles in the form of ice-cubes. Men were spitting on her or trying to get on the podium and groping her. Louise bravely battled on, the best way that she could. She ducked and swerved to avoid being touched by wandering hands or fiercely thrown objects.

The bar staff witnessed everything through dead eyes and did absolutely nothing to help. After about seven minutes of constant attack, Louise could stand it no longer. She jumped down from the podium and walked back to the 'dressing room´. I did not blame her. I could only hope that now, their wrath would not be projected onto me.

When I came off stage and returned to the corridor, I found Sharon consoling Louise who, not surprisingly, was crying. The manager saw what was happening and grabbed my arm.

"What is the problem?"

"What's the problem?" I replied incredulously. "The problem is this place! It's a DUMP!" I doubted he understood me, as he just nodded and smiled with a puzzled expression on his face.

"Now you change for next show. Start twelve-thirty, next disco, one o'clock."

"No, the second show is twelve o'clock!" I argued.

"Time change," he said and walked away.

I slumped down onto the bench with a sigh, next to my partners. We all felt the same - totally disillusioned!

After work, we walked home in silence. Sharon went out to find a phone and speak to Mr Lee, but she came back in tears.

"He doesn't want to know!" she sobbed.

Louise phoned Jim and she cried too, but strangely, for once, I did not. I felt like I had cried all the tears I could possibly cry in Korea. I was just angry, extremely angry.

* * *

The following day we were told that we would not be working for the next two evenings and we could not establish the reason why. Louise took this opportunity to go to Uijeonbu to see Jim. I had visions of being left alone in Chuncheon, but Sharon stayed behind. That afternoon, we went out for something to eat. While we both tucked into Om-rice, two young Korean guys approached us. They wanted to speak in English and they both had a good level. After the initial pleasantries, one of them leaned across the table with a conspiratorial expression on his face.

"So, how does it feel to be living so close to the DMZ?"

"Er, sorry but, what's the DMZ," I asked.

"You honestly don't know what the DMZ is?" he replied. Staring at me with such an incredulous expression on his face, he made me feel quite guilty for being so clueless as to our current geographical location.

"No...?" I said, but I had a sneaking suspicion that I was not going to like the answer.

"Well, some call it the Dead Man's Zone, but the real meaning is the Korean Demilitarized zone," he explained.

Not really being much the wiser, I looked across at Sharon who shrugged. She was as clueless as I was, so I asked him to elucidate.

"Don't you realise that you are living only a few minutes away from the border between North and South Korea?" He asked, surprised by our lack of knowledge.

"No way!" I interjected.

"Yes, the DMZ is a no man's land, which cuts the whole of the Korean peninsula basically in half."

"Wow!" I replied.

"You see, it's basically a war zone between the two Koreas," he continued, his smile broadening as my mouth gaped open in surprise. There is a strict protocol. If the soldiers consider that you are doing anything wrong, like taking photos, for example, you can be shot on sight!"

"Bloody Hell!" I replied.

"Yeah, there have been stories of stray bullets killing unsuspecting passersby..."

"Shit!" Sharon gasped, immediately looking overhead for roaming shrapnel.

"...We can take you there if you want!" he offered. "Would you like to go?"

"Er, thanks, but, no thanks!" I replied. "I think we'll give it a miss!"

Sharon gave a vigorous nod to show her assent. The thought of surviving six months only to be killed by a stray bullet was a daunting prospect and more than sufficient reason not to accept the invitation.

Little did we know that six months later, on March 3rd 1990, the fourth infiltration tunnel built by North Korea would be discovered not far from Chuncheon. Built to mount a surprise attack on the South, the tunnel had infiltrated South Korea by a mile and a half. It measured six feet wide by six feet high and was broad enough to fit lines of 3 men marching shoulder to shoulder. (Maybe the Korean's caterwauling in the karaoke bar had served a purpose after all. Perhaps their singing helped to disguise the excavation of the tunnel!).

* * *

The following day, out of sheer boredom, I sat on the roof with Sharon and sunbathed for three and a half hours. This caused me to commit a dancers' cardinal sin, as I fell asleep and forgot to take off my sunglasses.

"Bloody hell! You look like a negative of a giant panda!" Sharon scoffed when we got back into the rooms.

I eyed my reflection in the yeogwan mirror and shrugged.

"That's true, but I figure that, as we aren't working tonight, my suntan will have a chance to lessen slightly. And if it doesn't, who cares? We are dancing in the bloody dark anyway! I doubt that anyone will even notice."

On Monday evening, just after we had finished the first show which we performed to an audience of ten guys who were more interested in each other than in our show, Mr Lee paid us a visit in the dressing-room/corridor.

"I have many problems with you girls. Many problems!" he said, doing a double-take and squinting at my face, which was layered with several coats of foundation to hide my panda eyes.

"Huh! Believe me, you haven't got as many problems as we've got, working in this dump!" I replied.

"It's a shit hole!" Louise added.

Our agent was not in the mood to argue. He shook his head, wafted us away with annoying little hand gestures and walked out.

I felt strangely victorious. He was unable to counter-attack. It made me realise how much Korea had toughened me up. I had arrived barely muttering a word to anyone but over the past six months, I had had to learn to stand up for myself. I realised that the only way to survive in this male orientated world was to be confrontational. If not, the female sex would be constantly taken advantage of again and again; walked on; belittled and ignored.

An hour later, when the manager came to inform us that he had changed the time of our final disco spot from 1:00 am to 01:45 am, Louise and I both flatly refused to do it.

"No! You can't just change the time whenever you feel like it!" Louise argued.

"We're not doing it and that's that!" I counter attacked.

"I am manager!" he replied, laying down the law, stamping his foot and clenching his fists.

"And we don't care!" I answered.

Sharon, on the other hand, who probably thought we were about to lose our job, threw on a leotard and told him she would do it.

Looking rather dejected, the manager looked in my direction.

"Why are you always everyday madwoman?" he asked.

I wasn't sure if his use of 'mad´ referred to me being deranged, angry or both, so I played it safe by replying with my usual retort:

"Because this place is a dump! It's horrible, it's dirty, and YOU keep changing the times. I've had enough!"

"Well, maybe you go home!" He snapped, forgetting to smile for once.

"Fine by me!" I yelled. Then I stood my ground and stared him out until he turned on his heels and walked away.

As our head girl podium danced, Louise and I calmed down and decided to wait for her to finish so she would not have to walk home alone. I guess we both felt a little guilty that she had worked instead of us.

In hindsight, it turned out to be a good decision because, as we left the club, we found the manager waiting for us outside.

"Come, we talk," he said, smiling again.

We followed him as he trotted off down the street and I must admit I felt a little sorry for him. After all, I guessed that he was taking his orders from a higher authority and was only doing his job. He took us for a meal, supposedly to talk about the shows, but he became so drunk that we had serious doubts that all agreements would be remembered whenever he woke up the following day – most likely supporting a mega hangover!

* * *

Two days later on Wednesday 6th September, the three of us took a trip to the nearest bank to change some money. As soon as we entered the busy establishment, we felt like exhibits in a freak show. Everyone was staring, pointing and laughing behind their hands. Although this was a regular occurrence for us, for some reason, that particular day, I found it extremely annoying!

We approached the counter and I asked to change money. The female Korean bank teller, who for some unknown reason was dressed in traditional Korean garb, looked me straight in the face, giggled behind her hand and then ran away! As I heard more laughing behind me, I was seething.

"RIGHT!" I shouted. "I'll give you all something to gawp and laugh at!" Walking into the centre of the bank, I started to sing at the top of my voice.

"TWINKLE, TWINKLE LITTLE STAR, HOW I WONDER WHAT YOU ARE..."

A second bank teller ran towards the counter waving her arms up and down in a calming motion.

"Lady, lady, sit down please, wait a moment please!" she said, although she looked completely stressed out by my inappropriate antics!

"UP ABOVE THE WORLD SO HIGH..."

Sharon sat opened mouthed and Louise was laughing so much, I thought she was going to need the toilet!

"LIKE A DIAMOND IN THE SKY...."

A security guard approached me with caution and tried to take hold of my arm. I shrugged him off and continued singing.

"TWINKLE, TWINKLE LITTLE STAR..."

The second bank teller approached me and nervously thrust some banknotes into my hand.

"Lady, please! Here is your money!"

I snatched the cash and as I walked towards the open door, being escorted by the security guard, Louise and Sharon, I sang the final line:

"HOW I WONDER WHAT YOU ARE!"

I finished with a flourishing bow.

* * *

The next few days passed without event. I spent my days sunbathing or sewing one of my tapestries, and the evenings being spied on by the manager of the Karaoke bar, who continued to stalk us whilst constantly smiling.

As predicted, he had conveniently forgotten everything about our talk and continued to change the times of the shows and disco spots.

One evening, during one of the disco sessions, a guy walked over to me and handed me a 10,000₩ tip. Later, during the second spot, a different man handed me 20,000₩, so that particular day, the time changes seemed slightly more tolerable.

* * *

On the eleventh of September, the Karaoke bar hired a Korean disco dancer. This one had the biggest ego we had ever encountered in the female disco dancing community. She thought she was the bee's knees, and that anyone else around her was a mere minion.

Over the next few days, she bestowed us with condescending glances whenever she encountered us. In her eyes, she considered herself to be the most integral part of the karaoke bar employees. We, however, with our (by now) extensive knowledge of what a Korean disco dancer usually looked like, acted and wore, knew that this one paled in comparison.

After trying to monopolise the corridor/dressing-room, shouting at us for no apparent reason, and for three consecutive days, waiting until we were on stage to push all our costumes together in a heap, enough was enough. We wanted revenge. That evening, we waited until she went on stage to retaliate.

We threw all her clothes on the floor and broke her umbrella. A nervous tension permeated the walls of the corridor/dressing-room as we waited for her return and the expected backlash. I envisaged arguing and the possible throwing of something, but it did not happen. She entered the corridor and just stood there. She looked in disbelief at her belongings thrown on the soggy carpet, as we sauntered passed her, completely ignoring her, to get on stage.

From that moment on, she realised that she had taken on more than she had bargained for. Her attitude became much more subdued, and she left us to our own devices – which suited the three of us, just fine.

The following day, Sharon caught a bus to Seoul to try to catch the elusive Mr Lee in his office. She came back, after travelling all day, with the latest mail and the grand amount of one day's salary for each of us. She looked completely exhausted and more than a little fed up, so I vowed to phone our 'so-called' agent the following day.

"Mr Lee, we need money. I know it's a holiday tomorrow, so we'll expect to see you on Friday," I told him with an authoritative tone.

"No, the holiday is until Sunday. Now, all the banks are closed."

"Well, what do you expect us to do, Mr Lee? Starve?"

"Why didn't you tell me this yesterday?" he snapped, losing his cool.

"Because it's not my job to tell you, it's Sharon's. Anyway, she shouldn't have to ask you for our money, it's your job to give her it!"

"It's impossible! Impossible!" He replied.

"You have two choices, Mr Lee. If you bring the money on Friday, we will work. If you don't, we won't!"

"Oh well, fuck the job and I won't give you any money!" he yelled and slammed the phone down.

"I don't think he'll come," Sharon said when she thought I had calmed down a bit. "He doesn't like to be spoken to like that."

"Well, he came last time I had to talk to him like that," I replied, "when we were in Seoul."

"That's true," Louise confirmed.

Sharon sniffed.

The following day, our head girl received a phone call from Mr Lee telling her that he had spoken to the club manager and arranged for each of us to be given 20,000₩ (approximately £16). It was hardly a fortune, as twenty-one days had elapsed since the last full payment, but it felt like a victory to me.

This meant that we could finally eat a hot meal for the first time in five days.

* * *

Sunday 17th September marked our final day of work in South Korea. We had done more than 300 shows and over 150 disco spots. We were all in better moods as the final countdown to home drew even nearer.

Seeing the light at the end of the tunnel made everything, which would normally annoy or stress us out, seem trivial and unimportant. Even the Korean woman in the yeogwan, who had the habit of opening our bedroom door with the master key in the middle of the night to yell at us, wave and flap her arms about before going away, could not dampen our mood. We had no idea what she was shouting about anyway, so we just turned over and went back to sleep.

The only fly in the ointment was, as usual, our agent. He reminded me of the Grim Reaper: elusive and devious, a dangerous entity always in the background, waiting to darken our day. He had told us to be ready to leave Chuncheon on Monday at one o'clock in the afternoon. We sat in the yeogwan for six more hours before he finally arrived at seven o'clock in the evening. On arrival, he gave no explanation or apology and told us to hurry up - as though it was our fault that he was running late.

We travelled back to Seoul, assuming that we would be returning to the rat-infested Central Hotel again, but apparently, there was no room at the inn. Our driver drove to three different hotels where we went through the motions of unloading all our luggage out of the van only to be told to put it back in again, as Mr Lee could not strike a deal with the owners.

As we stopped for the fourth time, Louise and I decided to stay in the Bongo van instead of removing all our belongings yet again. Sharon accompanied Mr Lee to the reception of a yeogwan.

Louise and I were both watching him stride towards the entrance when BANG! He walked straight into one of the closed glass doors. His head rebounded off the glass and he staggered backwards. Sharon caught him, grabbed his shoulders from behind and manoeuvring him sideways, she pushed him through the opening, towards the reception. Even though we knew that he must have hurt himself, the two of us, plus the driver, found it highly amusing.

"Ha! That's karma, that is!" Louise laughed.

Consequently, our last few days in Korea were spent in our third yeogwan. Mr Lee paid us some more money, but we were still owed over $1,000. Nevertheless, this monetary boost gave us a chance to do our last bit of sightseeing.

We telephoned Amy and met in Itaewon to go on a boat trip down the Hanggang River. The ferries traverse through the heart of Seoul travelling from east to west, and as we sat in our seats, we travelled under bridges that held trains, we photographed the 63 building which would be our next stop on our excursion and took silly photos wearing the captain's hat and steering the ferry.

The 63 building, so-called for its 63 floors, stands 264 metres above sea level and is famous as one of Seoul's most renowned landmarks. The sixtieth floor held an observatory where we could take photos of Seoul. and there was a glass case with two life-size figures of a Korean man and women dressed in their traditional national costumes.

We visited the aquarium or sea-world centre in the base of the building. Once again, before I went inside, I was dubious about the welfare of the animals but I have to say that everything was in pristine condition. Apart from fish, we also viewed turtles, dolphins, seals and penguins. It was a lovely relaxing day - although, for me, the thought of not having to work that night had a lot to do with it.

Later that evening, we returned to Iteawon and visited the usual haunts. It was a decidedly bizarre experience for me, as it actually felt like we had come home.

As we wandered down the main street I heard: "Michele?"

Turning around I came face to face with a girl I had worked with on a summer season a couple of years before.

"Lisa, hello! How are you?"

"I'm fine."

"What are you doing here?"

"I'm dancing! We are a group of five girls. We've been here about a month. I'm having a great time," she said. "We are doing five and six shows a night."

"That's great!" I told her. "I'm about to go home. I can't wait. I've had enough! We seem to have had one bad experience after another!"

"The only bad experience we had was in our first hotel," she told me. "It was called the Central and it was horrible! We were in a really tiny room and we could hear scratching behind the walls. Someone had even written on the calendar in English, 'Don't stay in this room there are rats in it!'"

"That was me!" I exclaimed.

"You? No way! What a coincidence!" she said.

I had to agree that it was.

"Anyway, our agent moved us out of there straightaway and into another hotel," she explained.

(That was not so much of a coincidence!)

* * *

Two days later, we were packed and ready to fly back to England. All three of us were loaded down with luggage from our six months in Korea. Incredibly, despite all our negative experiences, we were all feeling a little dispirited at the thought of leaving the country.

Mr Lee appeared to take us to the airport and asked us for our identity cards. I had decided not to hand it over, as I had planned to keep it as a souvenir.

"I've lost it," I said. "I've no idea where it is."

"WHAT?" he exclaimed. "If you don't find, you can't leave Korea! It is very important document. Very important document!" He began walking up and down, apparently in a state of great apprehension.

"Oh look, here it is!" I said, miraculously finding it in two seconds flat in a side pocket of my holdall and reluctantly handing it over.

As we were driven to the airport, we sat in virtual silence, drinking in our last views of this incredible country. We said a curt goodbye to our annoying agent, who begrudgingly handed over the rest of the money that we were owed, and we turned and walked away from him forever.

* * *

Later as we sat in our seats on the jumbo jet and it began to taxi towards the runway, an English man sitting in front of us stuck two fingers up as he looked out of the window.

"What did you do that for?" we asked, laughing.

"Ugh! This place is the pits!" he said. "I've been here for two weeks and I've been living off my wife's sandwiches. The food is absolutely awful! How long have you been here?"

"Six months."

"SIX MONTHS! How on earth did you survive?"

We shrugged and laughed again.

"Wow! I admire you, I really do!" he said in awe.

If you only knew the whole tale, you would admire us even more! I thought.

Seventeen hours later as the plane touched down in England, I knew that, despite everything, I had had some amazing - if at times frightening and upsetting - experiences which I would never forget. My time in Korea had opened my eyes to a shady side of the entertainment world which I had never been a part of before and did not even know existed. It had introduced me to a different culture, tradition and attitude. Despite everything, I was grateful for the opportunity to have been able to live there.

Back at home, I proudly showed off my photos and souvenirs, explaining to a rapt audience (mum and dad) every experience in minute detail. I was back home, but part of me still wanted to be in Korea.

Three days later, I received a phone call from Marion, the English agent.

"I've got the perfect contract for you!" she said. "It's halfway up a mountain, in the middle of nowhere. You'll love it! It's on the island of Hokkaido in Japan!"

Hmm? I thought. *That sounds interesting. I've always wanted to go to Japan...*

THE END

Dear reader,

We hope you enjoyed reading *Fishnets in the Far East*. Please take a moment to leave a review, even if it's a short one. Your opinion is important to us.

Discover more books by Michele E. Northwood at
https://www.nextchapter.pub/authors/michele-e-northwood

Want to know when one of our books is free or discounted? Join the newsletter at
http://eepurl.com/bqqB3H

Best regards,
Michele E. Northwood and the Next Chapter Team

BIBLIOGRAPHY

AZ Quotes, (1998) AZ Quotes [on line] https://azquotes.com/ (accessed 22 July 2018)

Baum.L.F. (1900) 'The Wonderful Wizard of Oz', Chicago, George M. Hill Company.

Carroll, L (1865) 'Alice's Adventures in Wonderland', UK, Macmillan.

Dahl, R. (1964) *'Charlie and the Chocolate Factory' USA, Alfred A Knopf*

Good Reads (2011) Quote by Agatha Christie [on line] https//www.goodreads.com

Kyŏngju (1988) *'Kyŏngju, A Thousand-year Capitol',* Manri-dong, Chung-gu, Korea Textbook Co. Ltd.

Outlander, Season 3, 'The Doldrums'(2017) [TV] Channel 4, November 19th 2017

Taylor, J. (1806) 'The Star' later known as 'Twinkle, Twinkle little star', published in 'Rhymes for the Nursery' London. Original Publisher not known at this time, but the book is available at www. Amazon.co.uk

Post data:

'One of the oddest things in life, I think, is the
things one remembers.'
(Agatha Christie)

I was reminded of the above quotation when I discovered my original diary and sat down to read
it again. I found that, over the years, I had conveniently forgotten some of the more harrowing
times and only remembered the positive or funny
experiences.

Today, as a linguist with a First Class Honours
Degree in English and Spanish and being older
and wiser, I now look back on some of my diary entries with acute embarrassment. Some of
the ways in which I spoke to the Koreans with
whom I spent my time or how I treated them
were totally uncalled for. My only excuse is that
I was too young and foolish to really embrace the
culture, language and customs of that amazing
country. I suppose only experience and age help a
person to mature and see the error of their ways.
(Although... I would also argue that perhaps,
on occasion, some of my behaviour was called
for within the contexts of the situations in which
the Koreans -particularly the Korean men- placed
me). Let's hope that they also grew up and became better people.

As the writer, Freya Stark, once quoted: 'Good
days are to be gathered like sunshine in grapes, to
be trodden and bottled into wine and kept for age

to sip at ease beside the fire. If the traveller has
vintage well, he need trouble to wander no longer;
the ruby moments glow in his glass at will.'

With this in mind, my thanks go out to the real
'Louise', for her constant support throughout the
contract. Her character, wicked sense of humour
and general existence helped me through some
difficult times and provided me with some great
memories. I will always look back on our time in
Korea with fondness.

* * *

Thank you for taking the time to read my book. If
you have enjoyed it, please look out for the sequel:

"Fishnets and Fire-eating.
A dancer's true story in Japan."

Boat trip on the Hanggang River, Seoul.

The most interesting thing in Taejon, peppers
drying in the sun.

Eating kimchi for the first time.

Me, outside the Olympic Stadium.

GI Michele. On the American Army base.

Itaewon at night.

Me performing.

The James Bond routine.

On the street in Itaewon.

Me, my lunch and two tanks! My favourite
photo.

Fishnets in the Far East
ISBN: 978-4-86751-433-7 (Mass Market)

Published by
Next Chapter
1-60-20 Minami-Otsuka
170-0005 Toshima-Ku, Tokyo
+818035793528
15th July 2021